THE CATHOLIC DOCTRINE
OF
NON-CHRISTIAN RELIGIONS

STUDIES IN CHRISTIAN MISSION

GENERAL EDITOR
Marc R. Spindler (University of Leiden)

EDITORIAL BOARD
Jocelyn Murray (London)
Jean Pirotte (Université de Louvain)

VOLUME 7

THE CATHOLIC DOCTRINE
OF
NON-CHRISTIAN RELIGIONS

According to the Second Vatican Council

BY

MIIKKA RUOKANEN

E.J. BRILL
LEIDEN • NEW YORK • KÖLN
1992

25093696

BX
1787
·R86
1992

This series offers a forum for scholarship on the history of Christian missionary movements world-wide, the dynamics of Christian witness and service in new surrounds, the transition from movements to churches, and the areas of cultural initiative or involvement of Christian bodies and individuals, such as education, health, community development, press, literature and art. Special attention is given to local initiative and leadership and to Christian missions from the Third World. Studies in the theories and paradigms of mission in their respective contexts and contributions to missiology as a theological discipline is a second focus of the series. Occasionally volumes will contain selected papers from outstanding missiologists and proceedings of significant conferences related to the themes of the series.

Enquiries regarding the submission of works for publication in the series may be directed to Professor Marc R. Spindler, IIMO, University of Leiden, Rapenburg 61, 2311 GJ Leiden, The Netherlands.

Library of Congress-in-Publication Data

Ruokanen, Miikka.
    The Catholic doctrine of non-Christian religions according to the Second Vatican Council / Miikka Ruokanen.
        p.   cm.—(Studies in Christian mission, ISSN 0924-9389; v. 7)
    Includes bibliographical references and index.
    ISBN 9004095179 (hard)
        1. Catholic Church—Relations.   2. Christianity and other religions.   3. Vatican Council (2nd: 1962-1965)   4. Catholic Church—Doctrines.   I. Title.   II. Series.
    BX1787.R86   1992
    261.2—dc20   91-46332
                                                                      CIP

ISSN   0924-9389
ISBN   90 04 09517 9

© *Copyright 1992 by E.J. Brill, Leiden, The Netherlands*

All rights reserved. No part of this book may be reproduced or translated in any form, by print, photoprint, microfilm, microfiche or any other means without written permission from the publisher

Authorization to photocopy items for internal or personal use is granted by E.J. Brill provided that the appropriate fees are paid directly to Copyright Clearance Center, 27 Congress Street, SALEM MA 01970, USA. Fees are subject to change.

PRINTED IN THE NETHERLANDS

CONTENTS

HOLY SPIRIT LIBRARY
93 0585
CABRINI COLLEGE, RADNOR, PA.

1. INTRODUCTION

1.1. The Beginning of a New Way

Nostra aetate (NA), the declaration of the Second Vatican Council on the relation of the Church to non-Christian religions (De Ecclesiae habitudine ad religiones non-christianas, promulgated on October 28, 1965), marks an authoritative change in the Catholic approach to other religions. For the first time, there is recognition of non-Christian religions as entities which the Church should respect and with which Christians should enter into dialogue. The Council introduced a totally new atmosphere of respect towards other religions and their adherents.

The declaration is intended to be positive in tone: criticism of other religions is absent, with possible criticism being expressed by silence rather than by openly critical remarks. In the Council's discussion of religions, familiar terminology such as "pagan," "idolatry," "error," or "fallacy" is totally lacking. The NA declaration exemplifies the wisdom of prudence in ignoring elements in non-Christian religions that are repugnant to Christians and, instead, trying to find elements which unite all religions. The focus of the Council is on the possible spiritual and moral goodness of religions, in their expressing the value of human life and especially that of human dignity. Religions are seen as spheres of life contributing to the general progress of humanity and human culture. This is in accord with the Council's general tendency towards an *aggiornamento* of the Catholic Church in trying to find positive points of connection between Christianity and the modern world with its rapid cultural, scientific, technical, and social development.

When compared with the traditional approach of the Catholic Church towards other religions, the Council represents a real change. Characteristically, Catholic apologetics have defended the absoluteness and uniqueness of the Christian truth in the face of the error presumed to be present in other religions. Standard Catholic dogma teaches the natural cognition of God and his will: by virtue of creation, all people are able through their reason to know the existence of the Creator from his works and to understand natural moral truths on the basis of rational conscience. The classical biblical references are Rom. 1:20 in support of the general notion of God's existence and Rom.

2:14-16 in support of natural moral law.[1] Traditionally, however, supernatural revelation of the divine will and supernatural grace for salvation have been denied to other religions. Religious plurality was seen as the result of sin; the Church always strove to bring all non-Catholics into the realm of the Church, which alone possesses the proper means to salvation.[2]

Catholic theologians have welcomed the Second Vatican Council as a watershed which signifies a totally new approach by the Church to other religions. But there exist differences of opinion as to how far the Council has brought about a Catholic revaluation of non-Christian religions. The modernist critics of the NA declaration would say that basically nothing has changed – the NA document is mere rhetoric. Theologically conservative critics would accept that the document makes a compromise between the unique and absolute truth of the Christian faith and other "truths." There are some who maintain that the Council recognizes hardly any supernatural salvific function in other religions. Some interpreters argue that the Council affirms the possibility of revelation in such religions but denies their validity as paths to salvation.

But there are many commentators on the Council who would hold that the Catholic Church has recognized non-Christian religions as channels of supernatural divine revelation and salvation. Religions may also be seen as expressions of universal christological grace, even though this is less perfectly manifest in them than in Christianity. *Paul F. Knitter* summarizes: "The majority of Catholic thinkers interpret the conciliar statements to affirm, implicitly but clearly, that the religions are ways of salvation."[3] For instance, according to *Thomas F. Stransky*, the NA declaration "proposes that religions as such are not outside but within the history of salvation;" religions "incarnate sufficient 'religious beginnings' of a supernatural response to the revelation in Christ."[4] In *Pietro Rossano*'s interpretation of the Council, "Christ is seen as the origin, center, and destiny of the various religions, as the One who brought them to birth, takes them up, purifies

---

[1]   See *Schlette* 1964c, 37, and *Heislbetz* 1967, 51.

[2]   On the relation of the Catholic Church to religions in the past, see *Bouquet* 1958, *Eminyan* 1960, 167-181, *Allen* 1960, *Benz* 1961, 11-30, *Heislbetz* 1967, 30-38, *Türk* 1967, 18-22, *Müller* 1968, 12-34, *Schreiner* 1969, 378-389, and *Knitter* 1984, 50 & 1985, 121-123. *Schlette*, 1964c, 123-127, and *Heislbetz*, 1967, 223-231, offer exhaustive bibliographies on the Catholic discussion on religions before the Second Vatican Council. For a survey of pre-conciliar Catholic views (1912-1964) on the possibility of salvation outside the Church, see *Nys* 1966.

On the problem of the relation between Christianity and non-Christian religions as an ecumenical question, see *Shivute* 1980, 42-90, and *Mission Trends No.5* 1981. On the question of "cosmic christology" in ecumenical theological discussion, see *Bürkle* 1965.

[3]   *Knitter* 1984, 50.

[4]   *Stransky* 1985, 156-157.

them, and fulfills them." Consequently, "gifts of 'grace and truth' do reach or may reach the hearts of men and women through the visible, experiential signs of the various religions."[5]

1.2. The Aim of the Study

The aim of the present study is to analyze the Catholic doctrine of non-Christian religions as it is expressed by the Second Vatican Council, especially in the declaration on the Church's relation to non-Christian religions, *Nostra aetate*. When analyzing the theological teaching of the Council on religions, it is necessary to take into consideration the pre-conciliar development of the Catholic theologies of religions (Ch. 2.) and the concrete historical process by which the NA declaration came into existence (Ch. 3.).[6]

The declaration on non-Christian religions is closely linked to the dogmatic constitution *Lumen gentium*.[7] There are intimate links to other Council documents as well, especially to the missionary decree *Ad gentes* and to the pastoral constitution *Gaudium et spes*. The study presented here will therefore consider the integration of the NA declaration with all the final documents of the Council.[8] The present study will not, however, include post-conciliar developments in the issue of the doctrine of non-Christian religions. I do not intend to look at the general context in which we discuss interreligious relations today. An authentic scholarly interpretation of the teaching of the Council on non-Christian religions is not helped but actually hampered by reference to the later authoritative doctrinal evolution of the Church, not to mention the implementation of new ideas conceived by individual theologians.[9]

---

[5] *Rossano* 1981, 103, 108.

[6] The historical process of the outcome of NA is analyzed in Ch. 3., but the facts of that process are taken into consideration in later chapters whenever necessary for illustrating the crucial points of the Council's argumentation.

[7] This was implied, for instance, by Cardinal Bea in his relatio commenting on the draft for a declaration on November 20, 1964. AS III/VIII, 649.

[8] Thomas F. Stransky quite correctly noted: "I find much of the misinterpretation of NA in a lack of such integration." *Stransky* 1985, 155.

[9] For example, Stransky warns of interpreting NA through the post-conciliar documents: "Or worse, some authors have forced NA to say more than it intended in 1965 by reading into the texts later Roman Catholic development in thought - -" Stransky is also cautious about not "reading into conciliar texts the writings of some post-Vatican II biblicists and theologians who are going beyond this common teaching, or even against it." *Stransky* 1985, 155-156.

On the post-conciliar discussion on religions among Catholic theologians, see *Fahlbusch* 1969, *Waldenfels* 1970 *Bürkle* 1977, 25-33, *Knitter* 1985, 124-135, 249-251, and *Fisher* 1985.

It is certainly true that NA is not the final word of the Catholic Church about other religions. In 1981 *Gerald H. Anderson* described the after-effect of the new Catholic attitude towards religions: "- - Roman Catholic mission theology has undergone more radical change in these fifteen years than in the previous century. And there is obviously a great deal more ferment to come in the last fifth of the twentieth century."[10] However, an analysis of these latest trends is not included in my study.

When approaching the NA declaration, the basic questions which arise are: Is the new atmosphere of openness to non-Christian religions only a matter of rhetoric and diplomacy, or does the Catholic Church acknowledge in those religions vital aspects of truth and values which she truly sees as part of the truth as the Christian Church understands it? Do non-Christians and Christians share the same truth or at least some aspects of the same truth, and if so, what aspects of the divine truth and in what way? In other words, the crucial question must be as follows: Does the Second Vatican Council proceed from the standard dogma of the general notion of God and natural moral law through reason and recognize in other religions some aspects of supernatural divine revelation and supernatural or christological grace? And if so, how are these religions seen to mediate grace and to what extent?

When introducing a new draft of the declaration on non-Christian religions on November 20, 1964, Cardinal *Augustin Bea* spoke about "spiritual and moral values" (valores spirituales et morales) in non-Christian religions. (AS III/VIII, 651.) Does the Catholic Council indeed recognize both the proper religious or spiritual value of religions or is such recognition limited more or less to the sphere of the natural cognition of God and his will in natural moral law, which exists in all human beings as a result of creation? We must ask ourselves: In what way are non-Christian religions salvific in and through themselves?[11]

---

[10] *Anderson* 1981, 110.

[11] The English translation of the Conciliar texts used in the present study is that of *Vatican Council II, The Conciliar and Post Conciliar Documents*, edited by Austin Flannery. When referring to the documents, an abbreviation of the document, the number of the section and the number of the paragraph referred to within that section are indicated.

2. PRE-CONCILIAR CATHOLIC VIEWS ON NON-CHRISTIANS

The teaching of the Second Vatican Council on non-Christian religions has a dual background. On the one hand, the long tradition of the Church already includes fragments of theological teaching on this matter. On the other hand, since the 1930's interest has grown in a theological investigation of non-Christian religions in academic Catholic theology. In order to understand the Conciliar doctrine of non-Christian religions, we must take a look at the both aspects of its theological background.

2.1. A Brief History of the Catholic Teaching on the Possibility of Salvation extra Ecclesiam

Prior to the Second Vatican Council, the Catholic Church produced no positive official statements on non-Christian religions. Therefore, we must approach our theme indirectly by discovering what was taught about the possibility of salvation outside the Church. The history of Christian theology has been dominated, so to speak, by the *Heilspessimismus* of the North African fathers, *Cyprian* and *Augustine*.[1] According to their view, salvation is possible only by virtue of the *gratia increata*, the christological and pneumatological grace, offered through the sacramentally institutionalized mediation of the Christian Church. As is well known, Augustine denies the possibility of any natural inclination of man to acquire a position of grace in relation to his Creator; salvation is offered through the explicit means of grace exclusively to those whom God, in his eternal and hidden wisdom, has chosen to become one of the elected ones.

But in spite of the strict denial of the possibility of salvation *extra Ecclesiam*, the Patristic period of the Church does provide instances of the idea of God's universal grace. There are two aspects of this kind of grace;

---

[1] Karl Rahner blames Augustine and his followers for creating a theological mode of "Augustinischer Heilspessimismus" which prevailed in the Church for over a thousand years. *Rahner* 1978, 344. For a history of the Catholic teaching on the question of extra-ecclesiastical salvation, see *Congar* 1957 & 1961, *Eminyan* 1960, *Ricken* 1965, 352-366, and *Ratzinger* 1972, 152-166.

first, it is *gratia creata sive communis*, which means the gracious providence of the Creator of all beings. The very existence of the physical universe is an expression of the Creator's superabundant grace; all being flows from his infinite goodness. Furthermore, in his goodness God bestows his love upon all creation in sustaining the world and life, and in maintaining the moral consciousness for the good. Second, it is *gratia universalis* in the sense that God's specific saving grace is offered to all. God's universal grace covers the extension of the salvific christological grace and the call to salvation offered to all through the incarnation of the Son of God and through the proclamation of the gospel of Christ. For instance, *John Chrysostom* teaches about the universal grace that is poured out onto all creatures. *Irenaeus* goes as far as to state that, from the beginning of the world, Christ revealed his Father, the Creator of all, in a hidden way to all of creation. *Jerome* and *Cyril of Alexandria* hold the view that no human being is born without Christ. Some early teachers of the Church could see pre-Christian religions and philosophies as preliminary stages to the full truth revealed in Christianity.[2]

The Patristic doctrine of God's universal grace became possible because Patristic theology did not recognize any clear distinction between nature and grace, or between "natural" and "supernatural," as, in contrast, medieval theology did. The idea of universal grace is based on the Trinitarian dogma: *opera ad extra* of the Holy Trinity are indivisible. The creation of the world is God's first act of love, an expression of the Creator's creative grace, which, at the same time, represents both christological redemption and pneumatological sanctification. The Son and christological grace on the one hand and the presence of the grace-bearing *Spiritus Creator* on the other hand are inseparable from the work of the Creator (see Gen. 1:2; 2:7, and Col. 1, for instance). Consequently, the grace of the Triune God is a part of the ontological constitution of every human being, and all men have a supernatural vocation to share the eternal blessed life of the Holy Trinity.[3] Creative, redemptive, and sanctifying grace are inseparable; the creative love of the Creator is poured out upon all of his creation, the saving christological grace and the sanctifying pneumatological grace cannot be separated from God's creative grace. Without exception, it is, as Augustine

---

2   See *Korbacher* 1963, *Bsteh* 1966, and *Lubac* 1970, 190, 208.

3   Josef Heislbetz emphasizes "the central position of Christ in the act of creation." Grace which is inherent in every creature is inseparable from christological grace. Heislbetz depicts the classical Catholic doctrine: "Diese christozentrische Ausrichtung des ganzen Kosmos ist für den Menschen kein rein juridisches, dem Menschen äußerlich bleibendes Dekret Gottes, sondern eine real-ontologische Bestimmung des Menschen - - So ist nach der katholischen Dogmatik auch die Gnade des Urstandes schon Gnade Christi - -" *Heislbetz* 1967, 40-41.

would say, the vital ontological orientation of every man to love and enjoy (frui) the Triune God as his supreme good (summum bonum), and this inclination cannot become a reality except through *gratia increata* offered in Christ and becoming a living reality through the work of the Holy Spirit.

There is no reason to draw conclusions which move too far from the teaching of the fathers of the Church on universal grace. Although the fathers recognize the existence of universal Trinitarian grace, the Church has never accepted any doctrine about the eventual salvation of all human beings; the universal offer of grace does not mean the realization of the salvation of all. The idea of universal grace supports the universal claim for the uniqueness of the Christian gospel: Christ was sent for all people so that his universal grace may liberate from the bondage of universal or original sin anyone whom God the Creator of the universe wishes to call.[4] The influential early eastern theology, for instance, emphasizes the absolute transcendence of the Omnipotent. A clear dialectical distinction between the Creator and creation is maintained. The consummation of grace, i.e., the deification of man, is an eschatological rather than an immanent reality.[5]

The later course of the theological development of the Church led to the standard dogmatic position presented above (cf. 1.1.): all rational beings, created by the same God, are able to recognize the existence of their Creator through analogy with nature, and to understand basic moral truths on the basis of natural moral law engraved on their consciences. God may offer a special kind of grace for achieving eternal blessedness to such a man of "good will" who reveres God, seeks his truths, and is obedient to his voice heard in conscience.[6]

The principle of the natural rational knowledge of the existence of God and his will was most profoundly formulated by the great Scholastic *Thomas Aquinas.*[7] He developed a distinction between that which is natural as part of the creation, and that which is supernatural, consisting of the specific christological revelation and grace. Natural knowledge of God and the sphere of natural goodness and virtues of life are to be distinguished – though not separated – from the supernatural revelation and supernatural grace given to the world in Jesus Christ and mediated through the Church and its *media salutis*. Thomas introduced into Catholic theology the consistent use of the term pairs "nature - grace" and "natural - supernatural."

---

[4]   See *Bsteh* 1966, 187.

[5]   See *Fransen* 1973, 636-638.

[6]   For a description of the classical position, see, for instance, *Lubac* 1970, 191-192.

[7]   For a commentary on Thomistic and Scholastic concepts of grace and of the possibility of salvation outside Christianity, see *Morency* 1950, *Lais* 1951, *Lubac* 1965, 148-153, *Heislbetz* 1967, 56-57, *Ruini* 1971, *Lonergan* 1971, *Heck* 1971, *Hamm* 1977, and *Ruello* 1987.

Thomas teaches that all men may recognize the existence of God through reason, and that they know the general moral principles in their rational conscience. This notion of natural moral law is neither in contrast to nor separated from God's universal creative grace, but on the contrary, it itself is an "element of grace." According to Thomas, in order to fulfill the commandments, man needed God's grace even before the Fall; grace already belonged to the original, natural state of human beings. All nature as such is imbued by the presence of the graceful Creator, and even now, after the Fall, although the supernatural quality of *similitudo Dei* was lost, the natural goodness of man as *imago Dei* remained intact. On the basis of this, man is aware of God and of his moral law; man discovers his Creator's grace as implicit in the ontological constitution of his own being. In the human world, all that is natural already exists within the sphere of *gratia creata sive communis*.

Because mankind lost the supernatural quality of *similitudo Dei*, something divine, i.e., supernatural grace which is an additional gift (donum superadditum) or help (auxilium), is necessary for the healing, correction, and reinforcement of the wounded nature of human beings. This grace purifies and strengthens nature by elevating it to a share again in divine nature; in order to regain the lost status given to him in creation, man needs the gift of *gratia increata sive supernaturalis*, participation in the properties of the Triune God. Thus, in the Thomistic model, nature and grace, and respectively, natural knowledge of God and the relationship to God based on supernatural grace are inseparable. Supernatural grace purifies, strengthens and perfects that which is naturally good as a sign of the Creator's grace-bearing love. The well-known Catholic axiom runs: *gratia non tollit naturam, sed perficit.*[8] According to Thomas, as a rational being created in the image of God, man possesses a natural inclination to love God as the supreme being and a natural capacity to comprehend his call to participate in eternal felicity. But man's capacity to love is limited through sin, and his love cannot meet its infinite consummation unless perfected by the additional gift of supernatural grace. Man needs to be informed through the specific historical revelation and to be taken into the realm of supernatural grace through Christian baptism; this is a specific quality of grace which cannot be acquired *extra Ecclesiam*.

---

8   See, *Thomas, In II sententiarum* ds.9, qu.1, ar.8; Opera omnia 1, 152. For a commentary of the axiom, see *Stoeckle* 1962. In fact, Thomas has modified the principle already taught by Augustine: "Non quod per naturam negata sit gratia, sed potius per gratiam reparata natura." *Augustine, De spiritu et littera* XXVII, 47; Corpus Scriptorum Ecclesiasticorum Latinorum 60, 201, 19-20.

On the whole, in Thomism the grace of creation, the grace of redemption, and the grace of sanctification are brought consistently together. Thomas does not advocate any idea of natural religion, but he does locate the specific grace of God, based on the specific revelation, incarnation, and the work of the Holy Spirit, into the realm of the concrete ontological being of man. This supernatural grace is infused into man through the sacramental mediation of the Church. In accordance with the principle of incarnation, God does not present his specific grace directly but through the material element and through the socio-historical mediation within the Church. Thomas teaches the ontologism of grace: supernatural grace given through sacraments becomes integrated with the already existing created grace, and cooperates with the voluntary assent of its receiver; thus supernatural grace becomes an ontological property or the habitual grace, *gratia habitualis*, of its receiver. This habitual grace becomes a supernatural quality in man, initiated by God's supernatural grace and made effective by the cooperation of God and man. Grace does not alter man's nature, but it does gradually remove the disorder and weakness caused by sin and strengthen man's ability to love God and his will to do good. The natural constitution of man is drawn into an ever-progressive process of renewal, sanctification, and elevation. In the mutual process of causality or the chain of cooperation between the gracious God and the receiving man, stage by stage, grace makes man "a new creation."

The Thomistic model has had a great influence on the Catholic understanding – on both ecclesiastical doctrine and on individual thinkers – of non-Christians and of the possibility of salvation outside the Church. The basic feature of Thomas' theological thought, the inseparable relation of nature and grace, has always been an inexhaustible source of dynamic theological tension and thinking. This can also be seen in the way in which modern Catholic theologians have tried to develop a theological interpretation of non-Christian religions. Promoting a theory of perfection, some are biased towards the principle of "nature," whereas others construct their model more on the principle of "grace" (see below 2.2.).

Official statements by the Catholic Church on non-Christian religions and on the possibility of the salvation of their followers are scarce. The classical thought of *extra Ecclesiam nulla salus* has naturally provided the dominant line in interpretation. Even as late as 1442 the Council of Florence expressed the view of salvation as totally exclusive: an eternal fire awaits those who are outside the Catholic Church – Jews, heretics, and schismatics – not to mention ordinary pagans.[9] It is easy to see that the ideas of Thomas,

---

[9] "Firmiter credit, profitetur et praedicat, 'nullos extra catholicam Ecclesiam existentes, non

the great thinker of the 13th century, had yet to have much effect on the official teaching. The influence of Thomism was not really felt in the Catholic Church until the Council of Trent in the latter half of the 16th century; since then, Thomas has been the main single authority in the development of scholarly Catholic theology.

In the post-Reformation history of the Church there are signs of a slight relaxation of the rigorous attitude of the magisterium. For instance, in 1653 the pope condemned the ultra strict approach of *Cornelius Jansen*, who tried to find support for his exclusive views in Augustine. His argument, that in the natural postlapsarian condition of man there is no grace, was rejected. So too was his opinion that "it is Semipelagian to say that Christ has died and shed his blood for all human beings."[10] In rejecting the views of Jansen, the Holy Office passively allowed a small step towards the dogmatic recognition of the possibility of salvation outside the Church. The same line of development is seen in the condemnation of the opinion of *Paschase Quesnel* in 1713. The pope rejected Quesnel's proposition that no grace exists outside the Church.[11]

A new, more positive and active horizon of understanding for non-Christians was introduced into the official statements of the Church by *Pius IX* in 1863. Echoing some aspects of the Thomistic approach, and combining the aspects of nature and grace, the pope stated in his encyclical letter *Quanto conficiamur moerore* that if man follows the precepts of the natural law written in the human heart, i.e., is obedient to God, and leads an honest and right life, he may, by virtue of divine illumination and grace, acquire eternal life. Thus, if man does that of which he is capable as God's creature, he will receive the gift of divine grace and become acceptable to God. In line with the Catholic principle of *extra Ecclesiam nulla salus*, Pius IX emphasized that it is a condition for extra-ecclesiastical salvation that a person be ignorant through no fault of his own "of our most holy religion" and its mediation of grace.[12]

---

solum paganos', sed nec Iudaeos aut haereticos atque schismaticos, aeternae vitae fieri posse participes; sed in ignem aeternum ituros, 'qui paratus est diabolo et angelis eius' - -" DS 1351.

[10] Among the errors of Jansen were the sentences: "Interiori gratiae in statu naturae lapsae numquam resistitur." "Semipelagianum est dicere, Christum pro omnibus omnino hominibus mortuum esse aut sanguinem fudisse." DS 2002 & 2005.

[11] One of the condemned sentences was: "Extra Ecclesiam nulla conceditur gratia." DS 2429.

[12] "Notum Nobis vobisque est, eos, qui invincibili circa sanctissimam nostram religionem ignorantia laborant, quique naturalem legem eiusque praecepta in omnium cordibus a Deo insculpta sedulo servantes ac Deo oboedire parati, honestam rectamque vitam agunt, posse, divinae lucis et gratiae operante virtute, aeternam consequi vitam - - qui voluntariae culpae reatum non habeat." DS 2866.

The First Vatican Council (1869-1870), confronted with the rise of new scientific, industrial, social, and cultural challenges in Europe, gave new life to the Thomistic concept of the link between natural knowledge of God by reason and nature perfected by supernatural grace. There exists "a double order" of knowing God: natural reason and divine faith.[13] Referring to Rom. 1:20, the Council affirmed that God, the efficient and final cause of all creation, can be known with certainty (certo cognosci posse) from his works of creation by virtue of the natural illumination of human reason. In addition to this natural possibility of knowing him, God has instituted a supernatural means of knowing him by revelation in the Old and the New Covenants. Through the specific grace of revelation man can participate in the supernatural destination (finis supernaturalis) provided for him by a merciful God.[14]

The First Vatican Council spoke much about revelation, and what it had to say about the general knowledge of God applies to all non-Christians. From the point of view of our study, however, the Council provides a bare minimum of enlightenment; it had nothing positive to say about other religions nor about the possibility of extra-ecclesiastical salvation. On the contrary, it expresses itself quite negatively concerning those who, "led by human opinions, follow a false religion (religio falsa)."[15] The Council did not continue the promising initiative of Pope Pius IX in his teaching on the possibility of salvation outside the Church. In fact, the Council affirmed the ecclesiocentric view of salvation: without faith there is no justification and no eternal life; God instituted the Church in order to present the justifying faith to men.[16] The Church is a sign to all nations, calling them to herself.[17]

---

[13] "Hoc quoque perpetuus Ecclesiae catholicae consensus tenuit et tenet, duplicem esse ordinem cognitionis non solum principio, sed obiecto etiam distinctum: principio quidem, quia in altero naturali ratione, in altero fide divina cognoscimus." DS 3015.

[14] "Eadem sancta mater Ecclesia tenet et docet, Deum, rerum omnium principium et finem, naturali humanae rationis lumine e rebus creatis certo cognosci posse; 'invisibilia enim ipsius, a creatura mundi, per ea quae facta sunt, intellecta, conspiciuntur': attamen placuisse eius sapientiae et bonitati, alia eaque supernaturali via se ipsum ac aeterna voluntatis suae decreta humano generi revelare, dicente Apostolo: 'Multifariam multisque modis olim Deus loquens patribus in Prophetis: novissime diebus istis locutus est nobis in Filio'." DS 3004.

"Non hac tamen de causa revelatio absolute necessaria dicenda est, sed quia Deus ex infinita bonitate sua ordinavit hominem ad finem supernaturalem, ad participanda scilicet bona divina, quae humanae mentis intelligentiam omnino superant." DS 3005.

[15] DS 3014.

[16] "Quoniam vero 'sine fide - - impossibile est placere Deo' et ad filiorum eius consortium pervenire, ideo nemini umquam sine illa contigit iustificatio, nec ullus, nisi in ea 'perseveraverit usque in finem', vitam aeternam assequetur. Ut autem officio veram fidem amplectendi in eaque constanter perseverandi satisfacere possemus, Deus per Filium suum unigentium Ecclesiam instituit, suaque institutionis manifestis notis instruxit, ut ea tamquam custos et magistra verbi revelati ab omnibus posset agnosci." DS 3012.

[17] "Quo fit, ut ipsa (Ecclesia) veluti signum levatum in nationes et ad se invitet, qui nondum

It was not until the 1940's that the question of the possibility of extra-ecclesiastical salvation was again raised in the official documents of the Catholic Church. Twice *Pius XII* revealed a new line of thought. In his encyclical letter *Mystici corporis* of 1943, the pope stated that there is no certainty of salvation outside the Church,[18] but those who by some sort of unconscious desire or intention (inscio quodam desiderio ac voto) belong to the Church are part of the body of Christ.[19] Here again the emphasis lies on the mediation of salvation by the Church, but the idea of "the Catholic unity" is enlarged. The limits of the Church are not visible and strict. Those non-Catholics and non-Christians who are sensitive to God's call in their inner self are in a some secret manner latent members of that society to whom the explicit means of salvation are available.

Pius XII expressed his wider view of the possibility of salvation *extra Ecclesiam* for a second time in 1949 in his letter to the archbishop of Boston. In the letter, the Holy Office rejected the rigorous views represented by an American Catholic theologian, *Leonard Feeney*. Feeney had revived Jansen's insistence on a fully exclusive interpretation, according to which all who are outside the Catholic Church are denied salvation and eternal life. In his letter the pope makes a distinction between two paths to salvation. On the one hand, there is the way of *divina sola institutione*, salvation through the mediation of grace by the Church. On the other hand, there is the way based on the necessity of the subject-matter itself, *intrinseca necessitate*: it is an inherent part of human nature to wish to know God and to seek a relationship with him. The latter possibility becomes a reality when a person does not know the truths of Catholicism but, by his natural yearning for God, becomes a latent member of the Church through desire (voto et desiderio) and thus has an implicit desire or intention, *implicitum votum*, to conform his will to the will of God. Such a desire is man's free response to experiencing the presence of the grace-bearing Triune God in life and creation. According to Pius, God effects salvation by presenting supernatural faith (fides supernaturalis) to man on the basis of man's inherent desires.

---

crediderunt, et filios suos certiores faciat, firmissimo niti fundamento fidem, quam profitentur." DS 3014.

18 "- - ab eo statu se eripere studeant, in quo de sempiterna cuiusque propria salute securi esse non possunt." DS 3821.

19 "Quandoquidem, etiamsi inscio quodam desiderio ac voto ad mysticum Redemptoris Corpus ordinentur, tot tamen tantisque caelestibus muneribus adiumentisque carent, quibus in catholica solummodo Ecclesia frui licet. Ingrediantur igitur catholicam unitatem, et nobiscum omnes in una Iesu Christi Corporis compagine coniuncti - -" DS 3821. For a commentary on Pius' implementation of *votum*, see *Grillmeier* 1966, 196.

Such a person is associated with the Church and the realm of salvation – yet *solo voto implicito*.[20]

Pope Pius creates a kind of proleptic model: a person is already an implicit or latent member of the body of Christ, though not yet openly so. It is the mission of the Church to make her latent members corporate members of that salvific society in which the means of grace are fully deployed. A person is already inwardly a Christian, but he must become so outwardly as well. The model of fulfillment or perfection conceived by Pius does not lessen the urgency of the Church's mission; indeed, quite the opposite is the case. In an open statement, Pius condemns the opinion, according to which "people could be equally saved in all religions."[21] The pope refers to what he said in his previous encyclical letter of 1943. He also makes a reference to the Council of Trent, which introduced the idea of repentance "in voto" in its doctrine of the sacrament of penitence. Before the act of penitence itself has taken place, the desire and intention to make a confession are already accepted as conditions which meet the requirement for a correct relationship with God.[22] In an important way Pius XII widened his perspective from the notion of an implicit membership of the Church to that of an implicit relationship with God in conforming one's will to God's will. A man's implicit membership of the Church now means supernatural faith effected by God through man's intimate direct relationship with his Creator and doing what one knows to be right on the basis of one's conscience and the natural law inscribed upon it.

The official documents of the Catholic Church previous to the Second Vatican Council are very moderate in their views of the possibility of salvation *extra Ecclesiam*. There are no positive statements directly concerning non-Christian religions. The only extra-ecclesiastical way of salvation recognized is that of the direct relationship of man with his Creator

---

[20] "Infinita sua misericordia Deus voluit, ut illorum auxilium salutis, quae divina sola institutione, non vero intrinseca necessitate, ad finem ultimum ordinantur, tunc quoque certis in adiunctis effectus ad salutem necessarii obtineri valeant, ubi voto solummodo vel desiderio adhibeantur." DS 3869.

"Quandoquidem ut quis aeternam obtineat salutem, non semper exigitur, ut reapse Ecclesiae tamquam membrum incorporetur, sed id saltem requiritur, ut eidem voto et desiderio adhaereat. Hoc tamen votum non semper explicitum sit oportet, prout accidit in catechumenis, sed ubi homo invincibili ignorantia laborat, Deus quoque implicitum votum acceptat, tali nomine nuncupatum, quia illud in ea bona animae dispositione continetur, qua homo voluntatem suam Dei voluntati conformem velit." DS 3870.

"Quibus verbis providentibus tam eos reprobat, qui omnes solo voto implicito Ecclesiae adhaerentes a salute aeterna excludunt - - Nec votum implicitum effectum habere potest, nisi homo fidem habeat supernaturalem." DS 3872. The pope says with emphasis that those who know that Christ has instituted the Church for salvation and yet reject the Church cannot be saved. DS 3867.

[21] DS 3872.

[22] DS 1543.

through the illumination of reason and through obedience to conscience. Salvation, although containing the reality of supernatural faith, is defined in terms of the theology of creation and *gratia creata*. These are the means through which the creative grace of the Triune God works. Even in this case, those outside the Catholic Church are understood as being related, in a way hidden to us, to the mystical body of Christ, which is concretely visible in the Church. Thus they are saved as invisible members of the Catholic Church. The old strict principle of *extra Ecclesiam nulla salus* had changed into a new, more tolerant principle of *sine Ecclesia nulla salus*.

2.2. The Theological Interpretation of Non-Christian Religions

Modern Catholic theology has seen the rise of individual theologians endeavouring to find theologically sound and positive ways in which to understand salvation *extra Ecclesiam* and to establish some theological evaluation of non-Christian religions. During previous centuries such theologians made fragmentary comments concerning non-Christians, but failed to develop any profound theological approach to the problems involved. Undoubtedly, modern theological work had an impact on the teaching of the Second Vatican Council on non-Christian religions. The private theological thinking of individual Catholic theologians does not, of course, represent the official doctrine of the Catholic Church, though individual theologians do have some indirect influence on the development of Christian dogma as expressed in the official documents of the Church. It is impossible, however, to point out in what way and to whad extent this kind of influence takes place. At the very least we can note some of the changes taking place in academic theology as signs of a more general trend which will eventually emerge in the wider context of the life of the Church.

It is certain that both the pre-conciliar theological work and the Council itself were greatly influenced by global and by European political, scientific, cultural, social, economic, and other changes so rapidly occurring in the twentieth century. The Catholic Church was compelled to venture out of her own intellectual ghetto and to gaze at the world with a more open mind. It is the proper task of historians and sociologists to analyze the impact of historical changes on the Council. Some of these issues will be touched in Ch. 4., in relation to the Council's self-understanding of such historical changes. Examining church history, one sees the growth of internationalism and the rise of the ecumenical movement, having drawn the Protestant and the Orthodox churches closer to each other, certainly also increasing pressure on the Catholic Church to move in the direction of tolerance and dialogue.

In the following pages we shall take a look at the most prominent models created by Catholic scholars in the analysis of religions. It is no exaggeration to say that nearly all modern Catholic theology is at least to some extent influenced by Thomistic theology, and various models of the analysis of religions in the twentieth century all refer to Thomas Aquinas for their support, while emphasizing different dimensions of Thomism. These dimensions are then combined with certain modern approaches to theology, which result in modern types of Catholic theology.[23] From the viewpoint of theological analysis of religions, two key modes of thinking in modern Catholic (and also in Protestant) theology appear to rise above others: first, the emphasis upon the historicity of human existence[24] and correspondingly the historicity of God's salvation plan for mankind; and second, the role of theological anthropology, even anthropocentrism, in theological methodology. All the prevailing Catholic models for understanding theologically non-Christian religions contain an element which can be called either a historical fulfillment theory or a theology of sacramental perfection. Both say that, in a proleptic manner, seeds of the spiritual and moral truths can sprout outside Christianity. Such an approach combines the aspect of historical fulfillment with the idea of theological perfection.[25]

The scheme of fulfillment is taken from the basic biblical conception of God's salvation history: the Saviour was promised and prefigured in many ways in the Old Covenant, and the fulfillment of all those promises was consummated in the incarnation, crucifixion, and resurrection of Christ. The fulfillment theory became increasing important in theology in the early part of the twentieth century as a result of the rise of historical thinking and methodology which, under the impact of the modern scientific and cultural atmosphere of Europe, caused theological development to follow many new paths. Historical thinking and historical methods in theology created the concept of *Heilsgeschichte*, salvation history, which has been one of the key ideas for the development of both Catholic and Protestant theology in this century.[26] Most schools of thought in Catholic theology have adopted the

---

[23] It is not, however, my intention to show in the present study how or to what extent each school of the theology of religion is influenced by Thomism.

[24] Joseph Ratzinger says: "Die Entdeckung der relativierenden Weite der Geschichte, die uns in der klein gewordenen Welt geradezu physisch auf dem Leib gerückt ist, bildet mit der Entdeckung der unendlichen Weite des Kosmos, der jeder Anthropozentrik zu spotten scheint, das eigentliche Ferment der Krise des Glaubens, vor der wir stehen. Deswegen ist die Frage nach der Beziehung des Christentums zu den Weltreligionen heute zu einer inneren Notwendigkeit für den Glauben geworden." *Ratzinger* 1972, 178-179.

[25] For instance, Heinrich Fries is a typical conservative representative of the theory of fulfillment. He says that "religions are a presupposition for the Christian faith," but because "Christ is the completion of religions," Christianity means also "the end of religions." *Fries* 1965, 24-31.

[26] For an interpretation, see *Feiner* 1964, *Lubac* 1970, 219-223, and *Schlette* 1964c, 68-69.

idea of fulfillment combined with the notion of God's salvation history: non-Christian religions contain, to varying degrees, seeds of spiritual and moral truths and a certain kind of mediation of grace which have become completely clear and communicable in Christianity. Most often the idea of historical fulfillment is indivisibly combined with the Thomistic notion of ontic or sacramental perfection in the sense of infused grace: supernatural grace perfects the natural good already existing in human life.

Among the variety of theological approaches which have employed the idea of fulfillment is the relatively conservative school of theology which sees the possibility of non-Christians being saved in terms of "natural religion." These non-Christians may practice that love towards God and neighbor of which man is conscious because of his natural cognition of God and of natural morality. Christianity is thus seen as the perfection of man's intrinsic inclination to love. In the 1930's, *Otto Karrer* was a pioneer in further developing this traditional Catholic line of interpretation, being among the first Catholic theologians to discuss non-Christian religions with a truly open mind. Karrer's phenomenological comparison between the basic truths of Christianity and of other religions resulted in his favouring Christianity: the seeds of truth found elsewhere have been fully revealed only to Christians. Karrer clung to the idea of the positive natural religiosity of human beings, a natural religiosity which consists above all of the human ability to love; Karrer never mentions the possible seeds in religions of supernatural revelation or of grace. Instead he says all people have some natural knowledge of God (göttliche Kundgabe) which enables them to approach God and partially accomplish his will by means of practical love. Although other religions reflect in various degrees the divine phenomenon of love, the Catholic faith possesses the fullness of that love.[27]

This same idea of universal love present in all religions but perfected only in Christianity was extensively illustrated in 1950 in *Thomas Ohm*'s opus *Die Liebe zu Gott in den nichtchristlichen Religionen*. Referring to all the known religions of the world, Ohm tries to demonstrate that the theme of man's natural inclination to love God is expressed in all religions. Loving God belongs to the natural constitution of every rational creature; the Fall into sin has not totally destroyed man's natural ability to love God.[28] Ohm deals with the Catholic doctrine which teaches that after the Fall man is not

---

[27] See *Karrer* 1934, 239-392 & 1955.
[28] "Durch die Erbsünde ist diese natürliche Kraft zur Gottesliebe nicht vollkommen vernichtet worden. - - Der gefallene Mensch hat Fähigkeiten zum Guten im allgemeinen und zur Gottesliebe im besonderen." *Ohm* 1957, 46. "Auch die Liebe Gottes zu uns und die Verpflichtung des Menschen zur Gottesliebe vermag der Mensch aus eigener natürlicher Kraft zu erkennen." *Ibid.*, 44.

able to love God "in the supernatural way" required for justification, stating that even in the condition of sin, human nature retains the ability to receive supernatural love towards God. That supernatural love is not, however, found in religions; supernatural revelation and grace are also required.[29] This supernatural love of God is a gift to human beings from the true God.

But Ohm does not give to religions the specific role of mediating that love; religions seem to be merely expressions of the natural relation of man to his Creator, a relation which does not necessarily necessitate any religion at all. Consistently, Ohm clings to the idea that Christianity is the answer to the general human search for the truth through love.[30] He eventually arrives at a traditional solution: "The non-Christians must be emancipated from their religions."[31] Christianity is the perfection of the general search for a loving God, a search expressed by the religions of the world; Ohm does not specify what kind of possibility of eternal salvation exists among non-Christians.

Joseph Ratzinger is the probably the most prominent modern Catholic theologian carrying forward the line of interpretation of non-Christian religions based on the notion of natural moral law, and more specifically, on the idea of man's natural inclination to love. According to Ratzinger, non-Christian religions are valuable, because they contain elements "preparatory" for Christianity. In a proleptic manner they reflect that truth which became evident through the specific revelation of the Christian faith.[32] Ratzinger opposes the view that the mysticism present in non-Christian religions would serve as the point of connection with Christianity and thus be a route for receiving extra-ecclesiastical grace.[33] He is not at all fond of any non-historical idea of christology; instead, he prefers to emphasize the concrete historicity of revelation and salvation.

When dealing with the question of non-Christians, Ratzinger bases his argument on the concept of the promise of God realized as salvation history. The Church proclaims the promise of the coming of the Kingdom of God; Christianity has no monopoly on the Kingdom, though it does have the

---

[29] "Der Mensch ist aus sich auch nicht imstande, Gott als den Urheber und das Ziel der übernatürlichen Ordnung auf übernatürliche Weise zu lieben." *Ohm* 1957, 51.

[30] "Von allem Guten in der Welt führt ein streng notwendiger Weg zu einem Gott, der liebt, dem die Welt etwas bedeutet, dessen Herzen die Kreaturen nahe liegen. - - Von dieser (Liebe Gottes) wüßten wir bloß dank der übernatürlichen Offenbarung, dank der Heiligen Schrift oder sogar nur dank des Neuen Testamentes." *Ohm* 1957, 20-21.

[31] *Ohm* 1957, 463.

[32] "Hinsichtlich der anderen Religionen ist demgemäß eine doppelte Einstellung möglich: man kann sie als vor-läufig und insofern vor-läuferisch zum Christentum ansprechen und damit in gewissem Sinn positiv werten, soweit sie sich nämlich in die Haltung des Vor-läufers einordnen lassen." *Ratzinger* 1964, 289.

[33] See *Ratzinger* 1964, 304.

perfected means of proclaiming it and making present its reality. The Kingdom is greater than the Church; the main quality of that Kingdom is love.[34] Where fraternal love exists, there the quality of the Kingdom is present. When Ratzinger speaks of "the sacrament of the brother," the brother – or neighbor – represents the disguised presence of God. The way man treats his neighbor determines his salvation: striving to "save others" will save the saviour. Ratzinger says: "Who has love has everything. He is saved, he needs nothing else."[35] The notion of moral law is perfected by the reality of divine grace granted by the Creator of all: salvation is not merely based on the possibility of fulfilling the demands of God's law that we should love, but on God's promise of grace to those who do love.[36]

Ratzinger's view of the natural possibility of salvation – aided by God's creative grace – allows no specific role for non-Christian religions. The extra-ecclesiastical possibility of salvation is based on the theology of creation, the general revelation of God and his will to rational creatures. Ratzinger's solution is thus consistent with the traditional view of the Catholic Church. Furthermore, Ratzinger does not fail to give weight to the reality of sin: man is entangled with hubris and egoism and consequently needs the salvific media of the Church. Even in the case in which a man is ignorant of Christ and his Church, his possibility of salvation through obedience to God's law which commands one to love is implicitly connected with Christ and the Church.[37] Ratzinger's position adds nothing substantially new to what *Pius XII* had already said in the 1940's.[38]

The Catholic position in the interpretation of religions, as our study thus far shows, is an interpretation constructed upon the dimension "nature" rather than "grace." In this interpretation, non-Christian religions acquire no specific role in mediation between man and the divinity. These religions are neither demonized nor criticized; they are seen as a part of general humanity

---

[34] *Ratzinger* 1972, 168, 174-175, 191.

[35] "Das 'Sakrament des Brüders' erscheint hier als der einzig genügende Weg des Heils, der Mitmensch als jenes 'Inkognito Gottes', an dem sich das Schicksal eines jeden entscheidet. - - Wer die Liebe hat, hat alles. Er ist gerettet, er braucht nichts sonst." *Ratzinger* 1972, 169. "Der Mensch wird gerettet, indem er daran mitwirkt, andere zu retten. Gerettet wird man gleichsam immer für die anderen und insofern auch durch die anderen." *Ibid.*, 174.

[36] "Denn das Heil der Welt steht in Gottes Hand, es kommt aus Verheißung, nicht aus Gesetz." *Ratzinger* 1972, 192.

[37] "In jeder Rettung eines Menschen ist nach christlichem Glauben Christus am Werk. Wo aber Christus ist, da ist auch die Kirche beteiligt, weil er nun einmal nicht allein bleiben wollte, sondern gleichsam die doppelte Verschwendung geschieht, daß er und mitbeteiligt an seinem Dienst." *Ratzinger* 1972, 173-174.

[38] When dealing with the question of religions, Ratzinger refers frequently to other rather conservative Catholic theologians like Yves Congar and Hans Urs von Balthasar. Cf. *Congar* 1961 and *Balthasar* 1965.

and human culture. There exists, however, another line of interpretation of non-Christian religions in modern Catholicism which constructs its theory upon the sphere of "grace" rather than "nature," or it can be said to understand "nature" overwhelmingly through "grace." In developing this line of understanding, the categories of mystery, incarnation, sacrament, and cosmic grace are employed for understanding the status of non-Christians.

In the 1940's, the new approach of the papal magistrate to the question of non-Christians coincided with a new development of *nouvelle théologie* among individual Catholic thinkers.[39] It was the intention of the new theology slowly to dissolve the traditional distinction between grace as an inherent part of man's natural constitution as *imago Dei* and supernatural, non-created grace as the additional gift needed for redemption from sin and for sanctification in the process of elevation towards the supernatural goal of *similitudo Dei*. New theology emphasized that man is never "pure nature," but his nature is by definition graced nature; all human existence is influenced by the supernatural finality inherent in it. *Gratia universalis* is not just an offer of salvific christological grace, but it consists of the reality of supernatural, christological grace already existing within all humanity; this grace is unconditionally poured out upon all humanity everywhere. All human beings, created in God's image, are, by virtue of creation and incarnation, already partakers in supernatural divine light of revelation, and in the superadditional grace of the Triune God; innate *gratia creata sive communis* is supernatural christological and pneumatological grace as such. In the modern concept of grace, the independent theology of creation as focused on nature as well as the concept of natural moral law are weakened in favor of the theologies of redemption and sanctification. The aim of the modern reconstruction of the concept of grace seems to be to avoid any kind of split between nature and grace, and, on the basis of this reorientation, the Church is able to communicate with the modern world on an equal level of understanding and experience.

Henri de Lubac introduced in his famous *Catholicisme* of 1938 and then developed further in his *Surnaturel* of 1946 the idea that because all human beings are created in the image of God, merely on the basis of their humanity they are "anonymously" participants in the divine mystery. This is the "supernatural" dimension of every man, an inherent part of human essence.[40] Lubac's argumentation is founded on the positive use of the notion of humanity; neither the concept of general revelation nor natural moral law as such, but rather theological anthropology, is the focus most

---

[39] For a commentary, see *Rahner* 1950 and *Balthasar* 1962, 303-313.
[40] See *Lubac* 1970 (1938), 193-194.

useful for a proper theological understanding of the questions of human existence. Opposing all "personalistic atomism," Lubac treats humanity as an indivisible entity.[41] Lubac consciously intends to proceed from the foundation of the Patristic idea of universal grace: the Triune God has poured out his grace on all his creation. Furthermore, Christ has died for all men; his body comprises not only the members of the Church but all the members of the human family – all of whom he has redeemed. By extending the idea of *corpus Christi* to cover the whole of humanity, Lubac is able to speak of mankind's salvation: because the body is saved, all of its members are saved. In divergence from the traditional Catholic view, Lubac lacks interest in the salvation of individual non-Christians; he focuses on all of humanity.[42]

When developing his new approach, Lubac intends to reject any idea of *natura pura* in regard to humanity, and to introduce instead a concept of ontological sacramentalism. Seeing nature in contrast to grace makes supernatural grace something that is external, non-personal, moralistic, and non-historical; grace is not a "thing" outside man, but belongs inherently to humanity itself. Thus, Lubac wants to avoid any sharp distinction between the universal grace given in creation to all men, created in God's image, and the specific christological grace which has come to the world in the incarnation of Christ and in the historical revelation of God. Lubac understands the sacramental idea of universal supernatural grace in terms of finality and elevation: By virtue of creation, a supernatural destination, or "a positive ordination to the supernatural" belongs to the essence of every man. On the basis of this, every human being yearns "to see God." In revelation and, more specifically, in Christ's incarnation, grace has come down to human reality and history to meet and to fulfill this vocation of man towards divinity. By virtue of incarnation, all humanity, in a mystical and sacramental way, has been imbued by supernatural divine grace.[43]

Lubac's concept of grace leads to the understanding of all religions as united by the same finality: in the depth of human consciousness they all seek the answer to that divine mystical vocation of humanity of which man is unconsciously aware. All that is mystical in human life is of value in expressing the supernatural depth of existence; "the depths of God" are to be found in "the depths of humanity." Lubac creates a novelty in the

---

[41] *Lubac* 1970, 297.

[42] "Mag der Grad ihrer Erleuchtung und ihrer Funktionen noch so verschieden sein, es genießen doch alle Glieder der menschlichen Familie eine wesentliche Gleichheit vor Gott. - - Kurz, sie können gerettet werden, weil sie einen Wesensbestandteil der Menschheit bilden, die gerettet werden soll." *Lubac* 1970, 204. See also *ibid.*, 194-195.

[43] See *Lubac* 1946, 153, 161, 483-494 & 1965, 91-92, 117, 145, 150.

Catholic interpretation of religions: what unites Christians with non-Christians is not primarily the general notion of God discovered through reason or good life based on natural morality, but the shared mystical experience of life. Non-Christian religions can, however, answer only partially that universal longing for participation in divine life. They need Christ as an "educator" or a "physician" who can strengthen in them that which is good.[44] Lubac is fond of *Pierre Teilhard de Chardin*'s idea of the evolution of humanity. Both feel that religions can be seen as expressions of the different stages in man's evolution towards the fuller consciousness of himself and his divine vocation; a universally understood cosmic Christ is the point of "general convergence" uniting the truthful element in all religions.[45]

Lubac shares Teilhard's idea of the historical evolution of religion; Christianity is the perfection of the seeds of truth which exist in pre-Christian religions. In a proleptic manner, a non-Christian of "good will" is a latent member of the Church; as soon as he learns of the Church, he is obliged to join her.[46] Christianity will perfect and enrich that good effect of divine grace which is already at work in every religion.[47] Although divine grace is a mystical-sacramental reality, at the same time it is a historical-corporative reality incarnated in the Church. Lubac sees that, in accordance with the principle of incarnation, God uses the Church as the sign or sacrament of the world which sanctifies the whole of humanity by her mediation of explicit christological grace.[48] Through this sacramental mediation, the whole world becomes the Church: "The salvation of the world has been entrusted to the Church; in the final analysis, the Church is nothing else but humanity itself."[49] The question of the specific role of non-Christian religions in the realm of universal, incarnated supernatural

---

[44] *Lubac* 1965, 155-177 & 1966, 25-26, 38 & 1970, 224, 300-301.

[45] Lubac has written his own interpretation of Teilhard; see *Lubac* 1969. A central thesis runs: Teilhard has renewed the Catholic harmony between nature and grace. *Ibid.*, 190. Teilhard sees the incarnation of Christ as the "cosmic point of convergence" through which everything can be in touch with everything else in "the evolution of convergence" of the world. *Teilhard de Chardin* 1971, 87. "A general convergence of religions upon a universal Christ who fundamentally satisfies them all: that seems to me the only possible conversion of the world, and the only form in which a religion of the future can be conceived." *Ibid.*, 130. On Teilhard's basic modes of thought, see *King* 1981.

[46] *Lubac* 1970, 206-211, 219.

[47] Speaking about non-Christian religions, Lubac says: "Außerhalb des Christentums kommt nichts zu seinem Ziel, dem einzigen Ziel, nach dem unbewußt alle menschlichen Wünsche, alle menschlichen Bemühungen streben: in die umfangenden Arme Gottes in Christo. Die schönsten und mächtigsten dieser Bemühungen bedürfen also notwendig der Befruchtung durch das Christentum - -" *Lubac* 1970, 196.

[48] *Lubac* 1970, 205, 207, 211.

[49] *Lubac* 1970, 245.

grace is left open in Lubac's theology. What is the *modus gratiae* in religions?

Jean Daniélou adopted some of the ideas originally conceived by Lubac. Daniélou attempts to make a correction in the line of interpretation running through Lubac and Teilhard by laying more emphasis than they on the concept of salvation history. According to Daniélou, the prophetic nature of Christian revelation, a revelation connected with actual historical events in the here-and-now, is the main feature making biblical faith different from any other faiths.[50] On the basis of his historical interest, Daniélou attempts to find points of connection between Christianity and other religions by employing the classical method of typology. Just as there are many typological bridges between the Old and the New Testaments, there are also typologies between the Christian faith and any other religion. As one example, Daniélou mentions the Hindu theme of the cosmic three which can be interpreted as prefiguring the cross of Christ.[51] According to Daniélou, Christianity can adopt worthy symbols from other religions and give them a new reality without destroying their authentic meaning.[52]

Moreover, referring to the Patristic authors, above all *Irenaeus*, Daniélou shows his intention to combine two aspects of salvific revelation, the "dramatic" and the "historic," both representing the idea of fulfillment or perfection. By "dramatic," Daniélou refers to Christianity's perfecting the truth, the seeds of which truth are discernable in other religions; Christianity, which "marks the highest point of that (religious) evolution," "completes other religions and other civilizations."[53] Non-Christian religions contain many signs of grace, but those signs do not effect what they signify; therefore they are merely a prefigure or an indication of the grace fully available only through Christianity. Consequently, non-Christian religions must be "superseded" by the more advanced religion, which is the Christian religion.[54] Daniélou offers hints for the proper contextualization of the Christian faith among other faiths, but presents hardly any new insights into theory concerning the possibility of salvation of non-Christians.

The model for a theological analysis of religions which has been most discussed among modern Catholic theologians was initially represented by

---

50 *Daniélou* 1956, 128.

51 *Daniélou* 1962, 135-147. Daniélou quotes Hippolytus of Rome and Irenaeus, who knew the myth of the cosmic tree.

52 *Daniélou* 1962, 66, 70.

53 *Daniélou* 1962, 19.

54 "Therefore, what we find here is simply that species of universal sacramentalism which is a sort of deep intuition of the divine meaning of things, and which signifies grace, though it does not effect what it signifies. It is a sort of foreshadowing, a sort of call." *Daniélou* 1962, 69. See also *ibid.*, 20 & 1950.

Karl Rahner in his article *Das Christentum und die nichtchristlichen Religionen* in 1962.[55] In his theological theory of religions Rahner is very much in line with Lubac and *nouvelle théologie* in trying to overcome the gap between the natural and the supernatural, and in attempting to understand supernatural grace as inherent in all humanity. On the basis of this goal, it is Rahner's intention to break down the tradition of "pessimistic" Christian exclusiveness and to speak "optimistically of God and his saving will."[56] This *Heilsoptimismus* of Rahner is constructed on the foundation of his general theological framework. As a theologian influenced by both Thomism and German Idealism, especially by the latter's existentialistic model, Rahner links his view of religions with an idiosyncratic theological anthropology.

Rahner is a leader in a new way of thinking among Catholic approaches to other religions by emphasizing that non-Christian religions are not only reflections of man's natural cognition of God – they are not mere "natural theistic metaphysics" and natural moral law – as has been understood by mainstream Catholic interpretation of religions. According to Rahner, religions are something more than mere expressions of "natural religion," because they indeed include mediation of grace and thus add something to man's natural relation as creature to his Creator.[57] Rahner argues that a non-Christian religion "not only contains elements of natural knowledge of God," but "also supernatural instances of the grace which God presents to man because of Christ."[58] Rahner is, hereby, the first Catholic theologian who succeeds in relating the idea of extra-ecclesiastical grace to the concrete elements of non-Christian religions. His conception is founded on the solid principle of incarnation and of God's condescension to the level of his creation: God does not offer his supernatural grace "directly;" grace is always incarnated in matter, in the concrete element. God's universal grace must always take on historico-social flesh; in this sense grace is always of a sacramental nature.[59] Supernatural grace is never given without the

---

[55] The article is published in *Rahner* 1962, 136-158.

[56] *Rahner* 1962, 145-146.

[57] "Es geht jedenfalls nicht an, die nichtchristlichen Religionen nur zu betrachten als ein Konglomerat aus natürlicher theistischer Metaphysik und menschlich verkehrter Interpretation und Institutionalisierung dieser 'natürlichen Religion'. Die konkreten Religionen müssen Momente übernatürlichen, gnadenhafter Art an sich tragen und in ihrer Praxis konnte der vorchristliche Mensch die Gnade Gottes erreichen." *Rahner* 1962, 153.

[58] "- - enthält eine nichtchristliche Religion nicht nur Elemente einer natürlichen Gotteserkenntnis - - sondern auch übernatürliche Momente aus de Gnade, die dem Menschen wegen Christus von Gott geschenkt wird - -" *Rahner* 1962, 143.

[59] Agreeing with Rahner, Josef Heislbetz says: "Die Tatsache, daß übernatürliche Heil in und durch die Gnade im geschichtlichen Leben des Menschen sich ereignen muß, schließt noch nicht aus, daß dieses Gnadenereignis durch die Freiheit des Menschen vereitelt wird." *Heislbetz* 1967,

concrete natural *signum* of that grace, "nature" and "grace" in Rahner's model being inseparable. One could even say that religions are the *materia* used by the *forma* of the Triune God's universal supernatural grace.

Rahner expands the sacramental idea of the mediation of grace through concrete elements and historico-social forms of life. For the people who do not know the Christian mediation of supernatural grace, their own religions are "legitimate religions," i.e., God uses them as channels of his supernatural grace. Non-Christian religions contain "through and through supernatural instances of grace."[60] Later Rahner invented a concept of "categorical mediation" (kategoriale Vermittlung) to describe the role of religions as concrete links in the service of divine grace. Religions form a category of their own in transendentally linking man to God. It is interesting to observe that Rahner makes a clear distinction between atheists and adherents of other religions: atheists lack that "categorical mediation" or material incarnated medium of grace present in non-Christian religions.[61]

A non-Christian religion is thus the concrete mediator of salvific grace; it is a religious institution which a group of people at a certain time and place experience as being the correct way of relating oneself to God. Rahner refers to the analogy of the Old Testament: although the Old Covenant had not yet attained the perfection of God's revelation and grace, it served as the legitimate religion of that time, willed by God. The same principle can be analogously transferred to the non-Christian religions of today.[62] They are imperfect channels of salvation, but their lack of truth or their errors do not prevent them from being legitimate religions.[63] In the case of non-Christians, it is essential that they are open to God, seekers of the truth; this openness already demonstrates existence in a state of grace.[64]

It is important to note that Rahner constructs his theology of religions on the presupposition that any grace efficient in non-Christian religions is the same supernatural grace which has become perfected in the Christian religion. Rahner mentions no other grace except the grace of the Triune God which is fully efficient in the body of Christ, the Church. In accordance with

---

43. Similarly *Schlette* 1964c, 81.

60 "- - in den nichtchristlichen Religionen a priori durchaus übernatürlich-gnadenhafte Momente angenommen werden können." *Rahner* 1962, 143.

61 *Rahner* 1978, 347-348.

62 "Legitime Religion soll hier heißen: eine institutionelle Religion, deren 'Benützung' durch den Menschen zu einer bestimmten Zeit im ganzen als positives Mittel der richtigen Beziehung zu Gott und so zur Erlangung des Heiles angesehen werden kann und so in Gottes Heilsplan positiv einkalkuliert ist." *Rahner* 1962, 148. On Rahner's understanding of the Old Testament, see also *Evers* 1979, 527-529.

63 *Rahner* 1962, 143, 149.

64 Rahner depicts man's "openness for the unlimited being of God:" "Der Versuch, die Gnade der Erlösung und Gottesnähe derart einzuholen, höbe sie *als* Gnade auf." *Rahner* 1965, 547.

the theory of fulfillment which is characteristic of Catholic interpretation of religions, Rahner also clings to the idea of finality: Christ is the final cause of God's universal salvific will.[65] Consequently, Rahner creates the concept of an "anonymous Christian."[66] The sincere adherents of non-Christian religions are defined through Christianity; they are not-yet-perfected members of the same body of Christ as are Christians. The Church, in fact, should be seen as the "vanguard" (Vortrupp), as a historical and social entity expressing what also happens "as a hidden reality" outside the visible Church.[67] Non-Christian religions are provisional; they express the "seeking anticipation" of mankind,[68] their legitimacy lasting only until the more perfect revelation and mediation of grace becomes available. In this sense, Rahner shares the view of other Catholic theologians who represent the theory of historical fulfillment and sacramental perfection. Rahner's concept of anonymous Christians is a logical continuation of the principle expressed by Pius XII of the "implicit desire" of a non-Christian to conform to God's will.

Rahner's interpretation of religions is based on the overall structure of his theology. He does not adhere to any idea of universal or cosmic divine mystery; he starts "from below" by a rational analysis of the structure of individual human existence as such. According to him, all men are uniform, based on their ontological constitution. Rahner then concentrates on the transcendentals which belong to human existence, i.e., existentials, which make human existence what it is. His crucial argument runs: every human being has in his ontological constitution a spontaneous "supernatural existential" which enables one to have a supernatural connection and communication with God. This last instance of essence is throughout penetrated by habitual grace. The idea of the supernatural existential is Rahner's special way of expressing an idea of universal grace, the aspects of *gratia creata* and of *gratia increata* being united.

In order to have a relationship with God, man does not need first to find some "object" in which to trust or to believe. To know God is inseparable

---

[65] "-- wir Inkarnation und Kreuz als 'Finalursache' der mit dem Heilswillen gegebenen universalen Selbstmitteilung Gottes an die Welt sehen - -" *Rahner* 1977, 309. *Waldenfels*, 1984, 763, and *Knitter*, 1985, 128, also point to the Christ-centeredness of Rahner's theology of religions. The idea of finality is central in the theory of Johannes Feiner, too; see *Feiner* 1964, 325. On the whole, Feiner has very much in common with Rahner, because he also emphasizes that, in his universal salvation history, God is in no way restricted by the institutional media of grace within Christianity.

[66] *Rahner* 1962, 154. For an interpretation of Rahner's conception of "anonymous Christianity," see *Röper* 1963, *Riesenhuber* 1964, *Elders* 1965, *Christentum innerhalb und außerhalb der Kirche* 1976, *Weger* 1979, and *Schwerdtfeger* 1982.

[67] *Rahner* 1962, 156.

[68] *Rahner* 1977, 311.

from being aware of one's own existence; "being" and "knowing" coincide; thus God, a priori, elevates human consciousness to a supernatural level. To know God belongs spontaneously to the transcendental experience of every human being. From the ontological point of view, God is the "innermost substance" (entelekheia) of the world. Because of the essential presence of God in being, the human world has become habitually saturated with the grace of God. Consequently, ontologically every man exists under the influence of divine supernatural grace.[69] In fact, the idea of an anonymous Christian is founded on the presupposition of grace as an existential of human existence. The openness of man towards "the limitless being of God" creates a situation in which the final or utmost instance of man's existence can be defined as an essence saturated with habitual, infinite supernatural grace. The experience of "the unlimitedness of our transcendence" or of "the supernatural finality of our spirit" is an experience of divine revelation and of the infinity of God's grace. Rahner also calls this the primordial revelation of grace, on the basis of which an anonymous Christian has a *fides implicita* which gradually becomes explicit as he becomes aware of the fuller revelation entrusted to the Church.[70]

Thus, Rahner's conception minimizes the classical Thomistic distinction between the grace belonging to human nature as such, and the grace which is a supernatural gift and *auxilium* in the process of salvation. In Rahner's model, all grace is by definition supernatural grace. On the basis of this, he succeeded in creating a foundation for a new type of theological approach to non-Christian religions. The theoretical model he created does not, however, include specifics regarding the concrete religious material needed to define the *modus gratiae*, how supernatural grace is present in such material; instead, he left that work to others.

A student of Rahner, *Heinz Robert Schlette*, has attempted a further development of the theological understanding of religions, being among the first intentionally to employ the concept of the "theology of religions" (Theologie der Religionen). Lacking as profound and scholarly a general

---

[69] "- - jeder Mensch wahrhaft und wirklich dem Einfluß der göttlichen, übernatürlichen, eine innere Gemeinschaft mit Gott und eine Selbstmitteilung Gottes anbietenden Gnade ausgesetzt ist - -" *Rahner* 1962, 145. For an analysis of Rahner's theological anthropology and his concept of revelation, see *Speck* 1967, *Fischer* 1974, and *Greiner* 1978.

[70] *Rahner* 1962, 154-155 & 1965, 547-549 & 1978, 345. "Der Mensch erfährt in seiner Transzendentalität als Geist und Freiheit immer seine Verwiesenheit auf das unumfaßbare Geheimnis, das wir Gott nennen. Er erfährt in sich die Hoffnung, daß diese Verwiesenheit so radikal sei, daß sie ihre Erfüllung in der unmittelbaren Selbstmitteilung Gottes findet, von der übernatürlichen Gnade getragen, befreit und radikalisiert ist. Diese durch die Gnade radikalisierte Transzendentalität des Menschen ist aber als immer wenigstens anfanghaft reflektierte und als in Freiheit angenommene oder abgelehnte vermittelt durch die geschichtliche Erfahrung, an deren Inhalten der Mensch seiner eigenen Transzendentalität innewird." *Rahner* 1977, 311.

framework of theology as Rahner's, Schlette tries to develop further his teacher's view of religions, and in doing so, creates a rather radical theory of religions. On the basis of God's "universal history of salvation," Schlette describes non-Christian religions as the "ordinary" route to salvation, while Christianity, on the basis of the "special history of salvation," is the "extraordinary" route.[71] Schlette conducts an experiment to develop the traditional concept of salvation history by introducing a "history of epiphany" (Epiphanie-Geschichte).[72] Schlette transforms the traditional theory of fulfillment or perfection to fit his conception of religions. Christianity is the representative of the eschatological dimension within universal human history, a dimension which includes various possible ways to union with God. The Christian faith is the final "epiphany" of God's saving will, enlightening the entire world because it shows the finality, the *telos*, of the whole universe. The Church's mission is not to win conversions but to exist as the eschatological sign of the broad kingdom of God in all human history and in all cultures. For instance, Buddhists must not be converted into Christians but must be made better Buddhists; this is their normal means of salvation.[73] Schlette's use of the heuristic idea of epiphany as the mode of "God's self-revelation" produces no new information on the important question of the *modus gratiae* in religions.[74]

Hans Küng goes even further than Schlette. He clearly rejects Rahner's idea of anonymous Christians by calling it an offense to non-Christians to see them as latent or potential Christians. He wants to renounce totally the old self-sufficient conception of *extra Ecclesiam nulla salus*.[75] Küng, however, is content with rhetorical depiction without providing serious analytical support for his view; indeed, Küng does not create any new theory of religions which could be taken seriously in the Catholic theology of religions.

---

[71] "Wenn die Religionen die Heilswege der allgemeinen Heilsgeschichte sind, dann sind sie die allgemeinen Heilswege, und wenn gegenüber der allgemeinen Heilsgeschichte die Kirche – wie wir sahen – als specialis dispositio auf der Seite der speziellen Heilsgeschichte steht, dann darf man den Weg der Religionen als den ordentlichen und den Weg der Kirche als den außerordentlichen Heilsweg bezeichnen." *Schlette* 1964c, 85. See also *Schlette* 1964a, 63, 66 & 1970, 199.

[72] See *Schlette* 1964c, 66-112.

[73] "Die Kirche hat ihren Existenzsinn vielmehr von der ihr übertragenen Aufgabe her zu verstehen, die eschatologische Doxa Gottes zu bezeugen." *Schlette* 1964a, 67. Schlette speaks about the Church as "an eschatological sign" which "witnesses to the eschatological fulfillment which is still to come." *Schlette* 1964b, 312. Similarly *Schlette* 1970, 194-195.

[74] For an example of the line of argumentation, see *Schlette* 1964a, 64-65 & 1964c, 98.

[75] On Küng's theology of religions, see *Küng* 1974, 81-108. Küng asks ironically: "Und was würden die Christen sagen, wenn sie von den Buddhisten gnädig als 'anonyme Buddhisten' anerkannt würden?" *Ibid.*, 90. See also *Küng* 1965.

Before beginning an analysis of the Second Vatican Council's teaching on religions, we must note that the most recent development of the Catholic theology of religions has produced ever more radical views, especially among Third World theologians and those who in various forums have been practicing theological dialogue with non-Christians. In creating new theories of non-Christian religions, individual Catholic theologians are increasingly distancing themselves from the classical dogma. As *Paul F. Knitter* says, we have seen "a certain evolution from ecclesiocentrism to Christocentrism and, most recently, to theocentrism."[76] The post-conciliar development of the Catholic theology of religions has changed the whole paradigm of doing that theology, therefore, providing no enlightenment for the task left unfinished by Karl Rahner: to define more closely and analytically the *modus gratiae*, the sacramental way in which divine supernatural grace, fully mediated through Christianity, is present and efficacious in the religions of the world.

---

[76] Knitter gives an illustrative survey of the most recent radical development; see *Knitter* 1984, 53 & 1985, 130-135.

3. THE HISTORY OF *NOSTRA AETATE*

In order to explore the beliefs of the Catholic Church concerning non-Christian religions, we have to turn back to the official documents of the Church. The document whose importance exceeds all others' is naturally the *Nostra aetate* declaration of the Second Vatican Council. A proper understanding of the theological motives of that document requires historical analysis of the events surrounding the origin of that declaration.

3.1. The Need for Reconciliation with Jews

The history of the declaration begins with Pope *John XXIII*.[1] The recent horrors of the Holocaust in Christian Europe had made the need for reconciliation desperate. The pope, wishing the Council to issue a statement concerning Jews, asked Cardinal *Augustin Bea* to see that this be done. On September 18, 1960, the pope orally opened the Secretariat for Promoting Christian Unity, headed by Cardinal Bea, asking it to prepare a declaration on the relation of the Church with Jews. In the meanwhile, the pope received delegates and written appeals from the Jews who wanted the Catholic Church authoritatively to reject all biblical or other theological arguments used against Jews, for these had inspired all varieties of contempt and hatred towards Jews throughout history. One of the most important encounters was the meeting between the pope and the French Jewish scholar *Jules Isaac* on June 13, 1960. Isaac asked the upcoming Council to reverse all past teaching which approved elements of anti-Semitism. The American Jews were exceptionally active in striving for an impact on the content of the declaration which was impending.

---

[1] Among the commentaries on the NA declaration, Johannes Oesterreicher's exhaustively detailed account of the history of the declaration is in a class of its own. See *Oesterreicher* 1967. See also *Cottier* 1966, *Laurentin & Neuner* 1966, 18-47, *Becker* 1966, *Laurentin* 1967, 9-54, *Müller* 1968, 58-77, and *Rynne* 1964, 218-223, 235-239 & 1965, 31-35 & 1966, 160-166.

For general commentaries on the NA declaration, see *Masson* 1965, *Laurentin & Neuner* 1966, *Vatican II: An Interfaith Appraisal* 1966, *Vatican II, Les relations de l'Église avec les religions non chrétiennes* 1966, *La dichiarazione su "Le relazioni della Chiesa con le religioni non cristiane"* 1966, *Federici* 1966, *Laurentin* 1967, 57-83, *Müller* 1968, 78-164, and *Amstutz* 1973.

In 1961 the Secretariat produced the first draft of the schema on Jews, "Decretum de Iudaeis." In May, 1962, the text was passed to the Central Commission which would decide whether the schema was to be represented to the Council. Diplomatic manoeuvres and political speculation were growing around this whole project regarding the declaration on Jews. Pressure increased from the Arab countries which thought the Vatican planned a diplomatic recognition of the state of Israel. As a consequence, the Central Commission did not present their draft to the First Session of the Council, so the very first version of the declaration was never discussed by the Council fathers. For a while the whole project, it seemed, was to be withdrawn because of unfavourable political conditions.

In December 1962, Pope John appealed personally to Cardinal Bea not to drop the schema, expressed his approval and gave his advice for improving the text of the draft. It was also decided that the text be annexed to the schema on ecumenism as the schema's Chapter IV. This could possibly help calm the public stir inspired by a separate schema on Jews. But once the public interest was aroused, nothing could altere the situation: the declaration on Jews and non-Christians was to become one of the most thoroughly disputed documents of the Council. "No other conciliar document probably has been subject to so many influences and counterinfluences."[2] All of this was due more to political than to theological problems.[3]

The very first draft of 1961, which never reached the Council,[4] established a sound biblical, especially Pauline, doctrine of the relationship between the Old Covenant and the Christian Church; the text refers with emphasis to Rom. 11 and Eph. 2. According to the text, the election of the Church is rooted in the election of Israel. An unbroken continuation exists from the Old Covenant to the Church: all Christians are "sons of Abraham in faith." On the basis of all of this, the draft included mention of the hope of unity of all God's people. In addition to the Pauline doctrine of the mystery of Israel, the rest of the main bulk of argumentation in the first text concerned the attitude the Christians should take toward Jews. Because of God's fidelity, Jews must never be seen as a forsaken or a cursed people. The draft added that the Church deplores all of the contempt or persecution which Jews have suffered in the past or in the present.

The first draft introduced to the Council (Text I) was meant to be the fourth chapter of the ecumenism decree and was entitled "De Catholicorum

---

2 *Rynne* 1965, 33.
3 *Bea* 1966b, 293.
4 For the text, see *Oesterreicher* 1967, 426.

habitudine ad non-christianos et maxime ad Iudaeos" (AS II/V, 431-432). The two-page schema was presented to the 69th General Congregation on November 18, 1963, during the Second Session of the Council. Despite the title's including a reference to non-Christians, only three lines concerned non-Christian religions in general; all the rest of the text concerned Jews. The draft expressed the wish of the Church to hold discussions and cooperate with non-Christians on the topics of natural moral law and conscience. The African and Asian bishops were alarmed: three lines for two-thirds of the world!

The doctrine on Jews which was presented in the initial version was adapted and enlarged in Text I. The Pauline doctrine of the mystery of Israel and the idea of continuation were emphatically expressed: "omnes enim Christifideles, Abrahae filios secundum fidem;" the Church shares in the calling of the patriarchs of Israel. The text introduced a strong image of the common spiritual heritage of Jews and Christians: "Ecclesiae sit cum synagoga commune patrimonium." The text also expressed the hope of the unity of God's people in terms of Eph. 2; there is no notion of Christian proselytism of Jews.

In defining the Church's attitude towards Jews, Text I introduced strong new criticism of the attitude of hatred of Jews still prevalent even among committed Christians. The text denounced the idea of Jews as a "deicide" nation: "gens deicida." Not all Jews who lived in the days of Jesus were guilty of his death – the Jews who have lived since then even less so. Jews remain dear to God because of the fathers; they are neither a forsaken nor a cursed people. The draft urges that anything which might cause hatred or contempt against Jews must be excluded from catechesis and preaching in the Church. Instruction concerning the theological meaning of Israel was aimed at Christians, while "mutual understanding and appreciation" through common theological studies and "fraternal discussion" was recommended to both Christians and Jews. The text of the schema declared to all people that the Catholic Church deplores and condemns (deplorat et damnat) all hatred and persecution against Jews. In its achievement of reversing traditional theological rationale for anti-Semitism, this was the strongest version of the schema that ever existed. It was widely published in newspapers throughout the world, receiving widespread approval among Jewish communities and receiving increased Arab suspicion.

When introducing Text I, Cardinal Bea explained in his relatio (AS II/V, 481-485) that it was not the intention of the schema "to promote the recognition of the state of Israel on the part of the Holy See." Reasons for drafting the declaration were "pure religiosa." Because of the "grossly violent and criminal form" of anti-Semitism in Germany in the time of National Socialism, it was necessary that the Church dissociate herself from all anti-Semitic attitudes and slogans. The Christian faith had been misused in the propaganda against Jews; this must never again be possible. The Council had to defuse the notion of Jewish abuse of the Christian religion – a notion, Bea emphasized, which motivates condemnation of Jews as a God-cursed nation. With this statement, he exposed the profoundest initial cause for such a decree on Jews being necessary. In his relatio, the cardinal revealed that the late Pope John, who had died on June 6 of the same year, 1963, had half a year before his death personally expressed to the cardinal his approval of the initial text; "mihi plenam suam adprobationem significavit."

Text I was never discussed on the floor of the Council. The reason that Pope *Paul VI* wished to avoid a detailed debate on the Jewish problem was that it was too heated an issue and one which might have prejudiced the success of his Holy Land pilgrimage planned for January 1964. Between the Second and the Third Sessions of the Council, pressure from the Arab world was growing. On May 17, 1964, the Secretariat for Non-Christian Religions, headed by Cardinal *Paolo Marella*, was created.

A new draft of the schema on the Church's relation to non-Christians and Jews was delivered to the Council fathers in the 88th General Congregation on September 25, 1964. This schema was entitled "De Iudaeis et de non-christianis," and it was still meant to be a part of the ecumenism decree, inserted as sections 32-34. This Text II (AS III/II, 327-329) was nearly twice as long as the previous draft. The most visible change in this draft was a totally new text on non-Christian religions other than Judaism. The basic idea, which survived until the final declaration, was stated thus: the "opinions and doctrines" of other religions, although these differ greatly from Christianity, "nevertheless in many ways reflect a ray of that truth which enlightens all men." In order to strike a balance between Jews and representatives of other religions, Muslims were mentioned, and a clause appreciative of their monotheistic faith was introduced. Islam was included probably because it is the next closest religion to Christianity after Judaism. This addendum may also be seen as a concession to Arab pressure.

As they read the section of Text II concerning Jews, most of the Council fathers were badly disappointed. Although the basic theological insights were maintained as in Text I, the theme of hope in terms of Eph. 2 was dropped. The idea of the unification of God's people thus was considerably weakened. The most embarrassing change in the text for the participants of the Council was the omission of the formula "gens deicida" altogether. In his relatio (AS III/II, 558-564), Cardinal Bea gave an argument for that decision: bringing up the idea of deicide forcuses too much attention on the problem of the guilt of Jews; Christ died for all – therefore his death is a matter of collective guilt. In addition, the original rather firm renunciation of the habit of calling Jews "gens reprobata vel maledicta" was made milder, and the strong sanctioning of teaching anything which could cause "hatred or contempt" against Jews was softened by a condemnation of expressing ideas "that could alienate the minds of men from Jews."

As to the question of persecution, the focus was widened from a concern concentrated specifically on Jews to a general principle of renouncing strongly all forms of discrimination. The theme of denouncing discrimination was made forceful in the schema, as a means to ensure its remaining therein. As the theological foundation of this new, wider scope of the declaration, the text introduced a long biblical description of how all men are created in God's image and should, therefore, be "treated fraternally" (fraterne gerere). Denying this thus means denying God himself. The neutralization of themes concerning Jews can be understood as a concession to the diplomatic and political pressure exercised on the Vatican by Arabs. The pseudonymic author *Xavier Rynne* may well be correct when he says: "The sponsoring of this bastardized text was probably Pope Paul's single greatest mistake and gave rise to more misgivings about his intentions than anything else."[5]

The great discussion on the schema took place in the 89th - 91th General Congregations, September 28-30, 1964. Most of the speakers demanded that the formula "gens deicida" be reinstated. This wording must appear because it has been the very wording used in past centuries to curse Jews. The French Cardinal *Liénart* was the first to defend the deleted passages; for catechic and pastoral reasons it is necessary that the Holy Council clearly renounces the anti-Semitic terminology so commonly used by Christians throughout the world.[6] Liénart was supported by the North American cardinals *Léger, Cushing, Meyer,* and *Ritter*, and by the European cardinals *König* and *Frings*, among others.

Cardinal *Tappouni*, speaking for himself and on behalf of four other eastern patriarchs, suggested that the whole declaration should be dropped. According to the eastern fathers, if the Council said anything positive about Jews, it would be seen in the Arab countries as favouring the state of Israel. Consequently, Christian minorities in the Arabic countries would suffer. Confirming that their opposition did not mean opposing the Jewish religion, Tappouni said that if the declaration was to be accepted, it would cause "grave difficulties to our pastoral activity." (AS III/II, 582.) There were other opponents, as well. A small conservative faction, led by Cardinal

---

[5] *Rynne* 1966, 163. *Hebblethwaite*, 1984, 518, reveals that the famous pseudonymic writer was Fr. Francis Xavier Murphy.

[6] "Ideo ut catechesis et praedicatio nostra fideles sint, necesse est ut Sacra nostra Synodus explicite declaret quod ex hoc nunc a labiis nostris arceri oportet vocabula: 'reprobatum' et 'deicidii reum', in loquendo de Iudaeis." AS III/II, 581.

Ruffini, said that the formula of deicide should be abandoned because "no one can kill God." This faction also demanded that it also be mentioned that Jews should love Christians. Ruffini pointed to pejorative teachings about Christians in the Jewish tradition. (AS III/II, 585-586.) Furthermore, there were bishops from the Third World (as we are now accustomed to say) who emphasized that the Council must mention all non-Christian religions or none.

3.2. The Declaration Accomplished

Including all these emendations, the draft of the scheme on the Church's relation to Jews was revised according to the sense of the debate and rewritten by the Secretariat during the Third Session of the Council. The revised draft was introduced as a schema of its own, not as an attachment to the ecumenism decree, and was called a declaration on the Church's relation to non-Christian religions: "De Ecclesiae habitudine ad religiones non-christianas." This Text III (AS III/VIII, 637-641), beginning with the words "Nostra aetate," could no longer, because of the lack of time, be discussed during the Third Session of the Council. The text was voted on November 20, 1964, in the 127th General Congregation. The schema was accepted with 1651 *placet* against 99 *non placet* votes.

Text III had taken on a new form as an independent schema for a Conciliar declaration. A long section on religions in general and a section on Hinduism and Buddhism had been created. The section of Islam had been enlarged. But as these new themes were elaborated in such a late phase of the Council, they never really became an object of thorough theological discussion. Virtually only the section concerning Jews had been tested through arguments and the effects of changes of views by the Council fathers.

In the section on Jews, the idea of deicide was restored in the form "deicidii rea:" Jews are not to be considered guilty of deicide. The expression "gens reprobata vel maledicta," was reinstated, as well. Furthermore, the strong condemnation of arousing "hatred or contempt against Jews" was put back in the text. The theme of sternly judging all kinds of discrimination was retained and even fortified: the Church "severely reprobates" all injuries done against any people. But on the other hand, the lengthy positive description of human brotherhood was shortened. These changes indicate that the emendations of the majority of the fathers who spoke up in the great discussion of September were taken into consideration.

In his relatio (AS III/VIII, 649-651) introducing Text III, Cardinal *Bea* used the metaphor of how "a mustard seed grew into a tree" to describe how the originally concise schema on Jews had evolved into an overall survey of non-Christian religions, appreciating "those spiritual and moral values (valores spirituales et morales) which are present in each religion." Living in obedience to *recta conscientia* is, according to Bea, showing "implicit faith" which must be brought into "full participation of the riches of Christ" in the Church. Once again Bea emphasized the non-political character of the schema and saw a close affinity with the dogmatic constitution on the Church, *Lumen gentium* (which, in fact, was promulgated the day after Bea's speech).

During the interval between the Third and the Fourth Sessions of the Council, the schema for a declaration on the Church's relation to non-Christian religions was renewed in certain quarters. The reason for such a renewal is obvious: between the Sessions, a "holy war" raged against the schema. All possible means, diplomatic and undiplomatic, sympathetic and unsympathetic, were exploited in order that the schema would be dropped or at least altered.[7] Text IV was presented to the 149th General Congregation of the Council on October 14, 1965 (AS IV/IV, 690-696). The title of the schema was the same as in Text III. There was no great change in the amount of text; certain critical parts and details were refined. In the opening section, a sentence on the Church's concern for the unity of mankind was added. In his relatio, Cardinal Bea said the intention of the interpolation was to emphasize that which unites men (AS IV/IV, 722). The new sentence can also be seen in connection with the growing emphasis of the Council on the unity of the modern world, as it was to be expressed above all in the pastoral constitution *Gaudium et spes*. In other sections, the wording on Buddhism was made more accurate by describing some basic phenomena of that religion. Small elements emphasizing Christian witness in dialogue situations were introduced; this can be seen as meeting some of the conservative criticism of the schema.

Once again the focus of interest was on that part of the document which concerned Jews. Again came drastic alterations of the text. Above all, the tendency was to reformulate some expressions more carefully; in the opinion of many, these alterations watered down the sound intention of a clear and resolute renunciation of all theological roots of anti-Semitism. After so many painstaking procedures the famous formula of deicide was again dropped. Cardinal Bea explained that the alteration was made "in the light of pastoral prudence and evangelical charity" (AS IV/IV, 724). Furthermore, the strong expression that the Church "deplores and condemns (deplorat et damnat) hatred and persecutions against Jews" was deleted; the

---

[7]   On the details of that "holy war," see *Oesterreicher* 1967, 458-470.

word "damnat" was dropped altogether from the schema. The utterance "severe probans" was also deleted.

A new term, *antisemitismus,* was employed, and it was stated that the Church both "deplores" (deplorat) and "reprobates" (reprobat) all persecutions and manifestations of anti-Semitism. The verb *reprobare* was repeated at the end of the schema in which was expressed the renunciation of all forms of discrimination against any human beings. There are two reasons for changing "damnat" to "reprobat:" the verb *damnare* is normally used against heresies, and the Secretariat did not view anti-Semitism as a heresy – as some others would; and it had been the explicit wish of Pope *John XXIII* that the Council would not declare any condemnations. An additional, biblically documented clause mentioning the opposition of Jews to the gospel can be seen as a concession to the conservative wing of the Council. It was now understood that the Jews of New Testament times were partially responsible for the death of Jesus, which also explains in part the subsequent history of tension between Christianity and Judaism. In order to calm the criticism of the Arabic governments and peoples, an explicit clause was added stating that the Church deplores all manifestations of anti-Semitism, not for political but for religious reasons, "nec rationibus politicis sed religiosa caritate evangelica impulsa."

Text IV was voted upon in the 149th and 150th General Congregations on October 14 and 15, 1965. In the final vote on the whole text of the schema, of a total of 2023 Council fathers present, votes totalled 1763 *placet*, and 250 *non placet*, with 10 votes invalid. In comparison with numbers usual in the Council's voting, the number of *non placet* votes was relatively high. It must, however, be noted that it was not only the issue of Judaism which caused critical votes, there were also those not satisfied with the document's concise assertions on Hinduism, Buddhism, Islam, or animism. In addition, there were the theologically conservative, who feared that the document would lead to indifference to the Church's missionary zeal. This faction of the conservatives was led by Bishop *Carli*, who believed the declaration would "put an end" to missionary work by regarding all religions as of the same value.

Text IV was solemnly promulgated by Pope *Paul VI* as the Council's declaration "De Ecclesiae habitudine ad religiones non-christianas," starting with the words "Nostra aetate," in the 7th Public Session on October 28, 1965. In his speech following the promulgation, the pope did not take any position on non-Christian religions in general, but he did speak warmly about Jews.[8]

---

8   "Item eam respiciant sectatores aliarum religionum, impirimis ii, quibuscum propinquitate

In sum, we can state that the real discussion and dispute in the Council over non-Christian religions concerned Judaism. The initial aim of Pope John was accomplished: from that time forward no Catholic could quote the Bible to justify calling Jews an accursed or rejected people. The NA declaration ends a sad chapter in Christian history.[9] *Robert A. Graham* notes: "It has often been said, and rightly so, that if the present document had not been preceded by the earlier one, it would have been universally welcomed as one of the most important advances of the Council."[10]

We can conclude that the theological doctrine regarding the mystery of Israel and the close relationship between Jews and Christians was relatively easily accepted by the Council. The real points of controversy were not theological but political. Similarly, the doctrine concerning non-Christian religions other than Judaism also was accepted and received without any great dispute. But on the other hand, the more comprehensive text was created at a late stage of the Council, and the bureaucracy and the timetable of the Council could provide no more room for a thorough discussion on non-Christian religions, though there might have been a great need for such a discussion. On the whole, the situation is promising for anyone interested in the Council's doctrinal teaching about the nature of non-Christian religions. He will probably find a solid, well-argued and non-contradictory theology in the document. *Claud Nelson* concludes: "In the very long run, those sections of the Declaration dealing with Moslems, Buddhists, Hindus, and primitive religions may prove to be even more important than the section on the Jewish religion."[11]

The topic of Catholic doctrine on non-Christian religions, authoritatively taught by an ecumenical council or by a pope, is a novelty in the Church. As we saw above in 2.1., the history of Catholic theology has known since the Patristic times some positive theological thinking on religions. The relatio to Text III of November 1964 mentions *Irenaeus* in support of the idea of discovering "a ray of the truth" in non-Christian religions. (AS III/VIII, 645.) But the history of Christian theology has seen only sporadic occurrences of assertions concerning other religions, rather than any authoritative or comprehensive theological conception of the Church's

---

Abrahae coniungimur, maxime Hebraei, quibuscum sic agitur, ut non reprobentur neque iis diffidatur, sed ut erga eos reverentia et amor adhibeantur spesque in iis collocetur." AS IV/V, 563.

[9] Johannes Oesterreicher says: "Man kann kein wahrer Christ sein, wenn man die Juden, Christi Brüder und Schwestern dem Fleische nach, verachtet oder haßt, so besagt eine Botschaft des Dekrets." *Oesterreicher* 1964, 203.

For further studies on the Jewish-Catholic relationship, see *Lambert* 1964, *Bea* 1966a, *Lapide* 1967, *Cardinale* 1967, *Poncins* 1967, *Gilbert* 1968, *Oesterreicher* 1971, and *Lazar* 1978.

[10] *Graham* 1966, 658.

[11] *Nelson* 1966, 671.

relation to non-Christian religions. Consequently, the Council fathers had to exercise a capacity of theological initiative in creating the NA declaration, because they could not lean much on tradition.[12]

---

[12] There is only one reference to Catholic tradition in NA: note 5 refers to the polite letter of Pope Gregory VII to the Muslim king Anazir of Mauritania (from the year 1046). As positive documentation, the Council text might have referred to the beautiful treatment of Jews and Christ's death given in the Catechism of the Council of Trent for parish priests, published by the order of Pope Pius V in 1566. For some reason, though conscious of the existence of the Catechism, the creators of the document failed to mention it.

4. THE UNITY OF MANKIND

4.1. The Progress of Humanity

The idea of the progress of the cultural and social life of humanity is a theme very central in the papal addresses before and during the Second Vatican Council. In his encyclical letter *Mater et magistra* (May 15, 1961) Pope *John XXIII* developed a theme of *rationum socialium progressio*. The idea of modern progress of human life includes social, economic, scientific, and cultural evolution. Pope John evaluates modern developments as being beneficial to all mankind.[1] The paradigm of development was a theme also in Pope John's opening address in the First Public Session of the Second Vatican Council on October 11, 1962, when he expressed the Church's wish to contribute to human progress.[2]

In his first address to the Council, Pope *Paul VI* continued the line of his predecessor by speaking about the Church's task to serve the progress of humanity. In the Second Public Session on September 29, 1963, he uttered the opinion that the Church will by all means serve and contribute to the development of the modern world.[3] In his encyclical letter of 1964, *Ecclesiam Suam*, Paul affirmed the loyalty to and support of the Catholic Church in relation to changes in all spheres of human life. Such changes affect not only the external condition of life, but even the "inclinations of

---

[1] "Nemo sane dubitat, quin ex huiusmodi rationum socialium progressione complura proficiscantur commoda atque utilitates." AAS 1961, 416. "Rerum temporumque progressio magis magisque illud ostendit, ad iustitiae aequitatisque normas revocandas esse, non solum necessitudines inter opifices et moderatores societatum bonis pariendis, verum etiam rationes, quibus inter se coniungantur oportet simul varia rerum oeconomicarum genera, variaeque regiones aliae aliter ditatae, in una eademque natione; simul, in universa hominum communitate, plures variaeque nationes, quae in rebus oeconomicis et socialibus non uno modo profecerunt." Ibid., 431.

[2] "Hac de causa Ecclesia mirandis illis humani ingenii inventis doctrinarumque incrementis, quibus hodie utimur, non iners affuit, neque iisdem recte aestimandis impar evasit; sed haec omnia pervigili prosequens cura, homine admonere non desinit, ut super ipsam rerum aspectabilium speciem, oculos ad Deum omnis sapientiae et pulchritudinis fontem convertant - -" AS I/I, 171.

[3] "Probe noverit mundus se peramanter ab Ecclesia aspici, quae in ipsum sincera fertur admiratione sinceroque proposito movetur, non ei dominandi, sed serviendi, non eum contemnendi, sed dignitatem ipsius augendi, non eum damnandi, sed solacium et salutem ei afferendi." AS II/I, 197.

the souls" of men; and will inevitably affect the Church's life "like the waves of the sea."[4] In his address in the final Public Session of the Council, on December 7, 1965, Pope Paul revealed that it had been the intention of the Council deliberately to be optimistic concerning modern man.[5] The Catholic Church is seen as "the servant of the human race," serving mankind by contributing to the perfection of its good efforts (AS IV/VII, 660).

The *Nostra aetate* declaration is framed within a theological concept of the development of unity within mankind. The very opening sentence of NA contains the idea of men drawing more closely together, with the bonds of friendship being strengthened between different peoples. This unity is called the motivation for a closer examination of the Church's relation to non-Christian religions:

> Nostra aetate, in qua genus humanum in dies arctius unitur et necessitudine inter varios populos augentur, Ecclesia attentius considerat quae sit sua habitudo ad religiones non-christianas. (NA 1, 1.)
>
> (In this age of ours, when men are drawing more closely together and the bonds of friendship between different peoples are being strengthened, the Church examines with greater care the relation which she has to non-Christian religions.)

The idea of the progress of mankind in general and of the development of the unity of mankind in particular are an essential part of the theological thought in the Council documents. Yet, from Text I and Text II concerning Jews and non-Christians, the theme of the progress of human social and cultural life was still absent. The theme was instead consistently adopted into Text III, the revised draft declaration of November 1964. This theme was maintained and even confirmed with an additional sentence in the final form of the text (see below). In this respect, the history of the text is to be understood in the context of some of the main lines of Conciliar thought; the larger grew the document on Jews and non-Christians, the more it was connected with the major theological themes of the Council.

---

[4] "At pariter constat, humanam communitatem, quae hodie est, ad conversiones, perturbationes rerumque progressum procedere, quae non solum externas vitae consuetudines, sed ipsas etiam animorum inclinationes magnopere immutant. Hominum opiniones, eorumque mentis cultura ac spiritualis vita penitus afficiuntur sive magnis incrementis, quae multarum rerum scientia, technicorum artes et socialis vita sumpserunt, sive philosophiis, sive variis de moderantis republica doctrinis, quae in societate circumferuntur eamque pervadunt. Haec omnia veluti maris fluctus Ecclesiam ipsam obvolvunt et commovent." AAS 1964, 617-618.

[5] "Verum id est aperte fatendum, nostrum hoc Concilium, cum suum fecerit de homine iudicium, magis in serena hac eius fronte quam in tristi contuenda esse versatum; in quo quidem res omnes in optimam sane partem scienter esse interpretatum." AS IV/VII, 659.

The idea of human evolution is especially apparent in the pastoral constitution *Gaudium et spes*, and we must turn to that in order to understand Conciliar thinking on development. The constitution speaks of "profound and rapid changes" (GS 4, 2) and of "profound transformations" (GS 73, 1) that are taking place in human institutions, resulting in beneficial cultural, economic, and social development.[6] The Council appraises positively these changes which are taking place in the modern world; human development is profitable to all human beings and it also benefits the Church.[7] As a visible social structure, the Church has been enriched by the general evolution of social life (GS 44, 3).

The pastoral constitution confirms the permanent and universal validity of natural moral law with a declaration which expresses faith in the positive recognition of this law in today's world: "the conscience of mankind firmly and ever more emphatically proclaims" the principles of natural moral law.[8] The fathers of the Council believe in the positive implementation of natural moral law in modern social evolution, granted by the Creator of all peoples. Despite of the ever more apparent problems of the world, there exist seeds of good social evolution. The most evident positive element of modern "social dynamism" is the various forms of the progress towards unity (evolutio versus unitatem) in mankind.[9] In the pastoral constitution, the idea of social unification is seen as a matter of the utmost importance to mankind today. Social dynamism leading to the dependence of peoples on each other is the decisive factor changing the human world in modern times.[10]

The paradigmatic thought of the growing unity of mankind is also clearly discernable in the declaration *Dignitatis humanae*, where the sense of unity crosses the borders of cultures and even religions.[11] The paradigm of movement and change in mankind is also discernable in the *Ad gentes* decree. A "profound transformation which is taking place among nations" is

---

[6] "Nostris temporibus profundae advertuntur transformationes etiam in compagne et institutionibus populorum, quae ipsorum evolutionem culturalem, oeconomicam ac socialem consequuntur." GS 73, 1.

[7] "- - ipsa Ecclesia non ignorat, quantum ex humani generis historia et evolutione acceperit." GS 44, 1.

[8] "Deiectum istum humanitatis statum prae oculis habens, Concilium ante omnia in memoriam revocare intendit permanentem vim iuris naturalis gentium eiusque principiorum universalium. Ipsa generis humani conscientia haec principia firmiter magis magisque proclamat." GS 79, 2.

[9] "Ecclesia insuper agnoscit quidquid boni in dynamismo sociali hodierno invenitur: praesertim evolutionem versus unitatem, processum sanae socializationis et consociationis civilis et oeconomicae." GS 42, 3.

[10] "Quod vero hominibus magis in dies ab invicem dependentibus atque mundo magis in dies unificato maximi comprobatur esse momenti." GS 24, 2.

[11] "Manifestum est enim cunctas gentes magis in dies unum fieri, homines diversae culturae et religionis arctioribus inter se devinciri rationibus, augeri denique conscientiam propriae cuiusque responsabilitatis." DH 15, 4.

taken for granted (AG 11, 2). When giving advice to various institutions and individuals involved in the missionary task of the Church, the decree presupposes an idea of *progressus culturalis* or *progressus gentis* (AG 17, 2 & 21, 2).

The Council fathers do, indeed, trust in the ever-increasing sense of unity of the world and understand this unity to result in a clarification of natural moral law. The Church tries not to escape from modern challenges by protecting herself from the changes that are taking place in the world; in contrast, the classical notion of natural moral law is newly interpreted in accordance with the modern paradigm of development. For example, an intensified consciousness of human rights demonstrates positive evolution. The Church which proclaims the rights of men (iura hominum) "acknowledges and holds in high esteem the dynamic approach of today (hodierni temporis dynamismus) which is fostering these rights all over the world." The Church warmly welcomes this kind of dynamism and intends to "animate it by the spirit of the gospel." (GS 41, 3.) Modern social evolution is fully in accordance with the Catholic doctrine, states the Council.

The second sentence of NA declares that it is a special duty of the Church to foster the unity of mankind, fellowship among individuals and nations. All of this is firmly rooted in the natural moral law created by God. This particular sentence, intensifying the Church's mission in promoting the unity of mankind, was still missing from Text III in November 1964, and was added by the Secretariat to the text presented in the 149th General Congregation, October 14, 1965:

> In suo munere unitatem et caritatem inter homines, immo et inter gentes, fovendi, ea imprimis hic considerat quae hominibus sunt communia et ad mutuum consortium ducunt. (NA 1, 1.)
> (Ever aware of her duty to foster unity and charity among individuals, and even among nations, she reflects at the outset on what men have in common and what tends to promote fellowship among them.)

The final form of the declaration on the non-Christian religions, *Nostra aetate*, was created emphatically to express the idea of man's social development toward unity. The concept of unity is fully in accordance with the deepest theological intensions of the Catholic faith. The Holy Trinity himself is a model of unity between the three divine persons. Moreover, God created man to live in union with him, and Christ reconciled the fallen mankind in order to re-establish the union between God and man, and also in order to foster the integrity of the whole creation. God's Holy Spirit, using the means of grace, brings about divine grace and creates an intimate union of faith and love between man and the Triune God. Perfect unity with God will be the consummation of the Christian eschatological hope. Connected with these doctrines of God, creation, redemption, as well as soteriology and eschatology, Catholic moral theology contains a strong element of unity: the essence of Christian morality is love, and love is very much the same as a union of love among men.

The concept of unity belongs to the very essence of the Christian faith, and the idea of the natural created unity of all men is the fundamental basis for the Catholic doctrine of non-Christian religions as well. Before going into a deeper theological analysis of the substance of this doctrine, it is worth noting how the document ends with the same kind of theology, introducing the theme of *dignitas humana*. The growing recognition of human rights is connected with the recognition of human dignity.

4.2. Human Dignity and the Fraternity of All Men

The idea of defending "the sacred dignity of the human person" was a major theme in Pope *John*'s encyclical letter *Mater et magistra* of May 15, 1961.[12] The same line of argumentation was affirmed in his *Pacem in terris* of April 11, 1963. He makes the theological defense of *dignitas humanae personae* a theme of his letter.[13] The growing sense of human dignity in the world shall contribute to "the common good of all nations" (AAS 1963, 293). In developing his theme, Pope John frequently refers to the teaching of his predecessor Pope *Pius XII* who held views still relevant in the 1960's (see ibid., 260-267). Pope *Paul VI* consistently has carried forward his predecessor's aims in *Ecclesiam Suam* of August 6, 1964. The increasing "education of mind" and "exercise of conscience" inevitably strengthen the general consciousness of human dignity.[14]

---

[12] "E gravissimo huiusmodi principio, quo sacra humanae personae dignitas affirmatur et defenditur, praesertim superioribus hisce annis, Ecclesia sancta, sacerdotibus et laicis hominibus doctissimis operam ferentibus, luculente conclusit de re sociale praecepta, ad quae mutuae hominum necessitudines componantur - -" AAS 1961, 453.

[13] "Quodsi humanae personae dignitatem ex veritatibus divinitus traditis intuemur, tunc fieri non potest quin eam longe maiorem aestimemus; quippe homines sanguine Christi Iesu redempti sunt, superna gratia filii et amici Dei sunt facti, aeternae gloriae instituti heredes sunt." AAS 1963, 259.

[14] "Immo si haec educatio apte coniunctam habeat illam mentis conformationem, quae homo veritatem detegit ubi ea in rebus ipsis sane continetur, fieri etiam potest, ut ex hac inspiciendae conscientiae exercitatione quis possit se ipsum, suam ut hominis dignitatem, suasque ingenii vires agendique facultates magis magisque cognoscere." AAS 1964, 619.

The last paragraph of the declaration (NA 5) points to the firm foundation of human dignity and human rights (humana dignitas et iura) in the theology of creation. The historical background of the birth of the document is also clearly discernable there. The Church reproves (reprobat) all discrimination, in this statement being motivated, above all, by the need to judge all forms of anti-Semitism. Although this concept of discrimination was still missing from Text I, the Council's clearly critical attitude towards all forms of discrimination and violation of human dignity was introduced in Text II, which was presented and debated in the Council on September 28th and 29th, 1964. This element in the draft was unanimously accepted and remained virtually unchanged:

> Nequimus vero Deum omnium Patrem invocare, si erga quosdam homines, ad imaginem Dei creatos, fraterne nos gerere renuimus. Habitudo hominis ad Deum Patrem et habitudo hominis ad homines fratres adeo connectuntur, ut Scriptura dicat: 'qui non diligit, non novit Deum' (1 Io. 4, 8). Fundamentum ergo tollitur omni theoriae vel praxi quae inter hominem et hominem, inter gentem et gentem, discrimen quoad humanam dignitatem et iura exinde dimanantia inducit. Ecclesia igitur quamvis hominum discriminationem aut vexationem stripis vel coloris, condicionis vel religionis causa factam tamquam a Christi mente alienam reprobat. (NA 5, 1-3.)[15]
>
> (We cannot truly pray to God the Father of all if we treat any people in other than brotherly fashion, for all men are created in God's image. Man's relation to God the Father and man's relation to his fellow-men are so dependent on each other that the Scripture says 'he who does not love, does not know God' [1 Jn. 4:8]. There is no basis therefore, either in theory or in practice for any discrimination between individual and individual, or between people and people arising either from human dignity or from the rights which flow from it. Therefore, the Church reproves, as foreign to the mind of Christ, any discrimination against people or any harassment of them on the basis of their race, color, condition in life, or religion.)

In the text above, the brotherhood of all people is argued, irrespective of their race, colour, religion, or other conditions of life. There are two foundations for this: God is *omnium Pater*, and all human beings are created as *imago Dei*. This text obliges Christians to treat all men *fraterne* and to regard them as *homines fratres*. And moreover, for a Christian, treating other men with respect and love is a condition for his own relationship with God: if there is no love toward others, it is a sign that no relation of love with God exists.

---

[15] The version of Text II saw fraternal love as a basic motivation for valuing adherents of non-Christian religions: "Hac caritate erga fratres nostros compulsi, magna cum observantia consideramus opiniones et doctrinas - -" Text II, AS III/II, 329.

The theme of the brotherhood of all men, missing from Text I, was expressed at its strongest in Text II, as a section on non-Christian religions to be included in the ecumenism decree. In Text II it was forcefully introduced; Text II, with extensive biblical reference as well as rational evidence as support, declares the principle of *humana fraternitas*; he who denies the fraternity of all men, in fact denies God himself.[16] The same draft explicitly appealed to both biblical and rational evidence as support.[17] In his relatio of October 1965, Cardinal *Augustin Bea* noted that all the time the Secretariat quite intentionally meant to concentrate on that which unites men.[18]

Thus, in the draft of the declaration on Jews and non-Christian religions, the idea of brotherhood among Christians is enlarged into the general human principle of brotherhood. By so doing, the document lays special emphasis on the importance of a Christian's sincere search for unity in human matters, when encountering non-Christians. Basically, the idea of fraternity inspires exclusively Christian terminology in the Council documents, the terms *frater, fraterne, fraternitas* and *fraternus* being used in predominantly a clear Christian sense. Exceptions, however, occur: in a few places the idea of brotherhood is expanded and used as a concept for the theology of creation and is extended to cover the whole of mankind. The pastoral constitution speaks of the "vocation" of mankind to "form one family and deal with each other in a spirit of brotherhood," based on the "fatherly care" of the Creator and on the fact that all men are created in the likeness of God and called to the same end, to God himself. Thus the Council adheres to the principles of causality and finality, characteristic of Catholic theology – especially of Thomism.

Gaudium et spes is fully in accordance with NA 5 and clarifies the theme of the declaration on human fraternity.[19] Because God is the Father of all,

---

[16] This section was dropped from the later versions: "Ita enim arcte connectuntur habitudo hominis ad Deum Patrem et eiusdem habitudo hominis ad homines fratres, ut omnis negatio humanae fraternitatis negationem ipsius Dei, apud quem non est acceptio personarum (cf. 2 Par. 19, 7; Rom. 2, 11; Eph. 6, 9; Col. 3, 25; 1 Petr. 1, 17), secumferat vel ad eam ducat. Nam prius mandatum cum altero ita coalescit, ut nobis nequeant dimitti debita nostra, nisi nosmetipsi ex corde debitoribus nostris dimittamus. Iamvero in Lege Veteri dicitur: 'Numquid non Pater unus omnium nostrum? numquid non Deus unus creavit nos? quare ergo despicit unusquisque nostrum fratrem suum?' (Mal. 2, 10); idque in Nova Lege clarius affirmatur: 'Qui non diligit fratrem suum quem videt, Deum quem non videt quomodo potest diligere? Et hoc mandatum habemus a Deo ut qui diligit Deum diligat et fratrem suum' (1 Io. 4, 20-21)." Text II, AS III/II, 328-329.

[17] The sentence later dropped ran: "Dominus Iesus omnium hominum Patrem esse Deum, sicut iam Scripturae Veteris Testamenti statuunt et ipsa innuit ratio, luculenter confirmavit." Text II, AS III/II, 328.

[18] "Igitur magis attenditur ad ea quae homines coniungunt et ad mutuum consortium ducunt." AS IV/IV, 722.

[19] "Deus, qui paternam curam omnium habet, voluit ut cuncti homines unam efficerent

all men have a high divine vocation to belong to his people, the Church of
Christ, through which God himself purifies and perfects created nature
which has been vitiated by sin. This divine vocation is, however, in no way
contrary to the human vocation of each man; on the contrary, it purifies and
strengthens all the good qualities and pursuits of human beings. Above all,
the most profound vocation of men is universal brotherhood, which exists
on the basis of *humana et divina vocatio*.[20] The decree on the Church's
missionary activity, *Ad gentes*, declares that *fraterna concordia* of all men
is a part of God's plan of salvation in Christ and, consequently, is a part of
the Church's mission. And this "answers a profound longing in all men;"
i.e., the explicit work of salvation is in accordance with the natural
inclination of human beings to seek the truth in human life. The people of
God, the Church, expresses and promotes brotherly fellowship among all
men, a fellowship which brings about the realization of the created nature
of human beings as the image of God.[21]

The idea of *dignitas humana* appears in NA in the previously quoted
place (NA 5, 2). It occurs as well in AG 12, where the missionary work of
the Church is seen as a way *ad elevandam dignitatem humanam* (AG 12,
2). When teaching "the religious and moral truths, which Christ illumined
with his light," the disciples of Christ "seek to enhance the dignity of men
and promote fraternal unity" (eorum dignitatem et fraternam unionem
promovent; AG 12, 4). The concept also appears in GS, but most essential
it is for the declaration on religious liberty, *Dignitatis humanae*. This
declaration on religious liberty begins with a statement expressing faith in
the growing sense of human dignity in the modern evolution of social life:
"Contemporary man is becoming increasingly conscious of the dignity of
the human person."[22] By this statement the Council confirms the permanent
validity of natural moral law, given by the Creator of all. Granted that the
idea of human dignity is indeed recognized by conscience or by reason, at
the same time, this God-created reality of human life is further illumined

---

familiam fraternoque animo se invicem tractarent. Omnes enim creati ad imaginem Dei, qui fecit
'ex uno omne genus hominum inhabitare super universam faciem terrae' (Act. 17, 26), ad unum
eundem finem, id est ad Deum ipsum, vocantur." GS 24, 1.

[20] "Cum Deus Pater principium omnium existat et finis, omnes, ut fratres simus, vocamur. Et
ideo, hac eadem humana et divina vocatione vocati, sine violentia, sine dolo ad aedificandum
mundum in vera pace cooperati possumus et debemus." GS 92, 5.

[21] "- - quod sane, cum fraternam concordiam refert, intimo universorum hominum voto respondet.
Sic tandem consilium Creatoris, hominem ad imaginem et similitudinem suam condentis, revera
adimpletur, cum omnes qui humanam participant naturam, in Christo per Spiritum Sanctum
regenerati, unanimiter gloriam Dei speculantes, dicere poterunt: 'Pater noster'." AG 7, 3.

[22] "Dignitatis humanae personae homines hac nostra aetate magis in dies conscii fiunt, atque
numerus eorum crescit qui exigunt, ut in agendo homines proprio suo consilio et libertate
responsabili fruantur et utantur, non coercitione commoti, sed officii conscientia ducti." DH 1, 1.

and strengthened by the explicit divine revelation in Christ, "the very dignity of the human person is known through the revealed word of God and by reason itself." (DH 2, 1.)

Nature and grace, i.e., man's natural knowledge of the truths of the Creator, and the will of God revealed in his specific revelation of grace, belong together. As every human being has a double vocation, correspondingly human and divine, the value and dignity of human life is recognized on the basis both of natural moral law through reason and of Christ-centred revelation through faith. It is important to notice how the paradigm of the development of human social life works here: the demands of the dignity of the person "have become more fully known to human reason through centuries of experience."[23]

---

[23] When speaking of the theological foundation of religious freedom, the Council declares: "Quae de iure hominis ad libertatem religiosam declarat haec Vaticana Synodus, fundamentum habent in dignitate personae, cuius exigentiae rationi humanae plenius innotuerunt per saeculorum experientiam. Immo haec doctrina de libertate radices habet in divina Revelatione, quapropter eo magis a Christianis sancte servanda est." DH 9, 1.

5. RELIGIOUS OR MORAL TRUTH IN RELIGIONS?

The irenism concerning the Church's statements about her relation to the world, already recognizable in *John XXIII's Mater et magistra*, continues in the documents of the Council. The old terminology for pagan religions and their errors seems to be totally omitted from the documents of the Council.[1] When addressing the non-Christian religions, the opening paragraph of *Nostra aetate* employs two important tems, *religio* and *gens*. As for *religio*, it is important to note that the Council uses the concept of religion both in the sense of *religio christiana* and of *religio non-christiana*. The dogmatic constitution on the Church, *Lumen gentium*, is especially clear as to the positive use of *religio christiana*. The decree on missionary activity, *Ad gentes*, consistently uses both expressions, *religio christiana* and *religio non-christiana*. It seems that, on the level of terminology, the Council intends to see all religions as equal. All religions can be discussed seriously and with respect.

The respectful expressions *religio* and *gens* are normally used when speaking of the non-Christians. *Gens* is almost equivalent to *populus*. There is no counter-position between the Christians and the *gentes*; the only counter-position is the biblical distinction between *Iudaei et gentes* (see NA 4, 2; LG 6, 3 & 9, 1, e.g.). Thus *gentes* do not mean non-Christians but non-Jews. The word has the meaning of people in general as well as the meaning of all other people except the Jews. The Council, therefore, when speaking of the religions of the world, introduced a totally new atmosphere of respect and recognition.

5.1. Unity in Terms of Creation and in Terms of Teleology

The NA declaration begins a closer examination of the religions of the world by defining what is common to all people (omnes gentes):

---

[1] It is remarkable that the term *paganus* or its derivatives do not appear in the Council documents at all. Neither does the adjectival form *gentilis* occur. The term *idolatria* appears in the documents only once (AA 7, 3), and even then not in regard to non-Christian religions but when speaking of "an immoderate trust in the conquests of science and technology" which may "turn into a kind of idolatry of the temporal."

> Una enim communitas sunt omnes gentes, unam habent originem, cum Deus omne genus hominum inhabitare fecerit super universam faciem terrae, unum etiam habent finem ultimum, Deum cuius providentia ac bonitatis testimonium et consilia salutis ad omnes se extendunt, donec uniantur electi in Civitate Sancta, quam claritas Dei illuminabit, ubi gentes ambulabunt in lumine eius. (NA 1, 2.)

> (All men form but one community. This is so because all stem from the one stock which God created to people the entire earth, and also because all share a common destiny, namely God. His providence, evident goodness, and saving designs extend to all men against the day when the elect are gathered together in the Holy City which is illumined by the glory of God, and in whose splendor all peoples will walk.)

All peoples and all men have a common origin, because all are created by God. On the basis of this, all human beings live in the sphere of the Creator's providence and enjoy the goodness of created things. This is the fundamental locus of the theology of creation. But, in addition to this, God himself is the *finis ultimus* of all men, even though they may not be aware of it.[2] Through his *consilia salutis*, God offers the possibility of salvation and of citizenship in the eschatological Holy City. This is the fundamental soteriological-eschatological fact which is common to all men.

But there is a certain important difference between these two fundamental theological aspects which unite all human beings. The life of all is based on the fact of creation and providence. But the ultimate soteriological-eschatological destiny concerns only the elected (electi), those who have received God's offer of salvation through supernatural divine revelation and through the media of supernatural grace. So from the very beginning of the NA declaration, there seems to exist a certain duality of thought: on the one hand, all men live in the sphere of God's good creation; on the other hand, the means of salvation are extended to all, but reach their fulfillment only in the elected. However, it is important to note that the document does not, at least at this point, further define those who are elected. Irrespective of religion, anyone could be such one.

A similar idea of the duality of factors uniting mankind, or the double vocation of all human beings, is put forward clearly in the pastoral constitution *Gaudium et spes*. "All men are endowed with a rational soul and are created in God's image; they have the same nature and origin and, being redeemed by Christ, they enjoy the same divine calling and destiny."[3]

---

2   GS employs the word combination *finis ultimus* in a soteriologial sense: God as the ultimate destiny of man (GS 13, 1), and *mysterium Dei*, proclaimed by the Church, as *ultimus finis hominis* (GS 41, 1). The word pair is used without a soteriological notion in AA 7, 2 and GE 1, 1.

3   "Cum omnes homines, anima rationali pollentes et ad imaginem Dei creati, eadem naturam

On the basis of the theology of creation, the constitution emphasizes the common rational nature of all men, created in God's image. In addition to this common origin of creation, the document emphasizes the classical notion of *gratia universalis* in the sense of the soteriological or divine vocation of men: all human beings are redeemed by Christ and, therefore, enjoy the same divine calling and destiny. Conciliar theology is consistent with the principles of causality and finality; the first aspect is the fundamental fact of existence, the second aspect is a call (vocatio) which may become a reality in the life of any person.

In another context, the pastoral constitution emphasizes natural moral law as the factor common to all human beings. Adhering to the basic principle of *Thomas Aquinas'* teaching of moral law, the document says: "Deep within his conscience man discovers a law which he has not laid upon himself but which he must obey. Its voice, ever calling him to love and to do what is good and to avoid evil, tells him inwardly at the right moment: do this, shun that."[4] This is the law which God has inscribed in the heart of every human being. Conscience is "man's most secret core, and his sanctuary" where "he is alone with God whose voice echoes in his depths."[5] Through conscience Christians are joined to all other men, as the document concludes: "Through loyalty to conscience Christians are joined to other men in the search for truth and for the right solution to so many moral problems which arise both in the life of individuals and from social relationships." (GS 16,1.)

As these references to GS indicate, the voice of the Creator in the depth of human conscience is not limited to strictly moral questions, but conscience also touches the questions of religious truth. On the basis of creation and the Creator's voice in his conscience, every human being is also involved in the search for the religious truth; *notitia Dei* are discernable in all of creation. The missionary decree affirms that there are "elements of truth and grace" among all peoples; this is based on "the secret presence of God" in all his creation. (AG 9,2.) The decree expresses the classical idea

---

eamdemque originem habeant, cumque, a Christo redempti, eadem vocatione et destinatione divina fruantur - -" GS 29, 1.

[4] "In imo conscientiae legem homo detegit, quam ipse sibi non dat, sed cui odoedire debet, et cuius vox, semper ad bonum amandum et faciendum ac malum vitandum eum advocans, ubi oportet auribus cordis sonat: fac hoc, illud devita." GS 16, 1.

On the Catholic concept of natural moral law, see *Sertillanges* 1947, *Leclercq* 1955, *Armstrong* 1966, and *O'Connor* 1967. Cf. discussion on Thomism above in 2.1.

[5] "Nam homo legem in corde suo a Deo inscriptam habet, cui parere ipsa dignitas eius est et secundum quam ipse iudicabitur. Conscientia est nucleus secretissimus atque sacrarium hominis, in quo solus est cum Deo, cuius vox resonat in intimo eius." GS 16,1. Here the text refers to the classical biblical support, Rom. 2:14-16.

of God's *gratia creata sive communis*, recognized in the Patristic period: even the very fact of existence is an act of God's creative grace.

This line of thought becomes an explicit theme in the declaration *Dignitatis humanae*. Created by God, man is naturally a religious being, orientated to seeking a relationship to his Creator. Man's inclination to religion springs from the created goodness of nature.[6] In the same context, the DH declaration defines with special emphasis how man's religious inclination is firmly grounded in *lex divina, aeterna, obiectiva atque universalis*. The document states that, due to divine providence, man is able to progress in his knowledge of eternal religious truth.[7] In this context, no specific means of divine revelation or grace are presupposed – progress in the knowledge of the truth of religion takes place solely on the basis of natural cognition of God and natural moral law, both written by the Creator upon the rational conscience of man.

Man's inclination to religion grows out of the created goodness of nature. Man cannot avoid seeking the religious truth of existence; such an orientation towards religion is a part of his objective constitution as God's creature. According to NA 1, 2, this inclination witnesses to not merely the fact that all men are created by the same God, but also to the fact that all men meet the same final end. In the very humanity of every man there is a teleological orientation to seek participation in divine life. This destiny for eternal felicity becomes fulfilled through the *media salutis* present in the Church. Thus the Conciliar teaching places its understanding of the unity of mankind, expressed in man's universal search for religious truth, within the classical intellectual framework of both causality and finality (teleology), combined with a theory of perfection or fulfillment.

5.2. The Primacy of the Revealed Truth

Exploration of the duality of the factors which unite all men, Christians and non-Christians, proceeds further in NA 2, 2. The declaration appears to presume that in non-Christian religions not only moral but even some kind of religious truth exists:

---

6 "Secundum dignitatem suam homines cuncti, quia personae sunt, ratione scilicet et libera voluntate praediti ideoque personali responsabilitate aucti, sua ipsorum natura impelluntur necnon morali tenentur obligatione ad veritatem quaerendam, illam imprimis quae religionem spectat." DH 2, 2.

7 "Huius suae legis Deus hominem participem reddit, ita ut homo, providentia divina suaviter disponente, veritatem incommutabilem magis magisque agnoscere possit." DH 3, 1.

Ecclesia catholica nihil eorum, quae in his religionibus vera et sancta sunt, reicit. Sincera cum observantia considerat illos modos agendi et vivendi, illa praecepta et doctrinas, quae, quamvis ab iis quae ipsa tenet et proponit in multis descrepent, haud raro referunt tamen radium illius Veritatis, quae illuminat omnes homines. Annuntiat vero et annuntiare tenetur indesinenter Christum, qui est 'via, veritas et vita' (Io. 14, 6), in quo homines plenitudinem vitae religiosae inveniunt, in quo Deus omnia Sibi reconciliavit. (NA 2, 2.)

(The Catholic Church rejects nothing of what is true and holy in these religions. She has a high regard for the manner of life and conduct, the precepts and doctrines which, although differing in many ways from her own teaching, nevertheless often reflect a ray of that truth which enlightens all men. Yet she proclaims and is in duty bound to proclaim without fail, Christ who is 'the way, the truth, and the life' [Jn. 1:6]. In him, in whom God reconciled all things to himself, men find the fullness of their religious life.)

The relatio of NA in November 1964 explained the idea of "a ray of the truth" by referring to the Patristic theological tradition, especially *Irenaeus*, who, as we have already mentioned, has been quoted by many before.[8] The passage of NA quoted shows clearly that the Church recognizes "a ray of the truth" selectively on the basis of its own dogma, adding that the Catholic Church rejects nothing of what is true and holy in these religions.[9] Quite evidently, the use of term *sancta* implies a reference to the proper religious elements of non-Christian religions. The term pair *praecepta et doctrinas* includes both the moral and the religious aspects of truth. Text II of September 1964 used the term pair "opiniones et doctrinas" (Text II, AS III/II, 329). Later the ambiguous word "opiniones" was replaced by the more precise "praecepta." In the Council documents, the term *praeceptum* is used mainly with the mainly to mean moral precepts but also with the sense of the Christian doctrine. *Doctrina* is, of course, a term used to signify the proper content of the Christian religion.

Now NA 2, 2 declares that both the moral and other doctrinal contents of other religions may reflect a ray of the Christian truth: they "often reflect a ray of that truth (radium illius Veritatis) which enlightens all men." The term *radium* is a hapax legomenon in the Council documents; it appears only here in NA 2, 2. This speaks for the uniqueness of the present definition. But it is a definition which was employed with firmness in the early phase of drafting: Text II already expressed the same thought with the same words

---

8 "Hinc Ecclesia, secundum traditionem antiquam, cuius testis Irenaeus affertur, in diiudicandis religionibus et in practica relatione imprimis ea respicit, quae sunt falsa; in earum valoribus positivis veritatem agnoscit, quae ex Deo oritur, scl. radium luminis aeterni illuminantis omnes homines." AS III/VIII, 645-646.

9 Pope Paul VI expressed the idea of "a ray of the truth" very similarly in his Easter message on Italian radio, March 29, 1964. See AAS 1964, 394.

(Text II, AS III/II, 329). In this formula the Council fathers found a way of expressing their wish to say something positive about non-Christian religions. The term *veritas* referred to here is the Christian truth. This becomes clear in the following sentence which speaks about Christ as the truth. In the Council documents, *veritas* is a concept of the Christian truth; for instance: "Ipse Christus est veritas" (AG 8, 1). Christ himself is the embodiment of the truth, which is *veritas revelata* (LG 35, 4), *veritas catholica* (LG 25, 1), or *veritas evangelica* (NA 4, 6). The Christ-centred truth contains both religious and moral aspects: "veritates religiosas et morales quas Christus luce sua illustravit" (AG 12, 4). The Council documents employ the term *veritas* only twice to mean truth outside the revealed Christian religion: in the quoted text of NA 2, 2 and in AG 9, 2.[10]

The dogmatic constitution *Lumen gentium* gives more light on the issue: it takes as granted that all the temporal moral good found in nations' cultures, habits, religions, and so forth can be accepted by the Church. The Church "does not take away anything from the temporal welfare of any people." "Rather she fosters and takes to herself, in so far as they are good, the abilities, the resources, and customs of peoples. In so taking them to herself she purifies, strengthens, and elevates them."[11] The Catholic Church accepts "whatever good is found sown in the minds and hearts of men or in the rites and customs of peoples; these not only are preserved from destruction, but purified, raised up, and perfected for the glory of God, the confusion of the Devil, and the happiness of man."[12] *Ad gentes* speaks of "the riches of nations," including their *sapientia et doctrina*, to be given to Christ as an inheritance. (AG 22, 1.) In this manner the Council manages a modern implementation of the classical principle: *gratia non tollit naturam, sed perficit.*

NA 2, 2 proves ambivalent in regard to how much truth non-Christian religions contain. Without hesitation, it admits that in respect to *modi agendi et vivendi*, i.e., in respect to natural moral law, there is much truth in religions. But in regard to the secret of the supernatural divine mystery, the document is much more reserved, although it seems quite evident that the Council sees some kind of religious truth, the hidden presence of divine

---

[10] "Quidquid autem veritatis et gratiae iam apud gentes quasi secreta Dei praesentia inveniebatur - - " AG 9, 2.

[11] "- - Ecclesia - - nihil bono temporali cuiusvis populi subtrahit, sed e contra facultates et copias moresque populorum, quantum bona sunt, fovet et assumit, assumendo vero purificat, roborat et elevat." LG 13, 2.

[12] "Itaque quidquid boni in corde menteque hominum vel in propriis ritibus et culturis populorum seminatum invenitur non tantum non perit, sed sanatur, elevatur et consummatur ad gloriam Dei, confusionem daemonis et beatitudinem hominis." The same wording is given in LG 17, 1 and in AG 9, 2.

grace, to be found even outside Christianity. A continuity seems to exist between non-Christian religions and the Christian truth. A possibility of the presence of God's saving grace in other religions thus seems not to be totally excluded. The section ends with an explicit reference to Christ as "the way, the truth, and the life." In him God reconciled all things to himself. Consequently, plenitudo vitae religiosae is to be found solely in Christ. This expression was added to the text of the declaration no earlier than in Text IV, which became the promulgated version. This addition can be seen as a concession to those who feared that the declaration on non-Christian religions would lead to indifferentism to the Church's missionary endeavour. The growth of the missionary motive is present in the subsequent paragraph (NA 2, 3): the expression "prudentia et caritate - - christianam testantes" was added to Text IV. (On the missionary motives, see below Ch. 9.) The pressure in the direction of traditionalism is also documented by the fact that an expression in Text III in NA 2, 2 regarding the Church being taught by "the various dispositions of salvation" (de variis salutis dispositionibus edocta; Text III, AS III/VIII, 638) was dropped from the later version.

The Council is inclined to support the paradigm of interpretation, according to which religions contain religious truth only insofar as they reflect something of the Christ-centred truth, or have some sort of reference to the truth revealed in Christianity, or at least seek that truth which became plain in Christ. If there is therefore to be any development in religions towards "the fullness of religious life," it must be a movement towards Christ and his truth fully revealed in Christianity. Non-Christian religions thus seem to have no independent status as to revelation of the divine mystery; their religious truth must be related to the truth of Christianity. This is a line of interpretation which is a consequent expression of the perfection or fulfillment theory so usual in pre-conciliar Catholic analysis of non-Christian religions.

In our further analysis we must ask: how much and what kind of religious truth does the Vatican Council see in non-Christian religions? There seems to exist some tension between two views os these religions: On the one hand, the Church admits that there is much good in regard to common human morals in religions. As was shown above, optimism in respect to the growing moral consciousness of mankind is a framework within which the declaration on the relation of the Church to non-Christian religions was given. On the other hand, the Church admits that religions may contain a seed of religious truth concerning the supernatural divine mystery of reconciliation, but the degree of truth seems to be tested by the explicit Christian revelation. What aspects of the proper religious substance of non-Christian religions can be seen as exponents of the divine truth? Is there a way of salvation or a way of uniting man with God through non-Christian religions?

6. RELIGIONS AS AN INHERENT PART OF HUMAN CULTURE

6.1. The Council's Definition of Religion

Next we shall have a closer look at what is meant by religion. The *Nostra aetate* declaration itself gives a definition of the substance of religion by describing those elements which are common to all religions:

> Homines a variis religionibus responsum exspectant de reconditis condicionis humanae aenigmatibus, quae sicut olim et hodie corda hominum intime commovent: quid sit homo, quis sensus et finis vitae nostrae, quid bonum et quid peccatum, quem ortum habeant dolores et quem finem, quae sit via ad veram felicitatem obtinendam, quid mors, iudicium et retributio post mortem, quid demum illud ultimum et ineffabile mysterium quod nostram existentiam amplectitur, ex quo ortum sumimus et quo tendimus. (NA 1, 3.)
>
> (Men look to their different religions for an answer to the unsolved riddles of human existence. The problems that weigh heavily on the hearts of men are the same today as in the ages past. What is man? What is the meaning and purpose of life? What is upright behaviour, and what is sinful? Where does suffering originate, and what end does it serve? How can a genuine happiness be found? What happens at death? What is judgment? What reward follows death? And finally, what is the ultimate mystery, beyond human explanation, which embraces our entire existence, from which we take our origin and towards which we tend?)

The passage was presented to the Council in this form in November 1964 (Text III); the only later addition was the clause about sufferings (quem ortum habeant dolores et quem finem). Religions of the world thus have as their proper function attempting to answer the *aenigmata*, the unsolved riddles of human existence, riddles which cannot be solved by developments in scientific knowledge, technology, or the growing sense of moral consciousness.[1] NA 1, 3

---

[1] In addition to NA, the idea of *aenigma* appears elsewhere in the Council documents. *Gaudium et spes* says that in regard to death, the riddle of man (aenigma condicionis humanae) is shrouded in doubt (GS 18, 1). Furthermore, the pastoral constitution speaks about "vitae et mortis, culpae et doloris aenigmata" which remain unsolved for men (GS 21, 3) and about "aenigma doloris et mortis" which is enlightened by Christ (GS 22, 6). The *Ad gentes* decree states that the Church knows "vitae adspirationes et aenigmata" (AG 12, 1).

gives a depiction of those unsolved riddles of human existence with which religions deal. In addition to religion's concentration on the riddle of suffering and death, it is a function of religion also to try to answer the questions of who man is and what is the meaning and purpose of his life.

The idea of religion expressed here is very much a Catholic one, featuring the notion of the linearity of human existence in time, including the classical Thomistic dimension of causality and teleology or finality, as central. In religion, asking the meaning of *finis vitae* is essential. Religion must deal with the classical teleological problem of the eudaemonistic drive of man: how can genuine happiness be found? Furthermore, religion also treats the questions of finality which possibly terrify man: what is death, judgement, and retribution after death? The idea of causality, as well, is presumed in the concept of religion. NA 2, 1 states that in religion man searches for the power which lies behind the linear occurrence of events (cursus rerum).

It is worth noting that in its definition of religion, NA 1, 3 does not emphasize the question concerning moral good. The only sentence which implies moral aspects is that in which religion is said to struggle with the question: "What is upright behaviour (bonum), and what is sinful (peccatum)?" But even this question can be understood more widely than as a statement merely concerning morals; *bonum* and *peccatum* are factors determining the quality of the whole existence of man, good expressing the goal of the eudaemonistic search of man, and sin the bondage which hinders man from gaining the blessedness. Thus we are justified in concluding that according to the definition of religion in NA 1, 3, the essence of religion is something other than ethics or morals. As we have seen, NA strongly emphasizes the positive validity of natural moral law which unites all men. But the truths of moral law can be discerned by means of reason and conscience even if a specific religious inclination is lacking. Religions, however, do have a function in the sphere of natural moral law, as we shall see in our later analysis.

The Conciliar understanding of the phenomenon of religion becomes increasingly clear as we turn to the final statement of the definition in NA 1, 3: religion asks what is the ultimate mystery (ultimum et ineffabile mysterium), beyond human explanation, which embraces our entire existence? Here, again, the concept of linearity, in terms of causality and teleology, is present: it a mystery "from which we take our origin and towards which we tend." The idea of *mysterium* is very frequent in the Council documents. Twice in NA the term appears in a context involving truths other than the mystery of the Christian religion, once in the place quoted above and once in NA 2, 1 which states that "in Hinduism men explore the divine mystery." In all other cases in the documents of the Council, the term *mysterium* is used to mean the mystery of the true, i.e.,

Christian, religion. Above all, *mysterium Christi*, *mysterium salutis* and *mysterium Ecclesiae* are signified by "divine mystery". Even NA employs these common usages by speaking of *mysterium Ecclesiae* and *salutare Dei mysterium* in NA 4, 1. The adaptation of the idea of mystery into the definition of religion shows again how religion is understood in the classical category of the Catholic faith.

The following section of *Nostra aetate*, NA 2, 1, goes into an even deeper explanation of the foundation on which religions try to base answers to the profound questions and problems of human existence. This clarification reveals further how the nature of religion is understood by the Council:

> Iam ab antiquo usque ad tempus hodiernum apud diversas gentes invenitur quaedam perceptio illius arcanae virtutis, quae cursui rerum et eventibus vitae humanae praesens est, immo aliquando agnitio Summi Numinis vel etiam Patris. Quae perceptio atque agnitio vitam earum intimo sensu religioso penetrant. Religiones vero cum progressu culturae connexae subtilioribus notionibus et lingua magis exculta ad easdem quaestiones respondere satagunt. (NA 2, 1.)
>
> (Throughout history even to the present day, there is found among different peoples a certain awareness of a hidden power, which lies behind the course of nature and the events of human life. At times there is present even a recognition of a Supreme Being, or still more of a Father. This awareness and recognition results in a way of life that is imbued with a deep religious sense. The religions which are found in more advanced civilizations endeavour by way of well-defined concepts and exact language to answer these questions.)

There is no mention of the possible errors or fallacies in religions. In accordance with the fulfillment or perfection theory, the non-Christian religions of the world are seen as less perfect manifestations of the same truth which has become fully known in Christianity, meaning that there is a seed of truth in religions. Here we again see how religion is understood on the basis of a Christian *Vorverständnis*: Some religions have a certain awareness of the *prima causa* "which lies behind the course of nature and the events of human life;" here religions are measured by the western linear scopus of causality and finality.

More developed religions recognize the existence of a supreme being or a personal God or even of the Father (aliquando agnitio Summi Numinis vel etiam Patris).[2] The monotheistic idea of one personal God is presumed in the Council's thought about religion. The closer the concept of divinity is to the Christian view, the more developed is considered the religion in

---

[2]   In the documents of the Council, the idea of *Numen* appears only in NA 2, 2 and in DH 4, 2 where religion is defined as *cultus Numinis supremi*.

question. A further positive point of connection is seen in the sphere of the mystical dimension of religion: the awareness of God results in a life characterized by *intimus sensus religiosus*. Here the declaration recognizes the non-cognitive or the mystical elements of non-Christian religions; such a recognition is a logical consequence from the high esteem of the tradition of Christian mysticism.

The NA 2, 1 text seems to arrange religions into an order of rank: religions found in "more advanced civilizations" have developed an "exact language" with "well-defined concepts" to ask and to answer the profound questions of life. It seems that the Council values especially religions with a long literary tradition, i.e., religions which are similar to the Judeo-Christian tradition. The Council seems to rank the great world religions higher than it does any other religious phenomena of human life. The missionary decree notes that, of the population of the world, "some belong to one or other of the great religions (magnis religionibus), others have no knowledge of God." (AG 10, 1.) After a further analysis of NA 2, 1, we shall in Ch. 7. come back to the question of ranking religions.

6.2. Religions without Revelation

It is important to observe that NA 2, 1 quoted above does not use the concept of revelation (revelatio) at all. Theologically speaking, the general recognition of the supreme being or God does not belong to the sphere of revelation, it is a matter of the general cognition of God through reason. Astoundingly, the dogmatic constitution on revelation, *Dei verbum*, does not recognize any category of "general revelation." The concept of *revelatio* is absent except in regard to the explicit events and documents of salvation history, the history of Israel and of Christ and, correspondingly, of the Old and the New Testaments. Any idea of applying the concept of revelation to any instance outside Christianity is totally missing in the Council documents. When speaking of revelation, in all its documents the Council always means *revelatio divina* in the sense of *revelatio Veteris Testamenti* or *revelatio christiana*. In fact, the constitution on revelation offers nothing new about the natural knowledge of God; in this respect, the document only quotes the statement of the First Vatican Council about the natural recognition of God by reason through analogy in created nature. In the same context, the constitution refers to the classical biblical support, Rom. 1:20.[3]

---

[3] "Confitetur Sacra Synodus, 'Deum, rerum omnium principium et finem, naturali humanae rationis lumine e rebus creatis certo cognosci posse' (cf. Rom. 1, 20)." DV 6, 2. See DS 3004.

There is, in fact, no need to call the natural recognition of God "revelation," because the seeds of God's presence are perceived in all creation. That the providential influence of the Creator is present in all created beings and things can be grasped by human reason. Nothing specially religious is needed for that accomplishment. *Dei verbum*'s making no reference to non-Christian religions appears to be an expression of indifference in regard to religions as possible means of revelation. In other words, religions are neither a hindrance nor an advantage in regard to the natural cognition of God.

If there is no revelation in non-Christian religions, are all the notions of God to be understood solely in terms of the general cognition of the Creator? If so, the proper religious essence of any non-Christian religion, i.e., the attempt to solve the riddle of the *ultimum et ineffabile mysterium* of life, would have no independent value in itself. The highest criterion for evaluating any religious phenomenon would be man's rational consciousness of God and of natural moral law. The Council documents revere above all monotheistic features and moral values of a non-Christian religion. If, however, the idea of monotheism is understood mainly in the category of natural consciousness of God through reason, the proper religious value of any religion's expression of monotheistic ideas is radically lessened.

The process of evaluating religions primarily based upon the criterion of their search for the one true God and of their moral values was emphatically present in the first draft of the declaration on Jews and non-Christians.[4] The fact that the Catholic Church acknowledges above all the monotheistic features and the moral good contained in non-Christian religions becomes clear in some papal addresses, as well. In his address in the Second Public Session (September 29, 1963), Pope *Paul VI* said that the Catholic Church appreciates above all those religions which have a notion of the one Creator and which have organized their rituals and moral teachings in accordance with that notion.[5] The evaluation of the moral and social good in non-Christian religions is a theme also in Pope Paul's first encyclical letter *Ecclesiam Suam* of August 6, 1964.[6]

---

[4] The ending of the opening paragraph stated: "- - non-christianis, qui tamen Deum colunt, vel saltem bona animati voluntate, legem moralem hominis naturae insitam, pro conscientia servare student." Text I, AS II/V, 431.

[5] "Ultra igitur christiana castra oculos suos dirigit, et ad alias religiones respicit, quae servant sensum et notionem Dei, unius, creatoris, providentis, summi et rerum naturam transcendentis; quae Dei cultum exercent sincerae pietatis actibus; quae ex iis usibus et opinionibus morum et socialis vitae praecepta derivant." The Church accepts "quidquid veri, quidquid boni et humani apud ipsas reperiatur," i.e., the Church employs her own criteria for judging the value of religions. AS II/I, 198.

[6] Pope Paul states that a criterion for appreciating non-Christians is that they seek and adore

Does the Council recognize any salvific religious value in non-Christian religions? Thus far we cannot come to any final conclusion concerning this dilemma, but further analysis of the above-quoted text of NA 2, 1 offers us more material for discussion. The text says that *quaedam perceptio* and *aliquando agnitio* of the divine power or the supreme being "have imbued life with a deep religious sense" (intimo sensu religioso). Here it seems that the relevant religious phenomena are positively assessed by the Council. The noun *perceptio* and the verb *percipio* are used with the signification of perceiving religious, not moral, truth. Similarly, *agnitio* is a proper religious concept drawn from the Vulgate translation of Tim. 2:4 (agnitio veritatis).

In spite of the positive assessment of religious phenomena among nations, NA 2, 1 adds a statement which mitigates what was said previously. As religions are connected with the progress of culture (religiones cum progressu culturae connexae), they endeavour to answer questions about the mystery of life "with better defined concepts and more exact language." In other words, the ability of religions to face adequately the challenges and riddles of life is dependent on their relation to the progress of culture. The significance of religions is connected with the paradigm of the evolution of mankind towards the state in which the God-given natural moral law becomes more and more a reality in the lives of individuals and nations. The idea of such a positive development of the human world is the paradigmatic frame within which the NA declaration was set.

This line of thought lessens the value of non-Christian religions in contributing to the recognition of the religious truth or of the mystery of life. In spite of nice positive formulations which seem to express respect toward various religious elements of non-Christian religions, the Council seems to be biased on the side of "nature" rather than "grace."[7] Religions are valued in regard to their natural aspects, i.e., natural knowledge of the one personal Creator and natural moral law given by him, which are contained in these religions. Man does not necessarily need religion in order to understand the existence of God and natural moral law; on the contrary, plain reason and conscience may in some cases – if the religion which a person belongs to, does

---

the one God (Deum quaerant et adorent) who is known in "our true religion." After saying this he gives examples of those spheres of life which unite Christians and non-Christians: "Nolumus tamen reverenter non respicere bona spiritualia et moralia, quae in variis religionibus, christiano nomine non insignibus, insunt; una enim cum iis provehere iuvat ac tueri alta et praeclara, quae in campo libertatis religiosae, fraternitatis humanae, eruditionis ac doctrinae, beneficientiae socialis et ordinis civilis sunt communia." AAS 1964, 655.

7   Carl F. Hallencreutz comments on NA 2: "Theologically, these religions are interpreted with reference to how their answers fit the basic quest of man and of how divine truth is reflected in them. There is no specific attempt to explore further the question of these religions as 'ways of salvation'." *Hallencreutz*, 1977, 46.

not rank among the more "developed" religions – direct human beings better than religion can, in their search for that which is true and good in life.

This line of interpretation is further supported by various statements of the Council in documents other than NA. In the Council documents, a kind of idea of *logoi spermatikoi* can be found. The earlier-quoted sentence contained in *Lumen gentium* and *Ad gentes* speaks about the task of the Church to purify, elevate, and perfect whatever seeds of goodness are found in the hearts and minds of men, or in customs and cultures of peoples.[8] In the same context, AG clarifies the interpretation that the idea of *seminatum* includes the notion of truth and grace and, therefore, of the hidden presence of God.[9] It is important to note that AG 9 does not mention religion or religions at all, speaking instead of *gentes*; but this, as we have seen, is not a religious but a general term meaning people or nation. The secret presence of God, hidden like a seed, is not solely in religion but exists in all kinds of human cultural phenomena.

The term *semen* is also employed for the definition of the secret presence of God in human cultures. Most often the term is used as the biblical image of the seed of God's word, but in some cases it means the seed of the secret presence of truth in cultures. AG 18, 2 speaks about the seeds sown by God in the traditions of asceticism and contemplation outside Christianity.[10] Here again, the document speaks extensively about cultures, not particularly about religions. AG 12, 2 mentions the seeds of God's word which lie hidden in national and religious traditions of peoples.[11] Here religious traditions are set on an equal level with other cultural traditions like "national traditions." GS 3, 2 speaks about "divinum quoddam semen in homini insertum" in the context of natural moral law. The main point of this section is "the noble calling of man" (altissima vocatio hominis) which obliges all to foster brotherhood among men. There is no specific reference to religion. GS 18, 1 mentions "the seed of eternity" (semen aeternitatis) in man which makes man rebel against death.

The Second Vatican Council does see the hidden presence of the Creator in the various forms of human life. For instance, every part of the human family possesses in itself and in its good traditions some portion of the

---

[8] "Itaque quidquid boni in corde menteque ominum vel in propriis ritibus et culturis populorum seminatum invenitur, non tantum non perit, sed sanatur, elevatur et consummatur ad gloriam Dei, confusionem daemonis et beatitudinem hominis." LG 17, 1 and AG 9, 2.

[9] "Quidquid autem veritatis et gratiae iam apud gentes quasi secreta Dei praesentia inveniebatur - -" AG 9, 2.

[10] "- - traditiones asceticae et contemplativae, quarum semina iam ante Evangelii praedicationem nonnunquam antiquis culturis a Deo indita sunt - -" AG 18, 2.

[11] "- - traditionibus nationalibus et religiosis; laete et reverenter detegant semina Verbi in eis latentia." AG 12, 2.

spiritual treasure entrusted to men by the Creator of all.[12] According, however, to the Council, God's hidden presence is in no way more intense in non-Christian religions than in other cultural traditions of nations. And vice versa: religions are in no way worse media than other cultural forms of life for expressing the mysterious presence of the Creator in all life. Religions are on the same level with all the other modes of human cultural, social, or moral life.

The Council gives a definition of culture in GS 53: "The word 'culture' (cultura) in the general sense refers to all those things which go to the refining and developing of man's diverse mental and physical endowments. He strives to subdue the earth by his knowledge and his labour; he humanizes social life both in the family and in the whole civic community through the improvement of customs (progressu morum) and institutions; he expresses through his works the great spiritual experiences and aspirations of men throughout the ages - -" (GS 53, 2.) In the following section, religion and morals, among others, are mentioned as equally valid manifestations of human culture.[13] Religions are, therefore, seen as an inherent part of human culture on the whole, without receiving any special status either in a negative or in a positive sense.

According to Conciliar theology, religions are human cultural phenomena which belong to the natural goodness of life based on *gratia creata sive communis*; but as such, they consist neither of *revelatio specialis* nor of *gratia increata sive supernaturalis*. Consequently, we must ask: What does the Council teach about the great world religions? As the Council documents seem to place more value and emphasis on the more developed religions, i.e., those religions which contain elements which can be understood in harmony with Catholic faith, what is the role of these religions in expressing something of the divine truth?

---

[12] "Quaelibet autem humanae familiae pars in seipsa et in suis melioribus traditionibus aliquam partem thesauri spiritualis a Deo humanitati concrediti secumfert, etsi multi nesciunt ex qua origine procedat." GS 86, 6.

[13] "Ex diverso enim modo utendi rebus, laborem praestandi et sese exprimendi, religionem colendi moresque formandi, statuendi leges et iuridica instituta, augendi scientias et artes atque colendi pulchrum, diversae oriuntur communes vivendi condiciones et diversae formae bona vitae componendi." GS 53, 3.

7. THE VALUE OF THE WORLD RELIGIONS

When speaking about the historical religions of the world, the *Nostra aetate* declaration presents the religions in a sequence of three groups. First come Hinduism, Buddhism, and "other religions" (ceterae quoque religiones) together. The reference to other religions includes a ranking of religions from lesser historical religions with literary tradition to animism. Second comes Islam, and third Judaism, which naturally, from the point of view of the history of the NA document, occupies the most space in the document. The amount of attention paid to each of these religions testifies to the amount of respect the Council has for each of them.

In evaluating the religions of the world, the NA declaration ranks them in four groups. First, the most respected religion is Judaism, which is not only historically but also theologically intimately connected with Christianity. Furthermore, taking into consideration the birth-process of this document, it is natural that Judaism occupies much more space in NA than does any other religion. The second in rank is Islam, a strictly monotheistic book-religion which has borrowed from Judaism and Christianity. The great religions of eastern Asia acquire the third position in rank. They are not monotheistic religions, but they contain wisdom and values for human life which can be appreciated by Christians. In addition, their wisdom is preserved in sacred scriptures, which demonstrates each of these religions' cultural capacity. It is remarkable that the Council says makes no mention of the great ancient Chinese and Japanese religions. It may well be that the Council saw those religions as cultural, not properly religious, institutions to such an extent that they fall into the fourth and last category of rank.

All the rest of the religions of the world fall into the fourth broad category of rank. During the process of drafting the declaration, there were voices which demanded that animism should be mentioned. But it was decided to keep to the traditional idea of the great world religions and to mention all the rest in a general summary.[1] This ranking implies that it is probably easier for a Christian to discover traces of true faith and moral goodness in the so-called world religions which, for instance, have a long tradition of

---

[1] The relatio of October 1965 explained: "Animismus vero non explicite nominatur cum non sit una religio, sed potius typus communis plurium religionum, quae in variis gentibus inveniuntur." AS IV/IV, 700.

holy scriptures. This order of rank also implies, as a comment on the religions of the world, that the criteria of evaluation clearly are those of western Catholic Christendom. The Council admits that truth is revealed at various stages in different religions. But it is significant to note that the concept of grace, *gratia*, is never employed for the evaluation of other religions. They are not measured in regard to how and to what extent they possibly contain seeds of divine grace.

7.1. Hinduism and Buddhism

About Hinduism, NA 2, 1 says:

> Ita in Hinduismo homines mysterium divinum scrutantur et exprimunt inexhausta fecunditate mythorum et acutis conatibus philosophiae, atque liberationem quaerunt ab angustiis nostrae condicionis vel per formas vitae asceticae vel per profundam meditationem vel per refugium ad Deum cum amore et confidentia.
>
> (Thus, in Hinduism men explore the divine mystery and express it both in the limitless riches of myth and the accurately defined insights of philosophy. They seek release from the trials of the present life by ascetical practices, profound meditation, and recourse to God in confidence and love.)

Hinduism is not mentioned in the Council documents outside the above quotation. The Council text selects certain key elements of Hinduism without attempting the impossible task of describing in a short space the complex nature and the various schools of that religion.[2] Two basic conclusions are to be drawn from the above quotation. First, Hinduism is a religion which deals with the proper religious questions. It is orientated to the exploration of *mysterium divinum*, and expresses its search "in the limitless riches of myth and the accurately defined insights of philosophy." In its endeavour to express the divine mystery in a mythical and in a rational language, Hinduism resembles Catholic theology. Furthermore, the Hindus seek release from the anxieties of our present life "by ascetic practices, profound meditation and recourse to God in confidence and love" – here the text echoes the idea of the three ways taught by the oldest Veda literature.

---

[2] *Papali*, 1967, 478, comments: "Diese Worte des Konzils sind nicht als Beschreibung des Hinduismus gedacht, sondern als Hinweis auf einige seiner hervorstechenden geistigen Werte, die als Ausgangspunkt für den Dialog mit ihm dienen können." For a commentary on the NA statements on Hinduism and Buddhism, see also *Laurentin & Neuner* 1966, 89-91.

In so doing, the Hindus are in fact resorting to the same kind of religious practices as do devout Catholic Christians.

Second, the Council text says nothing about what the Hindus have found in the divine mystery or what kind of relationship they have to it. The essential terms used are "scrutantur," "quaerunt," and "refugium ad." All this indicates clearly that the Hindus are indeed seekers after divine truth.[3] The Council admits that they may be directing their exploration and questioning in the right direction, *ad Deum*; but this is the utmost that the document can admit, no further acquisition of religious truth is recognized. And even when admitting the correct direction for exploration, the NA declaration refers to the Christian concept of God in the singular, without recognizing the validity of the polytheistic nature of Hinduism.

Similar statements, in which the Council admits that the members of other religions are seeking God, can be found in other Conciliar documents as well. Meaning any religion, LG 16, 1 says that "God is not remote from those who in shadows and images seek the unknown God" (neque ab aliis, qui in umbris et imaginibus Deum ignotum quaerunt, ab huiusmodi Deus ipse longe est). AG 3, 1 speaks about the various efforts of men, explicitly including the religious ones (etiam religiosa), "through which they in many ways seek God" (multipliciter Deum quaerunt). The adherents of non-Christian religions are seekers but not yet discoverers of the truth of the *mysterium divinum* which lies behind our existence as human beings.

The Council's statement concerning Buddhism underwent a significant amendment between Text III and Text IV. One mention of the variety of the forms of Buddhism was added, and a general remark about the content of that religion (se abnegando et purificando a rebus transitoriis liberari et statum permanentis quietis attingere valeant; Text III, AS III/VIII, 638) was replaced by a more refined depiction of the content of the religion. Buddhism is not mentioned by name outside NA 2, 1 in the Conciliar documents. Combining some basic features of both Theravada and Mahayana, NA 2, 1 states:

> In Buddhismo secundum varias eius formas radicalis insufficientia mundi huius mutabilis agnoscitur et via docetur qua homines, animo devoto et confidente, sive statum perfectae liberationis acquirere, sive, vel propriis conatibus vel superiore auxilio innixi, ad summam illuminationem pertingere valeant.[4]

---

[3] Cardinal Karol Wojtyla, in a book originally written before he became Pope John Paul II, interpreted the Council's view on Hinduism and Buddhism in a similar way: "- - the main emphasis is laid on the search for God which for man is the core of religion, and which seems to constitute the basis of 'ordination' between the People of God." *Wojtyla* 1980, 130.

[4] *Dumoulin*, 1967, 482, says about the statement: "Im zweiten Satzteil des Konziltextes sind

> (Buddhism in its various forms testifies to the essential inadequacy of this changing world. It proposes a way of life by which men can, with confidence and trust, attain a state of perfect liberation and reach supreme illumination either through their own efforts or by the aid of superior help.)

With positive intensity, the Buddhists make an attempt to reach the truth. Recognizing the essential inadequacy of this changing world, they are orientated towards searching for "a state of perfect liberation" and "supreme illumination." The methods of searching resemble those which are familiar within Christianity as well: "animo devoto et confidente," "through their own efforts or by the aid of superior (divine) help." The Council goes as far as to admit that Buddhism teaches the way of acquiring liberty and illumination; but the text makes no comment on the possible salvific effect or finality of such pursuits. An important concept introduced here is *illuminatio*; it is admitted by the Council that the Buddhists teach a way to "reach supreme illumination." This means that their direction and attempts are correct, although nothing is said of how this illumination could possibly be connected with divine grace or eternal salvation. The soteriological status of such an illumination is not expressed here.

In the Council documents, *illuminatio* (and, correspondingly, *illumino* and *illustro*) means a revelation of truth, either religious or moral; most often, the salvific content of illumination is clearly expressed by the Council. The concept belongs to the vocabulary of Christian revelation, the idea of illumination is not used to mean illumination outside Christianity except in the quoted NA 2, 1. For example, the dogmatic constitution on the Church, *Lumen gentium*, begins with a solemn statement: "Christ is the light of humanity; and it is, accordingly, the heart-felt desire of this sacred Council, being gathered together in the Holy Spirit, that, by proclaiming his gospel to every creature (cf. Mk. 16:15), it may bring to all men that light of Christ which shines out visibly from the Church."[5] The basic intention of the whole Second Vatican Council was to bring to all men that light of Christ which shines visibly from the Church. Through the Church and her members "Christ will increasingly illuminate the whole human society with his saving light" (totam societatem humanam suo salutari lumine magis magisque illuminabit). (LG 36, 2.)

---

die beiden buddhistischen Hauptzweige Theravada und Mahayana in ihrer Besonderheit gekennzeichnet."

[5] "Lumen gentium cum sit Christus, haec Sacrosancta Synodus, in Spiritu Sancto congregata, omnes homines claritate Eius, super faciem Ecclesia resplendente, illuminare vehementer exoptat, omni creaturae Evangelium annuntiando (cf. Mc. 16, 15)." LG 1, 1.

After taking a position in relation to Hinduism and Buddhism, the NA text makes a general summarizing comment on other religions of a lower rank:

> Sic ceterae quoque religiones, quae per totum mundum inveniuntur, inquietudini cordis hominum variis modis occurrere nituntur proponendo vias, doctrinas scilicet ac praecepta vitae, necnon ritus sacros. (NA 2, 1.)
>
> (So, too, other religions which are found throughout the world attempt in their own ways to calm the hearts of men by outlining a program of life covering doctrine, moral precepts, and sacred rites.)

Other religions, too, try to answer the basic questions causing anxiety in men. It is important to note that the text uses the term "religiones nituntur proponendo." Religions attempt to calm the hearts of men by proposing religious doctrines, moral precepts, and sacred rites. Thus religions are patterns for answering the general *aenigmata* (cf. NA 1, 3) of the human heart, i.e., they attempt to answer the genuine religious questions. They represent human endeavour in the search for God; the Council does not say anything about the teleological efficacy of this search, about the possibility of finding the truth in those religions.

7.2. Islam

The Second Vatican Council speaks explicitly about Islam in two connections, in the NA declaration and in LG 16. Islam is a non-Christian religion which is, after Judaism, next closest to Christianity.[6] The Council recognizes affinity between Islam and Christianity at several points. NA 3, 1 states:

> Ecclesia cum aestimatione quoque Muslimos respicit qui unicum Deum adorant, viventem et subsistentem, misericordiam et omnipotentem, Creatorem caeli et terrae, homines allocutum, cuius occultis etiam decretis toto animo se submittere student, sicut Deo se submisit Abraham ad quem fides islamica libenter sese refert. Iesum, quem quidem ut Deum non agnoscunt, ut prophetam tamen venerantur, matremque eius virginalem honorant Mariam et aliquando eam devote etiam invocant. Diem insuper iudicii expectant cum Deus omnes homines resuscitatos remunerabit. Exinde vitam moralem aestimant et Deum maxime in oratione, eleemosynis et ieiunio colunt.

---

[6] On the relationship between the Catholic Church and Islam in the past, see *Federici* 1966, 206-216.

(The Church has also a high regard for the Muslims. They worship God, who is one, living, and subsistent, merciful and almighty, the Creator of heaven and earth, who has also spoken to men. They strive to submit themselves without reserve to the hidden decrees of God, just as Abraham submitted himself to God's plan, to whose faith Muslims eagerly link their own. Although not acknowledging him as God, they venerate Jesus as a prophet, his virgin Mother they also honour, and even at times devoutly invoke. Further, they await the day of judgment and the reward of God following the resurrection of the dead. For this reason they highly esteem an upright life and worship God, especially by way of prayer, alms-deeds, and fasting.)

At the beginning of the NA 3, 1 passage the declaration places special emphasis upon the high regard of the Catholic Church for the Muslims. *Fides islamica* falls into a category different from the other religions mentioned above. The Muslims are strictly monotheistic; they serve the same God as the Christians, the Creator of all. The Catholic admiration of the consequent monotheism in Islam is also emphasized by Pope *Paul VI* in his encyclical letter *Ecclesiam Suam.*[7] In terms of the theology of creation, harmony exists between Islam and Christianity. Although the name Allah is not mentioned, the NA declaration refers to the God of the Muslims with respect as the true God, not as a god. Allah is no false god but "God, who is one, living and subsistent, merciful and almighty, the Creator of heaven and earth." In this sense, Allah is only another name of the same true God whom the Christians address in their prayers. A major element of Islam, however, is here overlooked: the role of Prophet *Muhammad* as the receiver of divine revelation.[8]

In the Text II version (September 1964) of the passage, the Islamic concept of God was depicted using a more specific and familiar terminology: the Muslims worship the "personal and recompensing God" (Deum personalem atque remuneratorem adorant). And this worship was qualified as "sensu religioso." (Text II, AS III/II, 329.) In the later versions, the additional attributes of God were left out, and the last-mentioned expression was used in regard to religions in general (NA 2, 1). This neutralization of the Islamic concept of God was necessary, because the Council was to create a declaration concerning all religions of the world.

---

[7] "Deinde de iis, qui Deum adorant religionis forma, quae monotheismus dicitur, maxime ea qua Mahometani sunt astricti; quos propter ea quae in eorum cultu vera sunt et probanda, merito admiramur." AAS 1964, 654.

[8] *Anawati*, 1967, 486, says critically about the NA statement on Islam: "Neben diesen Vorbehalten kann man sagen, die Konzilserklärung gebe mit einem Minimum an Worten das Wesentliche der muslimischen Theodizee, nicht aber das Wesentliche des muslimischen Glaubens wieder, zu dessen wichtigsten Elementen der Glaube an die Sendung Mohammeds gehört."

For this purpose, a new attribute of God, "misericors," was added to Text IV and to the final version. In addition, note 5 of the declaration was revised: the reference to *Irenaeus* was replaced by a reference to the very friendly letter of *Gregory VII* to Muslim king *Anazir* of Mauritania (of the year 1076) in Text IV of 1965.[9] The above shows how the fathers of the Council saw an affinity between Islam and Christianity and wished to express their good will towards Muslims.[10]

In addition to recognizing Islam in terms of the theology of creation in the NA declaration, the Council acknowledges Islam as a prophetic religion. In this respect, too, Islam is similar to Christianity and Judaism. The Muslims worship God "who has also spoken to men." It is interesting to note how the text speaks of God's "hidden decrees", i.e., non-revealed perception of God and his will, to which the Muslims "strive to submit themselves" (cuius occultis decretis submittere student). Islam is a religion of learning submission to Allah. But the Catholic Council does not concede that there exists *revelatio specialis* in Islam, i.e., concede that God has openly spoken to mankind in Islam or through Muhammad. Embarassingly, Muhammad, so important for the Muslim creed, is not mentioned at all by the Council; according to it, God's revelation is still *occulta* in *fides islamica*.

Points of connection are recognisable in the historical content of belief between the two prophetic religions, Islam and Christianity. Abraham, the archetype of faith for the Christians, represents to the Muslims an archetype of submission. The role of Abraham is the only element of revelation in Islam recognized by the Church; this element is accepted, because it is in common with Christianity. Jesus is venerated as a prophet in Islam, but, of course, "not acknowledged as God," as the text says. In this fact naturally lies the crucial point of difference between the two religions. Furthermore,

---

9   The Council text does not quote the text of the letter. In his letter, Gregory, in a very polite tone, thanks the Muslim king for liberating Christian prisoners. By so doing the king was inspired by God, the Creator of all: "Hanc denique bonitatem Creator omnium Deus, sine quo nihil boni facere, imo nec cogitare possumus, cordi tuo inspiravit; ipse qui illuminat omnem hominem venientem in hunc mundum (Ioan. I) in hanc intentione mentem tuam illuminavit." The pope emphasizes that Christians and Muslims have the same God although they believe in a different way: "Hanc itaque charitatem nos et vos specialibus nobis quam caeteris gentibus debemus, qui unum Deum, licet diverso modo, credimus et confitemur, qui eum creatorem saeculorum et gubernatorem huius mundi quotidie laudamus et veneramur." The pope wishes that, after a long life, the receiver of the letter would be taken into "the beatific bosom of the most holy patriarch Abraham." PL 148, 450-452.

10   Even the moral quality of Muslims was described with more detail in Text III: "Vitam quoque moralem tam individualem quam familialem et socialem in obsequium Dei ducere conantur." Text III, AS III/VIII, 639. The final version merely said: "exinde vitam moralem aestimant."

Mary is honored also by the Muslims. The very concept of history is even similar in Islam and Christianity. The Muslims, too, see history as linear: "they await the day of judgement and the reward of God following the resurrection of the dead."

The two religions also hold beliefs in common in regard to religious practice. The Muslims "highly esteem a morally upright life." In accordance with this appreciation of high morality, they "worship God especially by way of prayer, alms-deeds, and fasting." The terms used here belong to the Christian vocabulary: "oratio," "eleemosyna," and "ieiunium." A major concrete historical fact of Muslim spirituality, however, the central role of the sacred Mecca, is ignored by the Council. It is important, that for both religions, the idea of moral life is directly associated with worship of God. This means that the Council recognizes the connection between moral life and the essence of religion as valid in Islam. When discussing Islam, the NA declaration employs a vocabulary different from that used when speaking about the great religions of East Asia. The text twice says that the Muslims worship and serve the true God: "Deum adorant," "Deum colunt." These are expressions absent when the Council speaks about Hinduism or Buddhism, religions which, nevertheless, do "explore" (scrutantur) the divine mystery in the right direction, *ad Deum,* or in various ways seek to answer the deepest questions and problems of human existence.

The dogmatic constitution *Lumen gentium* makes an important contribution to the relationship between Islam and Christianity by stating: "But the plan of salvation also includes those who acknowledge the Creator, in the first place amongst whom are the Moslems: these profess to hold the faith of Abraham, and together with us they adore the one, merciful God, mankind's judge on the last day."[11] The constitution says that God's plan of salvation includes "those who acknowledge the Creator." This means that as a strict monotheistic religion, Islam has a special position in God's salvific plan. The Muslims "hold the faith of Abraham." The Council even goes so far as to admit that "together with us they adore the one, merciful God." It thus becomes unambiguously clear that the Council recognizes the validity of Islam as a religion whose faith and rituals express the authentic faith in the personal, omnipotent God. What is apparent to human reason has become an institutionalized religion in Islam. The criterion of the Catholic Council for evaluating the truthfulness of that religion is the Christian faith: the more Christian elements the religion has,

[11] "Sed propositum salutis et eos amplectitur, qui Creatorem agnoscunt, inter quos imprimis Musulmanos, qui fidem Abrahae se tenere profitentes, nobiscum Deum adorant unicum, misericordem, homines die novissimo iudicaturum." LG 16, 1.

the more truthful it is. Islam has many such elements. But the crucial point of divergence lies in the mystery of grace. It is admitted that the Muslims believe in the "merciful" God, but there is no incarnated means of revelation, reconciliation, and grace as in Christianity.

7.3. Judaism

Judaism appears in the Council documents more often than does any other non-Christian religion. This is, of course, natural because of the close affiliation between Judaism and Christianity.[12] Taking into consideration the birth process of the document, it is also natural that Judaism occupies much more space in the NA declaration than any other religion; there is a clear concentration upon that topic in NA.[13] It is remarkable how the Council fails entirely to recognize the points of connection between Judaism and Christianity in the sphere of morals or in the endeavour of Judaism to answer the *aenigmata* of the human heart. Judaism is evaluated on other premises than are the rest of the non-Christian religions. When speaking of Judaism, the Council goes directly into the essence of true religion itself.[14]

Lumen gentium 16, 1 , regarding those "who have not yet received the gospel," yet "are related to the People of God in various ways," gives to the Jews a prominent place: "There is, first, that people to which the covenants and promises were made, and from which Christ was born according to the flesh (cf. Rom. 9:4-5): in view of divine choice, they are a people most dear for the sake of the fathers, for the gifts of God are without repentance (cf. Rom. 11:28-29)."[15] The Jews are thus a people of covenants and promises given by the faithful God; they still are the elected people, dear to God for the sake of the fathers. God's plan of salvation in history has not been altered. There also exists a direct physical continuity from Judaism to Christianity: from them are the fathers, the prophets, Virgin Mary, Jesus,

---

[12] On the Christian-Jewish relationship, see also *Federici* 1966, 235-400, and *Laurentin & Neuner* 1966, 47-77.

[13] In the Conciliar documents, all references to Israel are made exclusively in terms of salvation history, whereas references to Jews also include the view concerning Jews living today. The Council fathers were cautious not to make political statements concerning the state of Israel.

[14] Paul VI said in his *Ecclesiam Suam* that, among those who "adore the one and supreme God whom we also serve," closest to Christians are Jews. "Mentionem scilicet incimus de filiis gentis Iudaeae, reverentia et amore nostro sane dignis, qui eam retinent religionem, quam Veteris Testamenti propriae esse dicimus." AAS 1964, 654.

[15] "In primis quidem populus ille cui data fuerunt testamenta et promissa et ex quo Christus ortus est secundum carnem (cf. Rom. 9, 4-5), populus secundum electionem carissimus propter patres: sine poenitentia enim sunt dona et vocatio Dei (cf. Rom. 11, 28-29)." LG 16, 1.

and his apostles. Both theologically and historically, Christianity is intimately and inseparably interwoven with Judaism.

The *Nostra aetate* declaration speaks at length about Judaism in NA 4. Most importantly, the theme begins with a confession of the deep spiritual dependence on Judaism of the *mysterium* of the Christian religion:

> Mysterium Ecclesiae perscrutans, Sacra haec Synodus meminit vinculi, quo populus Novi Testamenti cum stripe Abrahae spiritualiter coniunctus est. (NA 4, 1.)
>
> (Sounding the depths of the mystery which is the Church, this sacred Council remembers the spiritual ties which link the people of the New Covenant to the stock of Abraham.)

A concession to the mystery of religion itself is, in NA, made only in regard to Judaism. Since the text concerning Jews had to be modified here in regard to the formulas "gens deicida" and "damnat," as illustrated in Ch.3., the religious-spiritual element was emphasized. Thus, for example, the term "spiritualiter" was added to Text IV of October 1965. During the process of the emergence of the declaration, the biblical and spiritual emphasis continually increased as a reaction to Arab political pressure against the document. For instance, the first sentence concerning Jews, when compared with the final result, differed totally in Text I, where it read: "Maxime autem hoc valet cum de Iudaeis agitur, quippe qui cum Ecclesia Christi speciali ratione coniunguntur." (Text I, AS II/V, 431.) In the final text, this cool rationalization is replaced by the "mystery of the Church" spiritually connected with "the stock of Abraham."

The religion of the Jews is essentially linked with Christianity not only historically, but in the very substance of religion itself. As the dogmatic constitution on divine revelation, *Dei verbum*, says concerning the Old Testament scriptures: "in them, the mystery of our salvation is present in a hidden way" (in quibus tandem latet mysterium salutis nostrae). (DV 15, 1.) The NA declaration speaks of *revelatio Veteris Testamenti* (NA 4, 2). The sacred scriptures of the Jews are, from the point of view of Christians, nothing less than documents of divine revelation. The term *revelatio* is never used in regard to other non-Christian religions. There is a direct and virtual continuity in theology between the two religions, they both have received the *revelatio specialis divina*. In *Dei mysterium* the Catholic Church finds her origins and her election in the patriarchs, Moses, and the prophets of Israel; all the faithful of Christ are, at the same time, "sons of Abraham." This is the part of the declaration which was maintained nearly intact from Text I to the final version: this description of the biblical salvation history which forms the solid backbone of the Council's thought about the relationship between Christians and Jews:[16]

> Ecclesia enim Christi agnoscit fidei et electionis suae initia iam apud Patriarchas, Moysen et Prophetas, iuxta salutare Dei mysterium, inveniri. Confitetur omnes Christifideles, Abrahae filios secundum fidem, in eiusdem Patriarchae vocatione includi et salutem Ecclesiae in populi electi exitu de terra servitutis mystice praesignari. (NA 4, 2.)
>
> (The Church of Christ acknowledges that in God's plan of salvation the beginning of her faith and election is to be found in the patriarchs, Moses, and the prophets. She professes that all Christ's faithful, who as men of faith are sons of Abraham, are included in the same patriarch's call and that the salvation of the Church is mystically prefigured in the exodus of God's chosen people from the land of bondage.)

The NA declaration expresses the *heilsgeschichtliche* continuity between Judaism and Christianity by speaking about "the common spiritual heritage," *patrimonium spirituale*, of the Jews and the Christians: "Cum igitur adeo magnum sit patrimonium spirituale Christianis et Iudaeis commune - -" (NA 4, 5; see also NA 4, 7.) The relationship between the two religions is of a profound spiritual and theological nature. This term *patrimonium* is used to describe the treasure of the revealed truth in Christianity. It is *patrimonium sapientiae christianae*, comparable with *sacra revelatio*. The expression also appears in the decree on the Catholic eastern churches, *Orientalium Ecclesiarum*, when the Council refers to the heritage of faith common to Christians: the tradition of the eastern churches is "part of the divinely revealed, undivided heritage of the Universal Church" (partem constituit divinitus revelati atque indivisi Universae Ecclesiae patrimonii). (OE 1, 1. Similarly in OE 5, 1.)[17]

The concept *patrimonium* is used especially when the Council makes a statement in regard to the eastern churches. Such usage is also apparent in the decree on ecumenism, *Unitatis redintegratio* (see UR 17, 2, e.g.). In contrast, the term is also used, though more rarely, in reference to the common heritage of the Christians in general (see UR 4, 11). Now in NA, the strongly Christian theological concept of *patrimonium* is adopted into the vocabulary applied to the relationship between Judaism and Christianity. In fact the concept of *patrimonium* survived in the declaration from the very first version the fathers discussed (Text I) to the final one. Here again, the

---

[16] Johannes Oesterreicher expresses regret that the expression of the Church's thankfulness, "grato animo," of Text I was later omitted. *Oesterreicher* 1967, 471.

[17] For a commentary on *Orientalium Ecclesiarum*, see *Lilienfeld* 1969.

Council easily reached unanimity on the biblical-theological foundation of the Jewish-Christian relationship. A great common spiritual heritage exists between the two religions; Judaism is seen not as a religion of law, but of grace, based on divine election. This, of course, is a Christianized view of Judaism, but it may open a new perspective even for the self-understanding of Judaism among Jews themselves.

Consequent to this acknowledgement, the Council expresses the hope of reconciliation and of an eventual unification of the Christians and the Jews into one people of God:

> Credit enim Ecclesia Christum, Pacem nostram, per crucem Iudaeos et Gentes reconciliasse et utraque in Semetipso fecisse unum. (NA 4, 2.)
> (The Church believes that Christ who is our peace has through his cross reconciled Jews and gentiles and made them one in himself.)

Shortly after this biblical reference (Eph. 2:14-16), the Council text clarifies the topic:

> Una cum Prophetis eodemque Apostolo Ecclesia die Deo soli notum expectat, quo populi omnes una voce Dominum invocabunt et "servient ei humero uno" (Soph. 3, 9). (NA 4, 4.)
> (Together with the prophets and that same apostle, the Church awaits the day, known to God alone, when all peoples will call on God with one voice and "serve him shoulder to shoulder" [Soph. 3:9].)

Christian hope of the unification of Jews and Christians was most strongly expressed in Text II where it stated emphatically that the unification of the Jewish people with the Church is a part of the Christian hope.[18] Text I also was more specific about the idea of unity between the two parts of the people of God.[19] In the later versions of the declaration, statements about the eventual unification of Jews and Christians were somewhat mitigated. Faith in the reconciliation and unification of Jews and Christians is part of the eschatological hope of the Church. Here the Council expresses its faith in the apostle Paul's words in Rom. 11 in regard to the

---

[18] "Memoria insuper dignum est adunationem populi Iudaici cum Ecclesia partem spei christianae esse. Ecclesia enim, docente Apostolo Paulo (cf. Rom. 11, 25), fide inconcussa ac desiderio magno accessum huius populi exspectat ad plenitudinem Populi Dei, quam Christus instauravit." Text II, AS III/II, 328.

[19] "Credit insuper Ecclesia Christum, Pacem nostram, uno amore et Iudaeos et Gentes complecti et utraque fecisse unum (cf. Eph. 2, 14) atque amborum in uno corpore unione (cf. Eph. 2, 17) annuntiari totius orbis terrarum in Christo reconciliationem." Text I, AS II/V, 432.

faithfulness of God and the eventual renewal of Israel. (There appear significant references to Rom. 9 and 11 in NA 4 and in LG 16, 1.) There shall be *novus Israel* or *novus Populus Dei* which includes believers from among the Jews and the gentiles.[20]

As for reconciliation between the Jews and the gentiles "facta est et fiet," it is a fact of salvation history, but still its perfection and fulfillment are objects of eschatological hope. In the Council documents, the terms *reconciliatio* and *reconcilio* (employed in NA 4, 2) express the mystery of salvation in Christ; but, in addition, they are phrases used to express the ecumenical hope of the reunification of the Christian churches. For instance, UR 24, 2 asserts: "Further, this Council declares that it realizes that this holy objective – the reconciliation of all Christians in the unity of the one and only Church of Christ (reconciliandi Christianos omnes in unitate unius unicae Ecclesiae) – transcends human powers and gifts." This special Christian concept of christological reconciliation and of ecumenical endeavour is grafted onto the hope of reconciliation between Jews and Christians as well. This final observation demonstrates most convincingly – from the point of view of Christianity – how Judaism, compared with all the other religions of the world, is a religion *sui generis*.

---

[20] *Lumen gentium* asserts: "Quod foedus novum Christus instituit, novum scilicet testamentum in suo sanguine (cf. 1 Cor. 11, 25), ex Iudaeis ac gentibus plebem vocans, quae non secundum carnem sed in Spiritu ad unitatem coalesceret, essetque novus Populus Dei." LG 9, 1. Elsewhere LG expresses the hope of reconciliation between Jews and Christians: "Est Ecclesia *agricultura* seu ager Dei (1 Cor. 3, 9). In illo agro crescit antiqua oliva, cuius radix sancta fuerunt Patriarchae, et in qua Iudaeorum et Gentium reconciliatio facta est et fiet (Rom. 11, 13-26)." LG 6, 3.

8. ENCOUNTER BETWEEN CHRISTIANS AND NON-CHRISTIANS

The *Nostra aetate* declaration is not meant to be the final word of the Catholic Church concerning non-Christian religions. It is, instead, just the beginning, meant to lay the foundation for dialogue, for a new system of communication between people of different faiths; this is in accord with the Council's vision of the united humanity.[1] The Catholic doctrine regarding non-Christian religions is also present in the teaching of the Second Vatican Council on behaviour during encounters between Christians and believers in other faiths. The NA declaration gives an overall definition of such a methodology:

> Filios suos igitur hortatur, ut cum prudentia et caritate per colloquia et collaborationem cum asseclis aliarum religionum, fidem et vitam christianam testantes, illa bona spiritualia et moralia necnon illos valores socio-culturales, quae apud eos inveniuntur, agnoscant, servent et promoveant. (NA 2, 3.)
>
> (The Church, therefore, urges her sons to enter with prudence and charity into discussion and collaboration with members of other religions. Let Christians, while witnessing to their own faith and way of life, acknowledge, preserve, and encourage the spiritual and moral truths found among non-Christians, also their social life and culture.)

The expressions "prudentia et caritate" and "fidem et vitam christianam testantes" did not come into the text until Text IV of October 1965. This addendum is to be understood as a consolidation of the missionary aspect against the critics of the declaration. But instead, an expression of Text III, "salva integritate fidei catholicae," was dropped from the final version in order to allow more freedom in the encounters between Christians and non-Christians.

---

[1] In his relatio of October 1965, Cardinal Bea said that the purpose of the declaration is not be a complete exposition of religions but "to show that there is a bond between man and religions which is meant to be the basis of dialogue and collaboration." AS IV/IV, 722.

8.1. Three Strategies for Encounter

We can find three categories of strategy in the text. First, discussion or dialogue (colloquia) should be carried out, with *dialogus*¹ being a phrase applied in the Council documents to describe the ecumenical endeavour. (See UR 18, 1 & 19, 4 & 23, 3.) In addition to *dialogus oecumenicus*, *dialogus* is also used to illustrate the encounter between Christians and non-Christians. This is used especially in the *Ad gentes* decree. The expression *dialogus cum non-christianis* is used in AG 34, 1 & 41, 5. AG 11, 2 calls this kind of encounter "sincere and patient dialogue." AG 16, 4 goes so far as to see this kind of dialogue as "fraternal:" the clergy in the mission fields should be trained "for fraternal dialogue with non-Christians." It is thus evident that the concept of dialogue is applied to the methodology both of ecumenical encounters between the Christian churches and of inter-religious encounters between Christianity and other religions. It is "dialogue with our separated brethren and with non-Christians" (GE 11, 1). In addition, *Gaudium et spes* introduced an idea of universal dialogue among all men, in which the Church herself is "a sign of the spirit of brotherhood which renders possible sincere dialogue and strengthens it."²

The second strategy for encounter between Christians and non-Christians, according to the NA 2, 3 text, is collaboration (collaboratio) with members of other religions. This means cooperation in the field of social ethics. This is fully in accordance with the basic motive of the NA declaration, as indicated in Ch. 4., the idea of the growth of unity and consciousness of natural moral law among nations. Cooperation in the preservation and promotion of *bona spiritualia et moralia* found among non-Christians is a duty of every Christian. Among spiritual and moral good, special emphasis is laid upon *valores socio-culturales*. It is important to note that the Council text speaks about the "bona" and "valores" found among the non-Christians, showing that the values contained in religions, not the religions themselves, are recognized and appreciated. Spiritual or moral good is to be measured by the criterion of Christian revelation and natural moral law as understood by the Church. The Catholic Church or Christians in general are the source of the discovery (inveniuntur) of those values.

Several times in the documents of the Council the theme of cooperation between Christians and non-Christians in social-ethical matters appears. Concerning Christians' involvement in building a just society, in defending

---

² "Ecclesia, vi suae missionis universum orbem nuntio evangelico illuminandi et omnes homines cuiusvis nationis, stripis vel culturae in unum Spiritum coadunandi, signum evadit illius fraternitatis quae sincerum dialogum permittit atque roborat." GS 92, 1.

human dignity, and in promoting peace in the world, *Ad gentes* urges that Christians cooperate with non-Christian religions.[3] Similarly, *Gaudium et spes* expresses the joy of the Church over "the spirit of true brotherhood" between Christians and non-Christians in regard to efforts toward social progress and the prevention of wars.[4]

The third method of encounter, according to NA 2, 3, comprises Christians' "witnessing to their own faith and way of life" (fidem et vitam christianam testantes). Encounter with non-Christians is not only dialogue or social-ethical cooperation, it also includes Christian testimony about the salvific truth revealed in Christ. This is the crucial essence of religious truth which is lacking in the religions of the world, although they may contain "a ray of the truth" in themselves. Because the preceding evaluation is from the Catholic point of view, it therefore, is bound to be biased towards the uniqueness of Christianity.

Because of the essential inadequacy of non-Christian religions as ways of salvation, every encounter between a Christian and a non-Christian includes its missionary aspect. All forms of encounter with non-Christians should take place "with prudence and love" in order to help them towards the fullness of truth. This missionary motive is present even in the final sentence of the NA declaration:

> Proinde, Christifideles Sacra Synodus, vestigia Sanctorum Apostolorum Petri et Pauli premens, ardenter obsecrat ut, "conversationem inter gentes habentes bonam" (1 Petr. 2, 12), si fieri potest, quod in eis est cum omnibus hominibus pacem habeant, ita ut vere sint filii Patris qui in caelis est. (NA 5, 3.)[5]
>
> (Accordingly, following the footsteps of holy apostles Peter and Paul, the sacred Council earnestly begs the Christian faithful to "conduct themselves well among the gentiles" [1 Pet. 2:12] and if possible, as far as depends on them, to be at peace with all men and in that way to be true sons of the Father who is in heaven.)

---

[3] "In hac activitate fideles sociam operam suam prudenter praestare exoptent inceptis quae ab Institutis privatis et publicis, a guberniis, ab organis internationalibus, a diversis communitatibus christianis necnon a religionibus non-christianis promoventur." AG 12, 2.

[4] "In omnibus istis campis gaudet Ecclesia de spiritu verae fraternitatis inter christianos et non-christianos florentis qui enititur ut conamina semper intensiora fiant ad ingentem miseriam sublevandam." GS 84, 3.

[5] The Text II draft of the declaration, September 1964, concluded with the idea of loving enemies. In the context of non-Christian religions, this could have caused misunderstandings: non-Christians must not in any sense be seen as enemies.

8.2. *Encountering Muslims and Jews*

In addition to the general principles of encounter between Christians and non-Christians, the NA declaration deals specifically with the question of strategies when meeting Muslims and Jews. In NA 3, 2 the declaration gives an account on the methods of encounter between Christians and Muslims:

> Quodsi in decursu saeculorum inter Christianos et Muslimos non paucae dissensiones et inimicitiae exortae sint, Sacrosancta Synodus omnes exhortatur, ut, praeterita obliviscentes, se ad comprehensionem mutuam sincere exerceant et pro omnibus hominibus iustitiam socialem, bona moralia necnon pacem et libertatem communiter tueantur et promoveant.
> (Over the centuries many quarrels and dissensions have arisen between Christians and Muslims. The sacred Council now pleads with all to forget the past, and urges that a sincere effort be made to achieve mutual understanding; for the benefit of all men, let them together preserve and promote peace, liberty, social justice, and moral values.)

Three aspects of strategy can be found in this text. First, the existence of quarrels and dissension between Christians and Muslims during the past centuries is conceded to. Then the Council makes a plea "to forget the past." There is not one word of regret, no sign of asking forgiveness for past offences of the Christians against Muslims. The only words the Catholic Council has to say about the great controversies are "praeterita obliviscentes." Second, the Council recommends that "a sincere effort be made to achieve mutual understanding." The text does not encourage any high level of mutual appreciation between the adherents of the two religions. The document shows surprisingly disillusionment regarding any possibility of reaching unanimity in any area of proper religious truth. Realistically only a sincere effort towards understanding, in place of hostility, is hoped for. This is an adaptation of the general principle of dialogue presented above.

Third, in accordance with the general principle of collaboration in the field of social ethical efforts, the declaration emphasizes cooperation in social issues between Christians and Muslims. If there is little, or hardly any hope of reaching understanding regarding proper religious truth, it is quite natural that the emphasis of the Council is skewed towards the sphere of social ethics. For the benefit of all men, let Christians and Muslims "together preserve and promote social justice, moral values, peace, and liberty." In regard to Islam, the Council believes in the possibility of reaching some kind of understanding and cooperation regarding the theology of creation and in the sphere of natural moral law.

In contrast to the strategies for encounter between Christians and Muslims, any special strategy for encounter between Christians and Jews is lacking in a social-ethical aspect; concerning Jews, the emphasis of the Council lies in proper religious matters. It is not only a monotheistic concept of divinity or moral values that unites Jews and Christians, but the revelation of the divine plan of salvation. Consequently, in regard to Jews, the Council refrains from expressing any missionary motive. Referring to the common spiritual heritage of Jews and Christians, the Council commends "mutual understanding and appreciation" (mutuam utriusque cognitionem et aestimationem). "This can be obtained, especially, by way of biblical and theological enquiry (studiis biblicis et theologicis) and through friendly discussions (fraternis colloquiis)." (NA 4, 5.) When compared with other dialogues, dialogue between Jews and Christians is different in nature: Jews and Christians share elements of their holy scriptures; consequently, it is possible to recommend common biblical and theological studies. The Council does not mention anything similar in disucssing dialogue with any other non-Christian religion. The NA text does not, however, go so far as to recommend any cooperation in the sphere of liturgy.[6]

Something new and unique here is the Council's wish for mutual appreciation between Jews and Christians. The Council texts do not use the term *aestimatio* when speaking about other religions except Judaism; the idea of the special recognition of Jews can be inferred the main motivation of the Council fathers behind the NA declaration. As was indicated in 3.1., the Catholic Church felt it necessary, after the Holocaust of the Second World War, to try to reconcile Jews and European Christians. As the Church renounces "every form of persecution against whomsoever it may be directed," "all hatreds, persecutions, displays of anti-Semitism leveled at any time or from any source against Jews" are deplored and reprobated by the Council. (NA 4, 7.) The Council's condemnation of anti-Semitism is somewhat watered down by its reference to the general principle of opposing all kinds of discrimination "on the basis of race, colour, condition in life, or religion." (Cf. NA 5, 3.) This generalization lessens the intensity of the Council's deploring crimes committed specifically against Jews.

As was noted above, it is remarkable that, in spite of the need for reconciliation, no word of repentance or regret nor any sign of asking forgiveness is expressed in the Council documents.[7] Instead, the guilt of

---

[6] Recommendations concerning common elements of liturgy were later given in "Guidelines on Religious Relations with the Jews," December 1, 1974. See L'Osservatore Romano, January 4, 1975.

[7] Regretting the absence of any confession of guilt, Claud Nelson says that NA "misses any satisfying expression of warm human feeling." The declaration is "lacking the spirit of reconciliation." *Nelson* 1966, 669. *Eckert*, 1976, 11, says that the reception of the declaration among the Jews of the world was "quite cool."

Jews for killing Jesus is explored in detail, this enquiry resulting in the compromise described above in 3.2. The NA declaration draws the conclusion that teaching and preaching in the Church must be cleansed of all elements of scorn for or accusations against Jews. "Consequently, all must take care, lest in catechizing or in preaching the word of God, they teach anything which is not in accord with the truth of the gospel message or the spirit of Christ." (NA 4, 6.)

9. THE MISSIONARY MOTIVE OF THE COUNCIL

9.1. *The Evangelization of Non-Christians*

As we have seen in our analysis thus far, the *Nostra aetate* declaration does not recognize much religious truth as evident in non-Christian religions, except in Judaism and in the strict monotheism of Islam. In regard to *mysterium divinum*, non-Christian religions are still seeking the truth, but in regard to the general notion of God's existence – or the divine mystery of life – and in regard to morals, the Council has shown willingness to recognize the value of any religion. This basic line of interpretation is confirmed if we turn more specifically to the missionary motives which appear in Council documents other than NA.

Noting how the Council documents use the crucial word-construction *non-christianus* gives a hint of the fundamental missionary motive of the Council: most commonly this word-compound is connected with a clear motivation for mission and evangelization, intending the conversion of non-Christians.[1] AG 13, 1 points to the necessity of conversion of non-Christians,[2] and AG 15, 8 speaks of proclaiming Christ "through word and deed" to non-Christians. AG 39, 1 speaks about "spreading the gospel among non-Christians" and AG 40, 2 about "opening the minds of non-Christians to hear the gospel" and "witnessing among non-Christians to the majesty and love of God, and to union in Christ." AG 30, 2 & 39, 3 introduce the construction *evangelizatio non-christianorum*; AG 41, 7 mentions Christian lay-people who give their "witness to Christ among non-Christians." PO 4, 3 says that "in non-Christian territories or societies people are led by the proclamation of the gospel to faith and by the saving sacraments."

The second most common usage of the construction *non-christianus* occurs when the Council speaks about the dialogue between Christians and non-Christians. AG 16, 4 uses the expression "dialogus fraternus cum

---

[1] *Non-christianus* is a term used mostly in the decree on the Church's missionary activity, *Ad gentes*.

[2] "- - annuntietur Deus vivus et, quem ad omnium salutem misit, Iesus Christus - - ut non-christiani, Spiritu Sancto cor ipsorum aperiente (cf. Act. 16, 14), credentes ad Dominum libere convertantur - -" AG 13, 1.

non-christianis" when giving instructions as to the training of priests in the so-called young churches. AG 34, 1 mentions "dialogus cum religionibus et culturis non-christianis" when speaking of scientific preparation for missionary activity. Similarly, AG 41, 5 sees scientific study of religions as a preparation for dialogue with non-Christians. By such study scholars "help the preachers of the gospel." According to GE 11, 1, those who exercise the "intellectual apostolate" in the theological faculties will, for their part, promote dialogue with non-Christians. Thus, when the Council employs the term *non-christianus* with the idea of dialogue, even then the emphasis lies in preparation for a more efficient witness among non-Christians to the Christian truth.

The same term is also used when the Council speaks about cooperation between Christians and non-Christians in socio-ethical issues and problems. According to AG 12, 2, in defending and promoting all dimensions of social welfare, human dignity and world peace, Christians "collaborate in projects initiated by private, public, state, or international bodies, or by other Christian or even non-Christian communities." AG 41, 6 says that, in matters concerning "the structure of the earthly city," Christian lay people "should collaborate with Christians, non-Christians and especially with members of international associations." GS 84, 3 comments on international and regional organizations which "represent the first attempts at laying the foundations on an international level for a community of all men to work towards the solutions of the very serious problems of our times." "The Church is glad to view the spirit of true brotherhood existing in all spheres between Christians and non-Christians as it seeks to intensify its untiring efforts to alleviate the enormity of human misery."

Our investigation of the term *non-christianus* indicates that the Council uses the word construction predominantly with a missionary motivation. The term is not employed for a comparison of religions or a study of proper religious truth. But it is, however, positively used when the Council expresses its delight over the cooperation of Christians and non-Christians in the sphere of social ethics. This term *non-christianus* is used without a missionary motivation only when dealing with matters which belong to the sphere of natural moral law.

9.2. *The Possibility of Salvation extra Ecclesiam*

Our analysis of the NA declaration and related materials from the Council has shown that the Catholic Church can speak about non-Christian religions with sympathetic understanding and in a tone of goodwill. The Conciliar documents have frequently been embraced with enthusiasm in Catholic theology on the basis that now, for the first time, the Church officially recognizes an extra-ecclesiastical way of salvation through other religions; the hidden work of christological grace is acknowledged even in non-Christian religions.[3] This line of interpretation is, however, over-simplified and lacks support from any detailed analysis of the documents of the Second Vatican Council. Although the Council does fully acknowledge the spiritual and salvific reality among *fratres a catholica Ecclesia seiuncti*, it does not recognize the same reality in non-Christian religions.

The Council fully acknowledges the moral good which can be found in the doctrinal concepts and moral practice of religions. But in regard to *mysterium divinum*, non-Christian religions are still seekers of the truth, with in fact, only Judaism as an exception. Next we must ask if any way of salvation exists in non-Christian religions. Is salvation, according to the Council, to be found exclusively within Christianity? In order to find an answer to this question, we must turn to other Conciliar texts besides the NA declaration, because NA offers no answers regarding whether and how non-Christians could become partakers of salvation and eternal life.

The most outstanding theological document of the Second Vatican Council, the dogmatic constitution *Lumen gentium*, begins with a solemn declaration: "Lumen gentium cum sit Christus - -" (LG 1, 1.) Christ is the light of humanity, the light "which shines out visibly from the Church." The image of the Catholic Church as the light for all, contributing to the world with her "strength of supernatural unity," was expressed with emphasis by *John XXIII* in his speech in the First Public Session of the Council on October 11, 1962.[4] The mission of the Church is "to proclaim his gospel to every creature." It is significant that the Council sees the essence of the Church as a sacrament of communion with God and of unity among all men.[5] It is the universal mission of the Church to advance the natural unity of mankind, which is so evidently furthered by modern social, technical, and cultural bonds, and, above all, to work for communion of all men with Christ.[6]

---

[3] Cf. Introduction (1.1.) above and, for instance, *Küng* 1974, 89, *Türk* 1967, 29-38, and *Stransky* 1985, 156-157.

[4] "Quo fit ut de Ecclesia catholica, cuius lux omnia illuminat et cuius supernaturalis unitatis vis in universae hominum familia profectum redundat - -" AS I/I, 174.

[5] *Schillebeeckx*, 1968, interprets LG 1 as a sacramental motive of the Church's mission. Here the main theme of the Council is in full harmony with what Henri de Lubac has taught since the 1930's; cf. 2.2. above.

[6] "Cum autem Ecclesia sit in Christo veluti sacramentum seu signum et instrumentum intimae cum Deo unionis totiusque generis humani unitatis, naturam missionemque suam universalem, praecedentium Conciliorum argumento instans, pressius fidelibus suis et mundo universo declarare intendit. Condiciones huius temporis huic Ecclesiae officio urgentiorem vim addunt, ut nempe homines cuncti, variis hodie vinculis socialibus, technicis, culturalibus arctius coniuncti, plenam etiam unitatem in Christo consequantur." LG 1, 1.

The very intention of the Council is to supply dogmatic clarification and pastoral edification on the universal mission of the Church of Christ. This universal mission consists of the saturation of all human life with the truth of the gospel of Christ. All spheres of human life – individual human beings, families, institutions, organizations, peoples, culture, scientific and technical progress, social and political structures must be penetrated by the spirit of the gospel. And above all, the salvific message and the sacramental presence of the Church must be extended to all men so that the possibility of salvation and participation in divine life is offered to all. As the sacrament of the world, the Church has the task of illuminating the entire creation with that truth which "elevates human beings to share in God's own divine life" (homines ad participandam vitam divinam elevare decrevit). (LG, 2, 1.) LG 13, 4 emphatically teaches that all people of the world are "called to the Catholic unity of the People of God." The concept of grace is connected with the idea of the call: all mankind is "called by God's grace to salvation."[7] Vocation or call does not yet equal election; all are called, but not all are to be numbered among the elect. The dogmatic constitution speaks about the offer of grace, but the efficacy and finality of that offer is the secret of God about which even the Church must utter the very minimum.

Delving deeper into the meaning of the mystery of salvation, the *Lumen gentium* constitution does not compromise in regard to what the Catholic Church has taught in the past about the central role of the Church as the medium of salvation. "This holy Council first of all turns its attention to the Catholic faithful. Basing itself on Scripture and Tradition, it teaches that the Church, a pilgrim now on earth, is necessary for salvation (Ecclesiam necessariam esse ad salutem)." (LG 14, 1.) The Council believes that God's plan of salvation entails that he save men not as individuals but that he instead redeem a people for himself.[8] As "the universal sacrament of salvation" (universale salutis sacramentum), the Church is the indispensable mediator of redemption; the risen Christ "is continually active in the world in order to lead men to the Church (ut homines ad Ecclesiam perducat) and, through it, join them more closely to himself." (LG 48, 2.)

---

[7] "Ad hanc igitur catholicam Populi Dei unitatem, quae pacem universalem praesignat et promovet, omnes vocantur homines, ad eamque variis modis pertinent vel ordinantur sive fideles catholici, sive alii credentes in Christo, sive denique omnes universaliter homines, gratia Dei ad salutem vocati." LG 13, 4.

[8] "Placuit tamen Deo homines non singulatim, quavis mutua connexione seclusa, sanctificare et salvare, sed eos in populum constituere, qui in veritate Ipsum agnosceret Ipsique sancte serviret." LG 9, 1.

The pastoral constitution *Gaudium et spes* specifies that the calling of all men is one and the same for all: *vocatio divina*.[9] The Holy Spirit offers to all the possibility of being made, in a hidden way, partners in the paschal mystery: "For since Christ died for all, and since all men are in fact called to one and the same destiny, which is divine, we must hold that the Holy Spirit offers to all the possibility of being made partners, in a way known to God, in the paschal mystery."[10] Even this sentence does not, however, refer to the finality of salvation; the emphasis is on the idea of *gratia universalis* in the sense of *vocatio* and *offerre*. God calls men to be participants in his grace; by what means and with what effect is not here stated. Consequently, although GS 22,5 has been frequently quoted as a Catholic concession to the salvific efficacy of supernatural grace outside Christianity,[11] we must not read too much into this passage.

It is important to note the context in which the idea of participation in the paschal mystery was expressed: GS 22, 5 speaks about the problem of suffering and death as belonging to the great mysteries of human life; the suffering of Christ illuminates this mystery and provides hope and strength to endure the grief of life. The possibility of salvation outside the Church is defined in a larger context, appearing in a section in which the Council does not speak at all about other religions but only about human and ethical problems in terms of the theology of creation: the nature and dignity of man, sin, death, conscience, freedom, and atheism. God's hidden grace may work in those who, guided by their God-given conscience, seek the truth and strive for that which is truly good in human life. This fact applies even to atheists.

In fact, the central idea of GS 22,5, the call (vocatio) of all men to the unity of God's people, appears frequently in the Council documents. *Gaudium et spes* affirms the special soteriological vocation of all people, because they are created in God's image; because human beings have the same origin, they also have the same teleological call or destiny.[12] Furthermore, before speaking about this call, GS 22, 5 points to the larger

---

[9] "Cum enim pro omnibus mortuus sit Christus cumque vocatio hominis ultima revera una sit, scilicet divina - -" GS 22, 5.

[10] "Cum enim pro omnibus mortuus sit Christus cumque vocatio hominis ultima revera una sit, scilicet divina, tenere debemus Spiritum Sanctum cunctis possibilitatem offerre ut, modo Deo cognito, huic paschali mysterio consocientur." GS 22, 5.

[11] For an interpretation of "the paschal christology" of GS 22 as a form of "anonymous Christendom," see *Amstutz* 1982, 92-95. *Ratzinger*, 1968, 353-354, says that GS 22 is a more developed expression of the extra-ecclesiastical salvation than is LG 16, because here salvation is linked directly with the center of christology.

[12] "Cum omnes homines, anima rationali pollentes et ad imaginem Dei creati, eamdem naturam eamdemque originem habeant, cumque, a Christo redempti, eadem vocatione et destinatione divina fruantur - -" GS 29, 1. Similarly GS 24, 1 and AG 2, 2.

context of natural moral law. The text before the quotation presented above runs: "All this holds true not for Christians only but also for all men of good will in whose hearts grace is active invisibly."[13] Here grace means the universal grace poured upon all creation. The possibility of good will is based on natural moral law and it is sustained by the creative and providential grace, *gratia creata sive communis*, of the Triune God. Consequently, the possibility of salvation expressed here is through the way of grace inherent in creation and in providence rather than through the way of universal supernatural grace, i.e., the specifically revealed christological grace.

The decree on the Church's missionary activity, *Ad gentes*, reveals a resemblance to the Church-centered doctrinal teaching of *Lumen gentium*.[14] Similarly to the doctrine expressed in LG, the missionary decree also includes in the scope of the Church's mission both promotion of the created good in the modern progress of human life and a call to membership in God's family.[15] The Church possesses *plenitudo mediorum salutis*; consequently, it is her mission to contribute to drawing all humanity towards *plenitudo catholica* which is a sojourn on its way towards *plenitudo eschatologica* (AG 6, 2 & 9, 2). It is the basic aim of the Church to establish the bodily presence of the people of God, i.e., of the Church herself, among every nation and people, "that the whole human race might become one People of God, form one body of Christ, and be built up into one temple of the Holy Spirit." (AG 7, 3.) Until the final day, it is the mission of the Church to add people from all nations to the number of the people of God; "by missionary activity the mystical Body is enlarged until it reaches the mature fullness of Christ." (AG 9, 2.) In accordance with the incarnatory principle of the divine salvific truth, the missionary decree teaches that the visible embodiment of the Church of Christ among all peoples is necessary for the salvation of men. The divine mystery of religion or *mysterium salutis* is indispensably incarnated into the spiritual and physical reality of the Church.[16]

---

13 "Quod non tantum pro Christifideles valet, sed et pro omnibus hominibus bonae voluntatis in quorum corde gratia invisibili modo operatur." GS 22, 5.

14 The very opening sentence of the decree, referring to LG 48, 2, states: "Ad gentes divinitus missa ut sit 'universale salutis sacramentum' Ecclesia ex intimis propriae catholicitatis exigentiis, mandato sui Fundatoris oboediens (cf. Marc. 16, 16), Evangelium omnibus hominibus nuntiare contendit." AG 1, 1.

15 "In praesenti autem rerum ordine, ex quo nova exsurgit humanitatis condicio, Ecclesia, sal terrae et lux mundi (cf. Matth. 5, 13-14), urgentius vocatur ad omnem creaturam salvandam et renovandam, ut omnia in Christo instaurentur, et in Ipso homines unam familiam unumque Populum Dei constituant." AG 1, 2.

16 "Ecclesia, ut omnibus mysterium salutis vitamque a Deo allatam offerre possit, sese omnibus his coetibus inserere debet eodem motu, quo ipse Christus incarnatione sua se obstrinxit

In the documents of the Council, some statements appear which seem to suppose a possibility of salvation *extra ecclesiam*. LG 9, 1 says: "At all times and in every race, anyone who fears God and does what is right has been acceptable to him (cf. Acts 10:35)."[17] The text gives the impression that the Council sees a possibility of revering the true God outside Christianity. The possibility of doing good or justice is, of course, here admitted solely on the basis of the general knowledge of God and his will, knowledge which is the mark of the Creator's handiwork in every human being. The text quoted says that anyone who fears God and does what is right is "Deo acceptus." The very next sentence of LG 9, 1 states the previously quoted idea of God's intention to save not individuals, but a people.[18] This somewhat limits attempts to find a doctrine of an extra-ecclesiastical way of salvation in the dogmatic constitution.

The Council documents introduce the idea that there is a certain classification of non-Christians: There are two main groups of people who do not believe in Christ. In the first group are those who hear the Christian message and "know that the Catholic Church was founded as necessary by God through Christ," but consciously reject the Church; these cannot be saved.[19] In the second group of non-Christians are those who through no fault of their own, *sine culpa,* do not know the saving gospel and the incarnated institution of grace, the Church; here the Council repeats the principle already explicated by *Pius IX* in 1863. Speaking about those ignorant of the gospel, LG 16, 1 says that even they "are related to the People of God in various ways."[20] From the very start it is made clear that the divine grace efficacious outside the Church nevertheless has a relation to the Church, because it is the grace of Christ who is the head of his Body. But the *modus* of that relationship remains a mystery; the Council restrains from saying much about it.

After making a comment on Jews and Muslims, the LG 16, 1 treats the issue of grace and eternal salvation. The major teaching of the Second Vatican Council on the possibility of salvation *extra Ecclesiam* runs:

---

certis socialibus et culturalibus condicionibus hominum cum quibus conversatus est." AG 10, 1.

[17] "In omni quidem tempore et in omni gente Deo acceptus est quicumque timet Eum et operatur iustitiam (cf. Act. 10, 35)." LG 9, 1.

[18] "Placuit tamen Deo homines non singulatim, quavis mutua connexione seclusa, sanctificare et salvare, sed eos in populum constituere - -" LG 9, 1.

[19] "Quare illi homines salvari non possent, qui Ecclesiam catholicam a Deo per Iesum Christum ut necessariam esse conditam non ignorantes, tamen vel in eam intrare, vel in eadem perseverare noluerint." LG 14, 1.

[20] "Ii tandem qui Evangelium nondum acceperunt, ad Populum Dei diversis rationibus ordinantur." LG 16, 1. There is a reference to Thomas' *Summa Theologica*.

> Nor is God remote from those who in shadows and images seek the unknown
> God, since he gives to all men life and breath and all things (Acts 17:25-28),
> and since the Saviour wills all men to be saved (1 Tim. 2:4). Those who,
> through no fault of their own, do not know the gospel of Christ or his Church,
> but who nevertheless seek God with a sincere heart, and, moved by grace, try
> in their actions to do his will as they know it through the dictates of their
> conscience – those too may achieve eternal salvation. Nor shall divine providence
> deny the assistance necessary for salvation to those who, through no fault of their
> own, have not yet arrived at an explicit knowledge of God, and who, not without
> grace, strive to lead a good life.[21]

The Council thus establishes the possibility of an extra-ecclesiastical way
of salvation. This quotation stresses three conditions for that possibility.
First, the non-Christians must be people who through no fault of their own
(sine culpa) do not know the gospel of Christ or his Church. Second, with
a sincere heart and open mind, they seek God, i.e., the Creator whose
existence they may know by reason but whom they do not yet know as the
personal God revealed in Christ. Third, they try to do God's will as they
know it through conscience, i.e., on the basis of natural moral law, and thus
they "strive to lead a good life." That is what many men try to do through
and in their religions, as well as outside religions. These people are, indeed,
"moved by grace" (sub gratiae influxu) and are "not without grace" (non
sine divina gratia) in their striving to do what is God's will. And
furthermore, the Creator of all, "divine providence shall not deny the

---

[21] "Neque ab aliis, qui in umbris et imaginibus Deum ignotum quaerunt, ab huiusmodi Deus
ipse longe est, cum det omnibus vitam et inspirationem et omnia (cf. Act. 17, 25-28), et Salvator
velit omnes homines salvos fieri (cf. 1 Tim. 2, 4). Qui enim Evangelium Christi Eiusque Ecclesiam
sine culpa ignorantes, Deum tamen sincero corde quaerunt, Eiusque voluntatem per conscientiae
dictamen agnitam, operibus adimplere, sub gratiae influxu, conantur, aeternam salutem consequi
possunt. Nec divina Providentia auxilia ad salutem necessaria denegat his qui sine culpa ad
expressam agnitionem Dei nondum pervenerunt et rectam vitam non sine divina gratia assequi
nituntur." LG 16, 1. For a commentary on LG 16, see *Grillmeier* 1966, 205-207.

A similar line of argumentation is present in LG 9, 1 as well: "In omni quidem tempore et in
omni gente Deo acceptus est quicumque timet Eum et operatur iustitiam (cf. Act. 10, 35)." And
in DV 3, 1: "- - sine intermissione generis humani curam egit, ut omnibus qui secundum
patientiam boni operis salutem quaerunt, vitam aeternam daret (cf. Rom. 2, 6-7)." See also GS
14, 2.

The LG text refers in its note 19 to the letter of the Holy Office to the Archbishop of Boston on
August 8, 1949, in which the idea of the responsibility of man is present in that letter. Without
any reference to universal grace, the letter speaks about the "implicit calling" of those who are
obedient to the will of God. See DS 3867 & 3870 and 2.1. above. Commenting on the same section
of LG, Cardinal Wojtyla says: "This search for God, as we see, is expressed primarily in right
conduct and obedience to one's conscience." *Wojtyla* 1980, 130. The moral line of interpretation
was the dominant theme in a speech of Pope Paul VI when he made a comment on LG, 13: "through
their moral uprightness open to God's mysterious mercy" men may be associated with salvation.
L'Osservatore Romano, June 2, 1966.

assistance necessary for salvation" to them; non-Christians are saved, not through law, but through grace. The idea of *gratia creata sive communis*, in terms of creation and natural moral law, is clearly recognized here, though not further developed. These are the three premises the conclusion of which is that the merciful God, willing the salvation of all people, does not deny his grace to them, but they live under the influence of his mercy. The final result of all this is eternal salvation (aeterna salus). The line of argument represented here is reiterated twice in LG 16, 1, using varying expressions.

In regard to the concept of grace, the expressions are minimal: the text does not explain what created common grace consists of and how it operates, the question about *modus gratiae* is left open. When speaking about divine mysteries of which no explicit revelation exists, Conciliar terminology is precautious and minimalistic. So doing, the Council leaves room for the possible development of the dogma. In accordance with the classical dogma, even salvation *extra Ecclesiam* is understood as the work of the ·Triune God, because *opera ad extra* of the Holy Trinity are indivisible. All grace is simultaneously the creative grace of the Creator, the redeeming grace of Christ, and the sanctifying grace of the Holy Spirit; Conciliar theology, however, does not speculate about the various grades and modes of grace. The Triune God's grace may assist non-Christians in their search for the truth and right life, in a manner not clear to any human being, God's creative grace perfecting and strengthening that which is already given in human nature through creation. These non-Christians may therefore attain eternal life in a way hidden to us. The Council proved of humble prudence in saying so little about this mystery of which there is so little knowledge.

It is remarkable that the Council text of LG 16 omits any mention of the possible contribution of the proper religious truth of non-Christians' own religion to salvation. Non-Christians reflect the truth only insofar as their life is in accordance with natural knowledge of the one God and of natural moral law.[22] This means that in LG 16 the possibility of an extraordinary way of salvation is reduced to the sphere of theology of creation and to the general conception of God and morals included therein. All this confirms what we noted in the analysis of the NA declaration: the Catholic Church does not indeed believe that there is a way of salvation in any non-Christian religion as a religion, i.e., as an epiphany of *mysterium divinum*. In other

---

[22] *Brechter*, 1968, 346, remarks: "Sed Concilium indubitanter dixit non-christianis salutem non propter coniunctionem cum aliqua religione aliena tribui, sed uniuscuiusque iudicio conscientiae causari."

words, non-Christian religions do not add any supernatural dimension of revelation or grace to the natural condition of man.[23]

The theology of the Council is fully in line with the basic theological notions of Thomism. Each time man hears and obeys his conscience, God's hidden grace is operating; this kind of universality of grace is working in man on the basis of creation and has nothing to do with the idea of God's specific or supernatural grace in religions. God's hidden grace, about which the Council speaks, is effective irrespective of the possible religious orientation of man. Grace is a reality which is in no way bound to human religiousity, being is far above all religious manifestations of human culture. God's universal grace, based on creation and expressed in the goodness of nature, is itself the criterion on the basis of which the value of all the cultural expressions of human life, including religious phenomena, are to be judged.

The line of interpretation present in the Council documents was clearly articulated by Pope *Paul VI* in his first speech to the Council fathers at the Second Public Session on September 29, 1963. According to the pope, the Church passes beyond her own sphere "seeing those other religions which preserve the sense and notion of the one supreme, transcendent God, Creator and Sustainer, and which worship him with acts of sincere piety and base their morals and social life on their beliefs and religious practices."[24] The general notion of the Creator, his cult, and morals based on that are acknowledged.

Cardinal *Augustin Bea*, the major promoter of the NA declaration, also supports the line of interpretation represented here. He says that those who, through no fault of their own, do not know Christ can be saved on the basis of living obedient to the voice of their conscience. Referring to LG 16, Bea explains that the Church contributes to their salvation by clarifying natural spiritual and moral values.[25] Bea's line of thought was discernable in his relatio to Text III of NA in November 1964, as well.[26] Bea's views mean a

---

[23] *Hallencreutz*, 1977, 44, quite correctly commented on LG 16 by saying that "the dogmatic constitution of the Church does not attach any specific salvatory significance to different human religions as such." "Lumen gentium is more concerned with dialogue with men of living faiths than with the theology of religion."

[24] "Ultra igitur christiana castra oculos suos dirigit, et ad alias religiones respicit, quae servant sensum et notionem Dei, unius, creatoris, providentis, summi et rerum naturam transcendentis; quae Dei cultum exercent sincerae pietatis actibus; quae ex iis usibus et opinionibus morum et socialis vitae praecepta derivant." AS II/I 198.

[25] "Nach der katholischen Lehre können jene, die ohne Schuld von Christus nicht wissen, gerettet werden, wenn sie nach ihrem eigenen guten Gewissen leben. Wenn sich nun die Kirche bemüht, die geistigen und moralischen Werte zu fördern, die sich bei den Gläubigen nicht-christlicher Religionen finden, wirkt sie tatsächlich mit, damit diese, indem sie nach dem eigenen guten Gewissen ihr Leben einrichten, ihr Heil wirken." *Bea* 1966b, 306.

[26] When explaining the new draft of the schema, he said: "Illi autem nihilominus salvari

possibility of salvation on other than religious grounds – on the basis of man's obedience to the voice of the Creator he hears in his own heart and conscience. It is not the way of supernatural revelation or grace. The hidden universal grace of the Triune God may cause man to be obedient to this will of God which he hears in his conscience. Bea sees a continuity between this kind of grace and the explicit grace of Christ in his Church.[27] It is remarkable that not once does Bea combine the idea of God's hidden grace with any non-Christian religion; it is grace which is similarly available to every human being, because everyone is God's creature. Religions have no specific role therein.

That is all that *Lumen gentium* has to say about the extra-ecclesiastical way of salvation. Immediately after the above statements, the text of the dogmatic constitution, LG 16, 1, emphatically states that whatever good or truth is found amongst the adherents of non-Christian religions, it "is considered by the Church to be a preparation for the gospel." This *praeparatio evangelica* does not, however, in any measure lessen the urgency of the Church's missionary activity. Quite the contrary, it challenges the Church to make an even greater effort in her mission.[28]

The *Ad gentes* decree also acknowledges an extraordinary means to salvation. Through his secret ways, God can lead those "into that faith without which it is impossible to please him."[29] The text of the missionary decree does see a possibility of an extra-ecclesiastical way of salvation through faith which God has given man through media other than the Church and her proclamation and sacraments. But this extraordinary way of salvation is a secret of the omnipotent and just God. It is the very minimum that the Council teaches about this extra-ecclesiastical way to communion with God. God's secret, of which the revelation gives little if any information, remains hidden even to the holy Council of the Catholic Church. The possibility of salvation outside the Church does not allow either Christians or non-Christians to lull themselves into a false sense of security. The idea of the incarnated divine truth is in no way compromised by any other means to salvation; and, on the other hand, the specific

---

possunt, si conscientiae dictaminibus oboediant." AS III/VIII, 651.

[27] "Hi enim, qui secundum dictamen propriae rectae conscientiae vivunt, implicita fide - - cum Christo eiusque Corpore Mystico uniuntur - -" AS III/VIII, 651. "He remains always absolute master of his grace and is able to grant it as and to whom he wishes." *Bea* 1967, 127.

[28] "Quapropter ad gloriam Dei et salutem istorum omnium promovendam, Ecclesia, memor mandati Domini dicentis: 'Praedicate Evangelium omni creaturae' (Mc. 16, 16), missiones fovere sedulo curat." LG 16, 1.

[29] After repeating word for word the previously quoted sentence of LG 14, 1, AG 7, 1 states: "Etsi ergo Deus viis sibi notis homines Evangelium sine eorum culpa ignorantes ad fidem adducere possit, sine qua impossibile est Ipsi placere (Hebr. 11, 6) - -"

concrete fact of the historical incarnation of Jesus Christ cannot be absorbed into any vague cosmic christology based on a universal interpretation of incarnation, yet Christ's incarnation certainly has its universal dimensions. Neither the urgency of the Church's mission nor the necessity for non-Christians to hear the gospel and to join the people of God is in any way lessened.[30] On the contrary, when making the above statement regarding an extraordinary way to union with God, the AG decree again emphasizes the missionary activity of the Church.[31]

The Council succeeded in taking as positive an attitude as possible towards non-Christian religions. Any conceivable critical attitude is expressed by silence rather than by critical statements. This is to say that the Council has declined to give any negative definitions or comments on other religions, but it has not, despite polite diplomatic language used in relation to non-Christian religions, laid much positive value on the religious essence of those religions. Does any theological criticism or negative statements at all against non-Christian religions appear in the documents of the Council?

The answer is yes, but this criticism is given indirectly. Referring to Rom. 1:21 and 25, LG 16, 1 makes a general statement, without any reference to religion, that "very often, deceived by the Evil One, men have become vain in their reasonings, have exchanged the truth of God for a lie and served the world rather than the Creator."[32] Further, LG 17, 1 quotes the commandment which Christ gave his apostles in the last passage of Matth. 28. The object of description being *omnes gentes*, not any non-Christian religion in particular, the Council says a little later: "By her proclamation of the gospel, she (the Church) draws her hearers - - snatches them from the slavery of error - - The effect of her work is that whatever good is found sown in the minds and hearts of men or in the rites and customs of peoples, these not only are preserved from destruction, but are purified, raised up, and perfected for the glory of God, the confusion of the Devil, and the

---

[30] On the tension in Catholic missiology between the traditional ecclesiocentric model of mission (plantatio Ecclesiae) and the modern models leaning on the idea of the sacramental role of the Church, see *Rütti* 1972, 25-62. The Second Vatican Council seems to have adapted some of the modern thinking, but without forsaking the old theory.

[31] The above-quoted sentence continues: "- - Ecclesiae tamen necessitas incumbit (cf. 1 Cor. 9, 16), simulque ius sacrum, evangelizandi, ac proinde missionalis activitas vim suam et necessitatem hodie sicut et semper integram servat." AG 7, 1. A little earlier the decree had emphasized the necessity of being incorporated into the body of Christ, i.e., the Church: "Oportet igitur ut ad Eum, per praedicationem Ecclesiae agnitum, omnes convertantur, et Ipsi et Ecclesiae, quae Corpus Eius est, per Baptismum incorporentur." AG 7, 1.

[32] "At saepius homines, a Maligno decepti, evanuerunt in cogitationibus suis, et commutaverunt veritatem Dei in mendacium, servientes creaturae magis quam Creatori (cf. Rom. 1, 21 et 25) vel sine Deo viventes ac morientes in hoc mundo, extremae desperationi exponuntur." LG 16, 1.

happiness of man."[33] Through her mission, the Church liberates men from "the slavery of error" and purifies that which is good in the hearts and cultures of men "for the glory of God, the confusion of the Devil." A statement like this presumes that, before the missionary activity of the Church, *gentes* may, to some extent, live as slaves of error and under the influence of the Devil. But this is not because of their religion, but because of the original sin penetrating all human life.

AG 9, 2 repeats the clause of LG 17,1 which speaks about "the confusion of the Devil." Before this passage, however, the text adds a few negative remarks, the object of description again being *gentes*: "It (the missionary activity of the Church) purges of evil associations those elements of truth and grace which are found among peoples, and which are, as it were, a secret presence of God; and it restores them to Christ their source who overthrows the rule of the Devil and limits the manifold malice of evil."[34] The text thus assumes that Christ, the second person of the Trinity and coeffective in the act of creation, is the source of all elements of truth and grace found among peoples. These elements are contaminated by the manifold malice of evil under *imperium diaboli*. It is the very aim of the Church's missionary activity to overthrow this rule of the Devil over nations. The subject of the above sentence (liberat, restituit, evertit, arcet) is the same as in the two previous sentences: *activitas missionalis* of the Church,[35] indicating that there exists a clear contrast between the redemption and purification brought about by the mission of the Church and the existence of *gentes* in many ways still under the influence of *imperium diaboli*.

---

[33] "Praedicando Evangelium, Ecclesia audientes - - a servitute erroris eripit - - quidquid boni in corde menteque hominum vel in propriis ritibus et culturis populorum seminatum invenitur, non tantum non pereat, sed sanetur, elevetur et consummetur ad gloriam Dei, confusionem daemonis et beatitudinem hominis." LG 17, 1.

[34] "Quidquid autem veritatis et gratiae iam apud gentes quasi secreta Dei praesentia inveniebatur, a contagiis malignis liberat et Auctori suo Christo restituit, qui imperium diaboli evertit et multimodam scelerum malitiam arcet." AG 9, 2.

[35] "Activitas missionalis nihil aliud est et nihil minus quam propositi Dei manifestatio seu Epiphania et adimplementum in mundo et in eius historia - -" AG 9, 2.

10. THE GOSPEL AND CULTURE

According to the Council, as we have seen, religions are good insofar as they include in themselves seeds and elements of the natural goodness of creation. Religions are not acknowledged to be good as religions proper, but as expressions of human life created by the one God, the Creator of all. All natural goodness of life points to the deeper call of man, to his *vocatio divina* – even though an individual man himself may not be aware of that.

This vocation is made clear and perfected by the means of God's grace, through *plenitudo catholica* which tends towards the final consummation of the call of man, *plenitudo eschatologica*. As *sacramentum mundi*, the Church of Christ and all members of his Body have the divine mission of penetrating and saturating all spheres of human life with the light and grace of the gospel, thus contributing to the elevation, purification, and perfection of that which is naturally good in human life. Adapting the idea of fulfillment and perfection, the Council creates a beautiful implementation of the Thomistic theological notion: *gratia non tollit naturam, sed perficit*.

10.1. Praeparatio evangelica

All the good elements contained in the life of individual men and peoples are *praeparatio evangelica*, a preparation for the coming of the revealed truth, proclaimed and sacramentally represented by the Church. About the worthwhile values and virtues of nations, *Lumen gentium* asserts: "Whatever good or truth is found amongst them is considered by the Church to be a preparation for the gospel and given by him who enlightens all men that they may at length have life."[1] *Ad gentes* and *Gaudium et spes* express the same line of thought. According to the missionary decree, the search for God and truth in religions is preparation for the gospel.[2] The same texts go

---

[1] "Quidquid enim boni et veri apud illos invenitur, ab Ecclesia tamquam praeparatio evangelica aestimatur et ab Illo datum qui illuminat omnem hominem, ut tandem vitam habeat." LG 16, 1.

[2] "Hoc universale Dei propositum pro salute generis humani perficitur non solum modo quasi secreto in mente hominum vel per incepta, etiam religiosa, quibus ipsi multipliciter Deum quaerunt - - haec enim incepta indigent illuminari et sanari, etsi, ex benigno consilio providentis Dei,

on to insist that not only the religious search of men but also their longing for a fraternal society is fulfilled in the Christian gospel.[3] Nothing in human life can be purified and elevated, unless through Christ, through his assuming human nature: "The fathers of the Church constantly proclaim that what was not assumed by Christ was not healed." (AG 3, 2.) Sanctifying human life through his incarnation, Christ has made men participants in divine life.[4] The pastoral constitution confirms the idea of *praeparatio evangelica* and the doctrine of purification of natural goodness of life through the presence of Christ. The mission of the Church in the modern world not only unites men with God but also sanctifies and elevates human dignity and all the aspects and endeavours of social life.[5] After stating that truth, the Council text mentions "the talents and activity of individuals and of society as a whole" as "praeparatio Evangelii." (GS 40, 4.) GS 57, 6 says that examples such as the modern progress of science and technology, instances of international solidarity, a growing awareness of responsibility to help one's fellow men, an eagerness to improve the standard of living of all men, etc. are all "aliqua praeparatio ad nuntium Evangelii."

The documents of the Second Vatican Council are rich in expressing the theological thought of the gospel of Christ, i.e., the Christian revelation, which perfects the natural goodness of life. Such expressions concerning the positive evaluation of non-Christian religions are but a small portion of the total number of positive statements about the relation of the Christian truth to the cultures and cultural development of the whole of mankind. When one notes this, the special emphasis of the Council's appreciation of other religions seems somewhat diminished: its acknowledgement of the value of those religions for human life can thus be seen as merely part of the wholesale openness and friendliness of the Council towards human culture and its development.

As we saw in Ch. 4., the *Nostra aetate* declaration lies in the framework of the concept of the positive progress of human social and cultural life. As was indicated in 4.1., one of the main motives of the whole Second Vatican

---

aliquando pro paedagogia ad Deum verum vel praeparatione evangelica possint haberi." AG 3, 1.

[3] "Deus autem ad pacem seu communionem Secum stabiliendam fraternamque societatem inter homines, eosque peccatores, componendam, in historiam hominum novo et definitivo modo intrare decrevit mittendo Filium suum in carne nostra - -" AG 3, 1.

[4] "Itaque per vias verae Incarnationis processit Filius Dei ut homine divinae natura participes faceret - -" AG 3, 2.

[5] "Ecclesia quidem, proprium suum finem salutarem persequens, non solum vitam divinam cum homine communicat, sed etiam lumen eius repercussum quodammodo super universum mundum fundit, potissimum per hoc quod personae humanae dignitatem sanat et elevat, humanae societatis compaginem firmat, atque cotidianam hominum navitatem profundiore sensu et significatione imbuit." GS 40, 3.

Council was to find positive points of connection between Christianity and the rapid social, cultural, scientific, and technological evolution of mankind. But even though the Second Vatican Council proved to be of unforeseen openness to the progress and problems of the modern world, it did not make the least compromise in respect to the Catholic faith. All beneficial evolution in mankind is welcomed and saluted with approval. Despite that fact, however, all forms and developments of social and cultural life need to be purified, strengthened, and elevated by the revealed divine truth, given to the world in Christ and incarnated in and transmitted by his Church. The moral or cultural values of non-Christian religions can be no exception; they also must be perfected by the light of the divine revelation.

10.2. Grace Perfects Nature

On the basis of the mystery of incarnation, "nature" and "grace" – the natural and the supernatural – belong together; the revealed or incarnated truth of grace liberates from the bondage of evil, purifies and perfects that which is good in created nature. In this way theology of grace and theology of creation are inseparable; "God has willed to gather together all that was natural, all that was supernatural, into a single whole in Christ." (AA 7, 2.) It is easy to find a great number of quotations from the Council documents which illustrate the theological principle of perfection. The two most outstanding examples are those quoted above, LG 17, 1 and AG 9, 2. The classical principle of grace perfecting nature is combined with missionary motivation.

In the following, we shall look at some additional notable statements expressing the idea of fulfillment through perfection. *Lumen gentium* 36, 2 gives a profound assertion of how the world must be "filled with the spirit of Christ" and how, "through the members of the Church, Christ will increasingly illuminate the whole of human society with his saving light." All this will lead to a more efficient realization of such human aspirations as justice, peace, and cultural and technical progress: "The faithful must, then recognize the inner nature, the value and the ordering of the whole creation to the praise of God. Even by their secular activity they must aid one another to greater holiness of life, so that the world may be filled with the spirit of Christ and may the more effectively attain its destiny in justice, in love and in peace."[6] LG 13, 2 speaks about the "universal character" of

---

[6] "Fideles igitur totius creaturae intimam naturam, valorem et ordinationem in laudem Dei agnoscere, et per opera etiam saecularia se invicem ad sanctiorem vitam adiuvare debent, ita ut

the people of God, on the basis of which the Catholic Church "seeks for the return of all humanity and all its goods under Christ the Head." By expanding the revealed truth of the gospel over all humanity, the Church makes its true catholicity manifest.[7] Not only Catholic Christians or other Christians but "universally all men" are called to "that Catholic unity of the People of God which prefigures and promotes universal peace." LG 13, 4.

The decree on the Church's missionary activity, *Ad gentes*, states that missionary activity "is intimately bound up with human nature and its aspirations." "In manifesting Christ, the Church reveals to men their true situation and calling." In the Church's missionary activity, supernatural grace meets the natural condition of man perfecting its real nature.[8]

The pastoral constitution *Gaudium et spes* is especially rich in statements expressing the Council's doctrine of the Christian revelation which perfects the naturally good elements of human life. A few examples will suffice here. The address of the pastoral constitution is "ad universos homines." In its initial doctrinal statement, the constitution describes how the world, despite being in the slavery of sin, is liberated through Christ so that it might be transformed anew according to God's design. The Council "has in mind the whole human family seen in the context of everything which envelopes it."[9] The risen Christ works through his Spirit in the hearts of men, "not only arousing in them a desire for the world to come but he quickens, purifies, and strengthens the generous aspirations of mankind to make life more humane."[10] The pastoral constitution asserts that the Christian revelation

---

mundus spiritus Christi imbuatur atque in iustitia, caritate et pace finem suum efficacius attingat." The text continues: "In quo officio universaliter adimplendo laici praecipuum locum obtinent. Sua igitur in profanis disciplinis competentia suaque activitate, gratia Christi intrinsecus elevata, valide conferant operam, ut bona creata secundum Creatoris ordinationem Eiusque Verbi illuminationem humano labore, arte technica, civilique cultura ad utilitatem omnium prorsus hominum excolantur, aptiusque inter illos distribuantur, et suo modo ad universalem progressum in humana et christiana libertate conducant. Ita Christus per Ecclesiae membra totam societatem humanam suo salutari lumine magis magisque illuminabit." LG 36, 2.

7   "Hic universalitatis character, qui Populum Dei condecorat, ipsius Domini donum est, quo catholica Ecclesia efficaciter et perpetuo tendit ad recapitulandam totam humanitatem cum omnibus bonis eius sub Capite Christo, in unitate Spiritus Eius." LG 13, 2.

8   "Etiam cum ipsa natura humana eiusque adspirationibus activitas missionalis intimam habet connexionem. Christum enim manifestando, eo ipso Ecclesia hominibus genuinam eorum condicionis atque integrae vocationis veritatem revelat, cum Christus principium sit et exemplar huius humanitatis renovatae, fraterno amore, sinceritate et pacifico spiritu imbutae, ad quam omnes adspirant." AG 8, 1.

9   "- - mundum, quem Christifideles credunt ex amore Creatoris conditum et conservatum, sub peccati quidem servitute positum, sed a Christo crucifixo et resurgente, fracta potestate Maligni, liberatum, ut secundum propositum Dei transformetur et ad consummationem perveniant." GS 2, 2.

10   "Sua resurrectione Dominus constitutus, Christus, cui omnis potestas in caelo et in terra data est, per virtutem Spiritus Sui in cordibus hominum iam operatur, non solum venturi saeculi

greatly fosters the reality of natural social life.[11] The human tendency towards communal life is perfected by Christ. (GS 32, 2.) The Church is the physical manifestation and the incarnated sacrament of a "new brotherly communion" in the world, and a proleptic sign of the eschatological fulfillment of perfect communion. (GS 32, 4.)[12] The Council believes that the light of the revelation will best illumine the path of modern development in mankind.[13] On the level of individuals' own lives, Christian revelation maintains "the image of a universal man" (imago hominis universalis). This image consists of elements of personality which are naturally good being newly restored and elevated by Christ.[14]

When speaking of the influence of the gospel, the Church or Christian lay people on the purification, sanctification, and perfection of the human world, the Council texts employ the idea of leaven, *fermentum*. For example, the missionary decree says: "Even in the secular history of mankind the gospel has acted as a leaven (fermentum) in the interests of liberty and progress, and it always offers itself as a leaven (fermentum) with regard to brotherhood, unity, and peace." (AG 8, 1.) According to DH 12, 2, the leaven of the gospel has greatly contributed to the growth of the consciousness of human dignity.[15] According to GS 40, 2, the Church is a leaven which contributes to the renewal

---

desiderium suscitans, sed eo ipso illa etiam generosa vota animans, purificans et roborans, quibus familia humana suam ipsius vitam humaniorem reddere et totam terram huic fini subiicere satagit." GS 38, 2.

[11] "Ad hanc vero communionem inter personas promovendam, Revelatio christiana magnum subsidium affert, simulque ad altiorem vitae socialis legum intellegentiam nos perducit quas Creator in natura spirituali ac morali hominis inscripsit." GS 23, 1.

[12] GS 39, 3 depicts this eschatological hope: "Bona enim humanae dignitatis, communionis fraternae et libertatis, hos omnes scilicet bonos naturae ac industriae nostrae fructus, postquam in Spiritu Domini et iuxta Eius mandatum in terris propagaverimus, postea denuo inveniemus, mundata tamen ab omni sorde, illuminata ac transfigurata, cum Christus Patri reddet regnum aeternum et universale - -"

[13] "Ecclesia, quae depositum verbi Dei custodit, ex quo principia in ordine religioso et morali hauriuntur, quin semper de singulis quaestionibus responsum in promptu habeat, lumen revelationis cum omnium peritia coniungere cupit, ut iter illuminetur, quod humanitas nuper ingressa est." GS 33, 2.

On the whole, the message of Christ renews, guards, and purifies all the naturally virtuous riches of human life: "Bonum Christi nuntium hominis lapsi vitam et cultum continenter renovat, et errores ac mala, ex semper minaci peccati seductione manantia, impugnat et removet. Mores populorum indesinenter purificat et elevat. Animi ornamenta dotesque cuiuscumque populi vel aetatis supernis divitiis velut ab intra foecundat, communit, complet atque in Christo restaurat." GS 58, 4.

[14] "Attamen unicuique homini remanet officium retinendi rationem totius personae humanae, in qua eminent intelligentiae, voluntatis, conscientiae et fraternitatis valores, qui omnes in Deo Creatore fundantur et in Christo mirabiliter sanati et elevati sunt." GS 61, 1.

[15] Similarly, GS 26, 4 says: "Evangelicum autem fermentum in corde hominis irrefrenabilem dignitatis exigentiam excitavit atque excitat."

of human society in Christ.[16]

The term *fermentum* is used often when the Conciliar texts describe the mission of Christian lay people in the world. Their whole life is a witness to the truth of the gospel, both through words and deeds. Thus "being led by the spirit of the gospel, they contribute to the sanctification of the world, as from within like leaven." (LG 31, 2.)

The decree on the apostolate of lay people, *Apostolicam actuositatem*, makes very clear how lay Christians act as the leaven in the world. They work both for the evangelization of men and the sanctification of the world.[17] The role of lay Christians as a leaven is also of crucial importance in the missionary role when witnessing to the truth of the gospel among non-Christians.[18] Lay people must be familiar with the culture in which they live; they "must purify and guard it," they "must perfect it in Christ so that the faith of Christ and the life of the Church will not be something foreign to the society in which they live, but will begin to transform and permeate it," the missionary decree affirms. (AG 21, 3.)

10.3. The Principle of Contextualization

Thus far we have seen how the relationship between the gospel and culture is based on the theological idea of the purification and sanctification of created nature by the revealed truth. In the Conciliar documents, this relationship is also understood in terms of the incarnation or contextualization of the divine truth into human culture. A full acknowledgement of contextualization is a new feature in the official doctrine of the Catholic Church. This new principle was anticipated by Pope *Pius XII*'s encyclical letter *Evangelii praecones* (June 2, 1951) in which he stated that "ethnicorum doctrinas" and "peculiares populorum mores" are to be

---

[16] "Ita Ecclesia - - tamquam fermentum et veluti anima societatis humanae in Christo renovandae et in familiam Dei transformandae existit." GS 40, 2.

[17] "Apostolatum reapse exercent sua operositate ad evangelizationem ac sanctificationem hominum et ad rerum temporalium ordinem spiritu evangelico perfundendum ac perficiendum, ita ut eorum operositas in hoc ordine testimonium Christi manifeste perhibeat et salutem hominum inserviat. Cum vero laicorum statui hoc sit proprium ut in medio mundi negotiorumque saecularium vitam agant, ipsi a Deo vocantur ut, spiritu christiano ferventes, fermenti instar in mundo apostolatum suum exerceant." AA 2, 2. See also AA 4, 5 & 5, 1 & 14, 2.

[18] "Ipsorum enim proprium est, Spiritu Christi imbuti, fermenti instar res temporales ab intra animare et ordinare ut secundum Christum iugiter fiant. - - ad hoc praesens est, ut concivibus non-christianis Christum verbo et opere annuntiet eosque iuvet ad plenam Christi receptionem." AG 15, 7.

cleansed by the Church.[19] The idea of contextualization was furthered by Pope *John XXIII* in his encyclical letter *Princeps pastorum* (November 28, 1959). In that he gives detailed instructions regarding the means by which the peculiarities of national cultures should be taken into consideration in the missionary situation. (See AAS 1959, 843-844.)

The new principle is emphatically present in those parts of the Conciliar documents which deal with the Church's missionary doctrine and activity. This means an authoritative repudiation of the cultural imperialism of western culture. But on the other hand, when accepting the principle of contextualization, the Council is careful not to make the least compromise of the revealed truth of the Christian faith: various cultural forms are accepted and adapted by each local branch of the Church insofar as they are in accordance with the natural goodness of created things as understood by the Church. The principle of contextualization is most readily accepted in relation to the eastern churches (Ecclesiae Orientis). The Council speaks about "the legitimate diversity," not only regarding diversity in ecclesiastical organization or liturgy, but even concerning diverse expressions of theological doctrines.[20] The variety within the universal Church is not an obstacle to unity; "variety in the Universal Church, so far from diminishing its unity, rather serves to emphasize it." (OE 2, 1.) From the point of view of the Church's mission, a certain diversity is beneficial.[21]

The principle of contextualization is clearly present particularly in the missionary decree *Ad gentes*, where contextualization concerns the incarnation of the truth of Christ into the reality of non-Christian cultures. In accordance with "the economy of the incarnation," the young churches "take over all the riches of the nations given to Christ as an inheritance." They borrow from all spheres of culture to the praise of the Creator.[22]

---

[19] "Quamorbem catholica Ecclesia ethnicorum doctrinas neque despexit neque respuit, sed eas potius, a quovis errore et a quavis impuritate liberatas, christiana sapientia consummavit atque perfecit. - - Peculiares quoque populorum mores eorumque tralaticia instituta non omnino cohibuit, sed quodammodo sacravit." AAS 1951, 522.

[20] "Quae supra de legitima diversitate dicta sunt, eadem placet etiam de diversa theologica doctrinarum enuntiatione declarare. Etenim in veritatis revelatae exploratione methodi gressusque diversi ad divina cognoscenda et confitenda in Oriente et in Occidente adhibiti sunt." UR 17, 1.

In the decree on the Catholic eastern churches, *Orientalium Ecclesiarum*, the Council prepared for the possibility of a union by emphasizing the legitimate right of the eastern churches to hold to their particular traditions; a union would not alter the eastern rite: "Sciant ac pro certo habeant omnes Orientales, se suos legitimos ritus liturgicos suamque disciplinam semper servare posse et debere, ac nonnisi ratione proprii et organici progressus mutationes inducendas esse." OE 6, 1.

[21] "Cum autem unitati Ecclesiae minime obstet, immo decorem eius augeat et ad missionem eius implendam non parum conferat quaedam morum consuetudinumque diversitas - -" UR, 16, 1.

[22] "Equidem ad instar oeconomia Incarnationis Ecclesiae novellae in Christo radicatae Apostolorumque fundamento superaedificatae, in admirabile commercium assumunt omnes divitias nationum quae Christo datae sunt in haereditatem (cf. Ps. 2, 8). Ipsae e suorum populorum

Numerous similar expressions in AG refer to the adaptation of the cultural riches of nations into the life of the Church. For example, a Christian in a missionary situation should learn to know "the riches which the generous God has distributed among nations." (AG 11, 2.) Religious institutes of the young churches should consider how traditions of asceticism and contemplation, "the seeds of which have been sown by God in certain ancient cultures before the preaching of the gospel," "might be incorporated into the Christian religious life." (AG 18, 2.) When religious institutes are established in missionary territories, a witness among non-Christians to the majesty and love of God is given "in a manner adapted to the genuinely religious traditions of the people." (AG 40, 2.) The young churches must graft elements of the universal Church onto their own culture.[23]

An important programmatic implementation of the principle of contextualization is given in the constitution on the sacred liturgy, *Sacrosanctum Concilium* 37-40, under the subtitle "Normae ad aptationem ingenio et traditionibus populorum perficiendam." The idea of "legitimae varietates et aptationes" is to be accepted in the field of liturgy. This is commended "especially in mission countries." (SC 38, 1.) In regard to liturgy, the Church "respects and fosters the qualities and talents of the various races and nations." Anything which is not indissolubly bound up with superstition and error is preserved intact or even can be admitted into the liturgy itself. (SC 37, 1.) In addition, in mission countries, elements of initiation rites may be christianized (SC 65, 1) and national musical tradition should be given due consideration in worship (SC 119, 1). In a closer analysis, the significance of the apparent positive application of the principle of contextualization is, however, to some extent diluted. The constitution on liturgy excludes doctrinal matters from the realm of contextualization; the principle concerns only issues "which do not involve faith" (fidem non tangunt). (SC 37, 1.) This means that all the possible adaptations of the proper religious contents of cultures are by definition excluded.

In other documents where the principle of contextualization occurs, this concept appears to be only a modification of the principle of the purification of cultures by the Christian revelation and to concern natural created goodness in these cultures. AG 22, 2 continues to clarify the principle of "oeconomia Incarnationis" by stating unambiguously that contextualization

---

consuetudinibus et traditionibus, sapientia et doctrina, artibus et disciplinis, ea omnia mutuantur quae ad gloriam Creatoris confitendam, ad gratiam Salvatoris illustrandam et ad vitam christianam rite ordinandam conferre possunt." AG 22, 1.

[23] "Intima permaneat Ecclesiarum novellarum communio cum tota Ecclesia, cuius traditionis elementa culturae propriae adiungant ad augendam, mutuo quodam virium effluvio, vitam Corporis Mystici." AG 19, 3.

means studying how the customs, concept of life, and social structures of a people "can be reconciled with the moral standards proposed by divine revelation." Here contextualization concerns only the sphere of morals, only the moulding of the moral concepts of any nation to be uniform with the moral concept of natural moral law, as understood in the Catholic Church.[24]

Contextualization is, after all, a procedure of taking elements of a national or ethnic culture "up into a Catholic unity," after such elements have been "illumined by the light of the gospel."[25] Although a Christian witness must "learn of the riches which the generous God has distributed among nations," he must, above all, "endeavour to illuminate these riches with the light of the gospel." (AG 11, 2.) AG 22, 2 advises that the principles of contextualization applied should avoid every appearance of syncretism and false particularism. On the basis of our analysis, we can conclude that, for the Second Vatican Council, "syncretism" would include the acknowledgeing of any actual religious truth of a non-Christian religion not in accordance with the Catholic faith; it would, in addition, be "particularism" to deny the existence of the natural cognition of the existence of the Creator and of his presence in the moral, cultural, and social good among non-Christian peoples.

Examination of the relationship between the gospel and culture in the teaching of the Council has confirmed the line of interpretation presented in previous chapters: non-Christian religions do not have good and acceptable elements in themselves on the basis of what they are as actual religions, but rather on the basis of any good traces of the creation by the one and true God they comprise. In this sense, human cultures in general and non-Christian religions share an equivalent position.

---

[24] "Sic clarius percipietur quibus viis fides, ratione habita philosophiae vel sapientiae populorum, quaerere possit intellectum, et quibus modis consuetudines, vitae sensus et socialis ordo, cum moribus revelatione divina significatis, componi queant." AG 22, 2.

[25] "Hoc agendi modo omnis syncretismi et falsi particularismi species secludetur, vita christiana ingenio indolique cuiusque culturae accommodabitur, traditiones particulares cum propriis cuiusque familiae gentium dotibus luce Evangelii illustratis, in unitatem catholicam assumentur." AG 22, 2.

11. CONCLUSION

We have seen that the official documents of the Second Vatican Council do indeed contain a doctrine of non-Christian religions. The statements in various documents concerning the relationship of Christianity to other religions – and the nature of those religions – are not merely pastoral in their essence, but deeply dogmatic. This study has shown that the common interpretation of the Council documents as recognizing non-Christian religions to be capable of specific mediation of God's saving grace is invalid. Many of the modern interpreters of the Second Vatican Council propose a line of interpretation which cannot be supported by the Conciliar texts. There may be other authoritative documents, and certainly there is a legion of individual Catholic authors who recognize non-Christian religions as vehicles of divine revelation and salvation or as expressions of supernatural christological grace. But the official statements of the Council do not permit such a conclusion.

The teaching of the Second Vatican Council is a consistent development of the basic notions of Thomism and of all that the Holy Office had previously stated concerning non-Christians. On the whole, the Council reaffirmed the classical Catholic position, thus representing continuity in the Catholic doctrine. It made a consequent advance from the lines of interpretation promoted by Pope *Pius IX* in the 1860's and by Pope *Pius XII* in the 1940's; this line of interpretation was also rooted in the statements of the First Vatican Council on the general notion of God. In the last resort, the firm foundation of the official Catholic teaching on the possibility of salvation outside Christianity lies in the theological insights of medieval Scholasticism. The traditional concept of the twofold relation between man and his Creator was affirmed: general cognition of God through reason from his works (Rom. 1:20) and the universal validity of natural moral law (Rom. 2:14-16). The salvific universal grace of the Triune God is effective through both these modes of relationship.

The new structure of interpretation introduced by the Second Vatican Council was that the general knowledge of God and of his will was related to non-Christian religions: religions must be evaluated as displaying natural good reflecting the general notion of God and his will. And, as was pointed out by *Joseph Ratzinger* and his predecessors in their interpretation of non-Christian religions, the content of God's will is above all the double commandment of love. Religions and their doctrinal views and rituals are a part of human culture; as such they belong to human nature and to natural moral law in its wider scope. This approach to non-Christian religions is in accordance with the classical model of grace imbued in nature: a non-Christian can attain salvation as he fulfills his duty toward God as he understands divinity in his own culture and cult, and loves his neighbor. This is the way of creation and natural moral law. Every human being, every culture and every religion is graced, because man, the rational being and the image of God, capable of knowing and worshipping his Creator, is graced in the meaning of creative and providential universal grace, *gratia creáta sive communis*. But grace inherent in nature, including non-Christian religions, lacks the supernatural quality of grace needed for the re-establishment of the *similitudo Dei* lost in the Fall.

Consistent with the pre-conciliar tradition, the Second Vatican Council does not differentiate between aspects of or qualify *modus gratiae*. There are no statements concerning the manner in which common grace is efficacious in mankind. The emphasis lies on the human aspect of the receiver, defining in what condition a non-Christian may be acceptable to God. A threefold condition was declared: that a person be ignorant of the existence of the gospel entrusted to the Church (sine culpa), that he seek God or truth with a sincere and open mind, and finally, that he try to do God's will as he is aware of it through conscience. To such a person God will grant his saving supernatural grace. The Council does not, however, make any attempt to explain in detail what is meant by this mystery of grace in detail. The general reference to the *gratia communis* of the Triune God does not furnish any new insight, if compared with the Patristic or Scholastic teaching; the opera ad extra of the Holy Trinity are indivisible. The Council texts do not differentiate between creative, christological, or sanctifying grace when speaking as relevant to non-Christians. In that context, the usage of the concepts of grace remains vague – partly quite intentionally so, leaving room for a variety of interpretations and for the possible development of the dogma.

The qualified Conciliar teaching concerning Jews highlights the fact that if a religion has a specific function of revelation and grace as a proper religion, this function is indeed pointed out. The Jewish religion is the only one which the Council thus qualifies, no other non-Christian religion attains to such a status in the divine mystery of salvation. *Hans Waldenfels* came to the conclusion that, "in spite of speaking about 'the true and holy' in religions, the Council's concept of the salvific meaning of religions remains obscure."[1] We can respond: it is obscure because no specific salvific meaning even exists.

---

[1] *Waldenfels* 1984, 760. Commenting on NA, Waldenfels also asks: "Denn unbeantwortet bleibt die Frage: Was will Gott mit den Religionen? Sind die Religionen reines Menschenwerk, oder sind sie letztlich doch auch Gotteswerk?" *Waldenfels* 1970, 130.

It is important to note that when teaching of the possibility of salvation *extra Ecclesiam*, the Council refers to individual non-Christians. The idea of collective salvation of those outside the Church through universal or cosmic christological grace – the position promoted by *Henri de Lubac* and others – is not apparent in the documents. Sacramentalism is a very strong theological trend in the Council documents, but it functions mainly in the sphere of ecclesiology. The idea of sacramentalism was not extended to the Conciliar understanding of non-Christian religions, at least it was not implemented *expressis verbis*. On the other hand, there is no explicit refusal to extend the idea of sacramental universal grace to other religions. In this sense, the question remains somewhat open for later theological elaboration and development.

The Council did make an advance in its view of the Catholic relation to non-Christian religions in finding an abundance of positive points of connection between Christians and non-Christians. This totally new atmosphere is in itself a radical change and demonstrates progress in the Church's attitude towards those outside Christianity. But although the Council proved to show unforeseen openness to the progress and problems of the modern world, it did not make the least compromise in respect to the Catholic faith. The religious substance of non-Christian religions has no specific role as a medium of the supernatural revelation and grace. With good reason, we can say that the important novelty of the Second Vatican Council in relation to non-Christians was the implementation of the sympathetic language concerning them and the recognition of non-Christian religions as naturally good entities of human culture. The essence of the Catholic doctrine concerning the possibility of salvation *extra Ecclesiam* underwent no significant change.

A sincere seeker of truth and doer of good may be an adherent of any religion or of none. Non-Christian religions are neither demonized nor divinized; they are seen as naturally good. They are, however, neutralized and relativized: religions are a part of human life and culture, and as such they offer – if compared with other aspects of human culture – neither any particular hindrance nor any special advantage in a non-Christian's relation to his Creator. To varying degrees, religions express the cognition of and celebrate rituals of the one Creator of all; in any case they are manifestations of man's sincere search for God, and they contain moral truths common to all human beings. Depending on its "rank," a religion may assist man with his natural awareness of God and in understanding and fulfilling natural morals. It may even be stated by the Church that a religion is good only because of and only insofar as it may contain elements of natural cognition of God and of natural moral law. But stating this, we must be aware that we are already using Catholic concepts when speaking about the general knowledge of God and natural morals engraved on every man's heart. On this basis, for instance, the strictly monotheistic Islam is a religion of a high rank.

After all, non-Christian religions are considered good insofar as they teach what Christianity teaches about God, and they aid in the process of achieving universal human community. The Christianity-centrism of the Conciliar doctrine of non-Christian religions is demonstrated by the documents' teaching that even the moral good which may be found in cultures and religions is imperfect as such: it must be illumined, purified, and perfected by the salvific light of *revelatio specialis*. The moral, not to speak of the spiritual, good of a non-Christian religion is not independent but integrally linked with the divine truth revealed solely in Christianity.

The urgency of the Church's mission is in no way lessened by the Second Vatican Council: the Church has received the explicit revelation of divine grace in Christ; she possesses the *plenitudo mediorum salutis*, and, consequently, it is her mission to establish the bodily presence of the people of God – of the Church herself – among every nation and to add people from all nations to the number of the elected. The Council established its doctrine of non-Christian religions on the solid rock of the standard idea of fulfillment and perfection, most clearly formulated in the Scholastic theology of Thomism.

The position held by *Karl Rahner*, defining religions – in agreement with the Catholic idea of sacramental grace mediated through material elements – as the incarnated "legitimate" material mediation of saving grace, failed to gain Conciliar recognition. The ecclesiological emphasis of sacramentalism was not extended to the social and material elements of non-Christian religions. From the point of view of the Council's teaching, religious non-Christians when compared with atheists, have no advantage. Every sincere seeker of truth who is ignorant of the specific ecclesiastical way of salvation stands in an equal position before his Creator. Rahner himself -- though not all of his followers – noticed that the Council's definition of religions is much more cautious and conservative than his own theory. When commenting on the NA declaration, Rahner expressed his disappointment by saying that "the proper theological quality of non-Christian religions remains undefined."[2] With profound insight into the Conciliar teaching, Rahner notes that the text does not acknowledge any specific status of the salvific mediation in religions.[3] Rahner even expressed his open astonishment

---

[2] "In dieser Erklärung bleibt die eigentlich theologische Qualität der nichtchristlichen Religionen unbestimmt." *Rahner* 1978, 343.

[3] Rahner asks: "Vollzieht sich der eigentliche heilschaffende Glaube, den das Konzil an den anderen genannten Stellen auch im Heiden und Atheisten als grundsätzlich möglich anerkennt, nur außerhalb des Lebens dieser Religionen als solcher, etwa in der Treue gegenüber dem Spruch des Gewissens, in der Nächstenliebe usw., so daß Akte im Bereich dieser nichtchristlichen Religionen als solcher nicht heilswirksam wären?" *Rahner* 1978, 343.

at the Conciliar teaching when he asked how atheists can be in the same position as the religious non-Christians: how could "explicit, verbalized and institutional religiosity be superfluous in all human life for the relation of man to God?"[4]

In spite of the strong classical framework of theology backing the Conciliar doctrine of non-Christian religions, it was clearly the intention of the Council fathers to tolerate new perspectives of grace, and such ideas were given some legitimate room to exist within the Church and to await their further theological elaboration and maturing. *Vaticanum Secundum* was a gathering in the series of ecumenical councils; many of its concepts and lines of thought are ecumenical in the sense that they may comprise and tolerate trends of thought which may even seem to conflict with each other. Being an ecumenical Council, it aimed at the consensus of faith, trying to extract from the final documents any traces of open conflicts and contradictions.

The Council itself proceeded very much along the lines of traditional Catholic theology. But it is significant that the new ideas of supernatural universal grace, promoted above all by Henri de Lubac and Karl Rahner even before the Council, were by no means reprobated. The existence of new views was accepted in silence; many of the new developments in Conciliar theology may, in fact, be quite implicit, expressed by silence rather than words. In regard to the question of God's common saving grace, the Conciliar documents use precautious and minimalistic statements. This can be understood as a compromise which can be accepted by more conservative as well as by more progressive Catholic theologians.

The Council did not recognize the salvific efficacy of other religions in particular, but it did acknowledge the general salvific presence of the Triune God's grace in the universe he created. On the whole, the Council *expressis verbis*, while making some fragmentary remarks on the idea of the created grace effective in all human life, did not become specific concerning the *modus gratiae*, i.e., saying how this grace is present and operative in human life and culture. What the Council did explicitly state about the possibility of salvation *extra Ecclesiam* moves emphatically in the lines of traditional theology – especially of Thomism – in terms of the rational knowledge of God and of natural moral law.

At the beginning of our study we asked: In what way are non-Christian religions salvific in themselves? On the basis of our analysis, we must

---

4 "Aber da man nicht der Meinung sein kann, daß ausdrückliche, verbalisierte und institutionelle Religiosität für das Verhältnis des Menschen zu Gott in dem ganzen menschlichen Leben überflüssig sein könnte - -" *Rahner* 1978, 348.

answer: As proper or actual religions, they are not in any specific way salvific. If a non-Christian is saved, he is saved on the basis of his honest search for truth and his obedience to the voice of his Creator which he hears in his conscience. Such a non-Christian person, being taken into the realm of the salvific *gratia praeveniens,* receives the hidden grace of the Triune God in a proleptic manner. He is a latent member of Christ's body, and he has *fides implicita,* the salvific faith accepted by God; man cannot be saved through his own works, both grace and faith are needed for salvation even outside Christianity. We are compelled to conclude that the doctrine of the Second Vatican Council of non-Christian religions is rather conservative and faithful to the accepted Catholic dogma. The Council permitted no reinterpretation of its standard doctrine in christology and soteriology. There is no compromise in matters of the revealed truth of the divine mystery of supernatural grace.

In order fully to participate in the creative, redemptive, and sanctifying grace of the Triune God, all men need to receive the gift of *gratia increata sive supernaturalis* through the explicit means of grace entrusted to the Church of Christ. This is the superabundant gift of God's grace which cannot be obtained unless through conversion and Christian baptism. The urgency of the Christian mission – a mission which respects all dimensions and phenomena of human culture, including religions – was in no way diminished by the Council.

APPENDIX A

THE SUCCESSIVE VERSIONS OF *NOSTRA AETATE*

TEXT I

The fourth chapter of the ecumenism decree, November 1963: De Catholicorum habitudine ad non-christianos et maxime ad Iudaeos:

Postquam de Oecumenismi Catholici principiis tractavimus, silentio praeterire nolumus, quod eadem, habita ratione diversae condicionis, applicari debent, cum agitur de modo colloquendi et cooperandi cum hominibus non-christianis, qui tamen Deum colunt, vel saltem bona animati voluntate, legem moralem hominis naturae insitam, pro conscientia servare student.

Maxime autem hoc valet cum de Iudaeis agitur, quippe qui cum Ecclesia Christi speciali ratione coniungantur.

Ecclesia Christi grato animo agnoscit fidei et electionis suae initia, iuxta Dei salutare mysterium, iam inter Patriarchas et Prophetas inveniri. Omnes enim Christifideles, Abrahae filios secundum fidem (cf. Gal. 3, 7) in eiusdem Patriarchae vocatione includi et in populi electi exitu ex terra servitutis Ecclesiae salutem mystice praesignari confitetur. Nequit Ecclesia, nova in Christo creatura (cf. Eph. 2, 15), oblivisci se continuationem esse populi illius quocum olim Deus ex ineffabili misericordia sua Antiquum Foedus concludere dignatus est.

Credit insuper Ecclesia Christum, Pacem nostram, uno amore et Iudaeos et Gentes complecti et utraque fecisse unum (cf. Eph. 2, 14) atque amborum in uno corpore unione (cf. Eph. 2, 17) annuntiari totius orbis terrarum in Christo reconciliationem. Etsi populi electi magna pars interim longe a Christo, iniuria tamen diceretur populus maledictus, cum Deo maneat carissimus propter Patres et dona eis data (cf. Rom. 11, 28), vel gens deicida, quia omnium hominum peccata, quae causa fuerunt passionis et mortis Iesu Christi, Dominus passione et morte sua luit (cf. Lc. 23, 34; Act. 3, 17; 1 Cor. 2, 8). Mors tamen Christi non a toto populo tunc vivente, et multo minus ab hodierno populo adducta est. Ideo caveant sacerdotes ne quid dicant in instructione catechetica neque in praedicatione, quod in cordibus auditorum, odium aut despectionem erga Iudaeos gignere possit. Neque obliviscitur Ecclesia ex hoc populo natum esse Christum Iesum secundum carnem, natam esse Mariam Virginem, Christi Matrem, natos esse Apostolos, Ecclesiae fundamentum et columnas.

Quare cum tantum Ecclesia sit cum synagoga commune patrimonium, Sacra haec Synodus utriusque mutuam cognitionem et aestimationem, quae studiis theologicis et colloquiis fraternis obtinetur, omnino fovere et commendare intendit et insuper, sicut iniurias hominibus ubicumque inflictas severe reprobat, ita etiam magis odia et persecutiones contra Iudaeos, sive olim sive nostris temporibus perpetratas, materno animo deplorat et damnat.

TEXT II

Sections 32-34 of the ecumenism decree, September 1964: De Iudaeis et de non-christianis:

32. *(De communi patrimonio Christianorum cum Iudaeis.)* Ecclesia Christi libenter agnoscit fidei et electionis suae initia iam apud Patriarchas et Prophetas, iuxta salutare Dei mysterium, inveniri. Confitetur enim omnes Christifideles, Abrahae filios secundum fidem (cf. Gal. 3, 7), in eiusdem Patriarchae vocatione includi et in populi electi exitu e terra servitutis salutem Ecclesiae mystice praesignari. Quare nequit Ecclesia, nova in Christo creatura (cf. Eph. 2, 15) et populous Novi Foederis, oblivisci se continuationem esse populi illius, quocum olim Deus ex ineffabili misericordia sua Antiquum Foedus inire dignatus est, et cui revelationem in Libris Veteris Testamenti contentam concredere voluit.

Neque obliviscitur Ecclesia ex populo iudaico Christum natum esse secundum carnem, natam esse Christi Matrem, Mariam Virginem, et natos esse Apostolos, Ecclesiae fundamentum et columnas.

Verba quoque Apostoli Pauli semper habet et habebit prae oculis Ecclesia de Iudaeis "quorum adoptio est filiorum et gloria et testamentum et legislatio et obsequium et promissa" (Rom. 9, 4).

Cum igitur tantum patrimonium Christiani ex Iudaeis acceperint, Sacra haec Synodus mutuam utriusque cognitionem et aestimationem, quae et studiis theologiciis et fraternis colloquiis obtinetur, omnino fovere vult et commendare, atque insuper, sicut iniurias hominibus ubicumque illatas severe reprobat, ita enim odia et vexationem contra Iudaeos deplorat et damnat.

Memoria insuper dignum est adunationem populi iudaici cum Ecclesia partem spei christianae esse. Ecclesia enim, docente Apostolo Paulo (cf. Rom. 11, 25), fide inconcussa ac desiderio magno accessum huius populi exspectat ad plenitudinem populi Dei, quam Christus instauravit.

Ideo curent omnes ne, sive in catechesi impertienda et Verbi Dei praedicatione sive in quotidianis colloquiis, populum iudaicum ut gentem reprobatam exhibeant, neve aliud quid dicant aut faciant, quod animos a Iudaeis alienare possit. Caveant praeterea ne Iudaeis nostrorum temporum quae in Passione Christi perpetrata sunt imputentur.

33. *(Omnes homines Deum ut Patrem habeant.)* Dominus Iesus omnium hominum Patrem esse Deum, sicut iam Scripturae Veteris Testamenti statuunt et ipsa innuit ratio, luculenter confirmavit. Nequimus vero Deum omnium Patrem vocare vel orare, si erga quosdam homines, ad imaginem Dei creatos, fraterne nos gerere renuimus. Ita enim arcte connectuntur habitudo hominis ad Deum Patrem et eiusdem habitudo hominis ad homines fratres, ut omnis negatio humanae fraternitatis negationem ipsius Dei, apud quem non est acceptio personarum (cf. 2 Par. 19, 7; Rom. 2, 11; Eph. 6, 9; Col. 3, 25; 1 Petr. 1, 17), secumferat vel ad eam ducat. Nam prius mandatum cum altero ita coalescit, ut nobis nequeant dimitti debita nostra, nisi nosmetipsi ex corde debitoribus nostris dimittamus. Iamvero in Lege Veteri dicitur: "Numquid non Pater unus omnium nostrum? numquid non Deus unus creavit nos? quare ergo despicit unusquisque nostrum fratrem suum?" (Mal. 2, 10); idque in Nova Lege clarius affirmatur: "Qui non diligit fratrem suum quem videt, Deum quem non videt quomodo potest diligere? Et hoc mandatum habemus a Deo ut qui diligit Deum diligat et fratrem suum" (1 Io. 4, 20-21).

Hac caritate erga fratres nostros compulsi, magna cum observantia consideremus opiniones et doctrinas quae quamvis a nostris in multis discrepent, tamen in multis referunt radium illius Veritatis quae illuminat omnem hominem venientem in hunc mundum.

Sic amplectamur imprimis etiam Musulmanos qui unicum Deum personalem atque remuneratorem adorant et sensu religioso atque permultis humanae culturae communicationibus propius ad nos accesserunt.

34. *(Omnis species discriminationis damnatur.)* Fundamentum ergo tollitur omni theoriae vel praxi quae inter hominem et hominem, inter gentem et gentem discrimen quoad humanam dignitatem et iura exinde dimanantia inducunt.

Abstineant ergo necesse est omnes bene cordati homines et praesertim Christiani a quavis hominum discriminatione aut vexatione propter stirpem eorum, colorem, condicionem vel religionem. At contra Christifideles Sacra Synodus ardenter obsecrat ut "conversationem inter gentes habeant bonam" (1 Petr. 2, 12) si fieri potest, quod in eis est, cum omnibus hominibus pacem habeant (cf. Rom. 12, 18); immo eisdem praescribit ut diligant, non tantum proximum suum, sed et inimicos, si quos se habere censeant, ita ut vere sint filii Patris qui in caelis est et qui solem suum oriri facit super omnes (cf. Mt. 5, 44-45).

TEXT III

Declaration, November 1964: De Ecclesiae habitudine ad religiones non-christianas:

1. *(Prooemium.)* Nostra aetate, in qua genus humanum in dies arctius unitur et necessitudines inter varios populos augentur, Ecclesia attente considerat quae sit sua habitudo ad religiones non-christianas.

Una enim communitas sunt omnes gentes, unam habent originem, cum Deus omne genus hominum inhabitare fecerit super universam faciem terrae,[1] unum etiam habent finem ultimum, Deum, cuius providentia ac bonitas testimonium et consilia salutis ad omnes se extendunt,[2] donec uniantur electi in Civitate Sancta, quam claritas Dei illuminabit, ubi gentes ambulabunt in lumine eius.[3]

Homines a variis religionibus responsum exspectant de reconditis conditionis humanae aenigmatibus, quae sicut olim et hodie corda hominum intime commovent: quid sit homo, quis sensus et finis vitae nostrae, quid bonum et quid peccatum, quae sit via ad veram felicitatem obtinendam, quid mors, iudicium et retributio post mortem, quid demum illud ultimum et ineffabile mysterium quod nostram existentiam amplectitur, ex quo ortum sumimus et quo tendimus.

2. *(De diversis religionibus non-christianis.)* Iam ab antiquo apud diversas gentes invenitur quaedam perceptio illius arcanae virtutis, quae cursui rerum et eventibus vitae humanae praesens est, immo aliquando agnitio Summi Numinis ac Patris. Religiones vero cum progressu culturae connexae subtilioribus notionibus et lingua magis exculta ad easdem quaestiones respondere satagunt. Ita in Hinduismo homines mysterium divinum scrutantur et exprimunt inexhausta foecunditate mythorum et acutis conatibus philosophiae, atque liberationem quaerunt ab angustiis nostrae conditionis per formas vitae asceticae, per profundam meditationem, necnon per refugium ad Deum cum amore et confidentia. In Buddhismo radicalis

---

[1]   Cf. Act. 17, 26.
[2]   Cf. Sap. 8, 1; Act. 14, 17; Rom. 2, 6-7; 1 Tim. 2, 4.
[3]   Cf. Apoc. 21, 23-24.

insufficientia mundi huius mutabilis agnoscitur et via docetur qua homines, animo devoto et confidente, se abnegando et purificando a rebus transitoriis liberari et statum permanentis quietis attingere valeant. Sic ceterae quoque religiones, quae per totum mundum inveniuntur, inquietudini cordis hominum variis modis occurrunt proponendo vias, doctrinas scilicet ac praecepta vitae, necnon ritus sacros.

Ecclesia catholica nihil eorum, quae in his religionibus vera et sancta sunt, reicit. Annuntiat enim indesinenter Christum, qui es "via, veritas et vita" (Io. 14, 6) et in quo Deus omnia Sibi reconciliavit.[4] De variis salutis dispositionibus edocta,[5] sincera cum observantia considerat modos agendi et vivendi, praecepta et doctrinas, quae quamvis ab iis quae ipsa proponit in multis discrepent, referunt tamen radium illius Veritatis quae illuminat omnes homines.

Filios suos hortatur igitur, ut per colloquia et collaborationem cum asseclis aliarum religionum, salva integritate fidei catholicae, illa bona spiritualia et moralia necnon illos valores socio-culturales, quae apud eos inveniuntur, servent et promoveant.

3. *(De Musulmanis.)* Cum aestimatione quoque Musulmanos respicit Ecclesia qui unicum Deum adorant, viventem et subsistentem, omnipotentem, Creatorem caeli et terrae, homines allocutum, cuius occultis etiam decretis toto animo se submittere student, sicut Deo se submisit Abraham ad quem fides musulmana libenter sese refert. Iesum, quem quidem ut Deum non agnoscunt, ut Prophetam tamen venerantur, matremque eius virginalem honorant Mariam et aliquando eam devote etiam invocant. Diem insuper iudicii expectant cum Deus omnes homines resuscitatos remunerabit. Exinde Deum colunt maxime in oratione, eleemosynis et ieiunio; vitam quoque moralem tam individualem quam familialem et socialem in obsequium Dei ducere conantur.

Quodsi in decurso saeculorum inter Christianos et Musulmanos non paucae dissensiones et inimicitiae exortae sint, Sacrosancta Synodus omnes exhortatur, ut, praeterita obliviscentes, se ad comprehensionem mutuam sincere exerceant et pro omnibus hominibus iustitiam socialem, bona moralia necnon pacem et libertatem communiter tueantur et promoveant.

4. *(De Iudaeis.)* Mysterium Ecclesiae perscrutans, Sacra haec Synodus meminit vinculi, quo populus Novi Testamenti cum stirpe Abraham coniunctus est.

Ecclesia enim Christi grato animo agnoscit fidei et electionis suae initia iam apud Patriarchas, Moysen et Prophetas, iuxta salutare Dei mysterium,

---

[4] Cf. 2 Cor. 5, 19.
[5] Cf. S. Irenaeus, Adv. Haer., IV, 28, 2; PG 7, 1062.

inveniri. Confitetur omnes Christifideles, Abrahae filios secundum fidem,[6] in eiusdem Patriarchae vocatione includi et salutem Ecclesiae in populi electi exitu de terra servitutis mystice praesignari. Quare nequit Ecclesia oblivisci se a populo illo, quocum Deus ex ineffabili misericordia sua Antiquum Foedus inire dignatus est, Revelationem Veteris Testamenti accepisse et nutriri radice bonae olivae, in quam inserti sunt rami oleastri Gentium.[7] Credit enim Ecclesia Christum, Pacem nostram, per crucem Iudaeos et Gentes reconciliasse et utraque fecisse unum.[8]

Semper quoque prae oculis habet Ecclesia verba Apostoli Pauli de cognatis eius, "quorum adoptio est filiorum et gloria et testamentum et legislatio et obsequium et promissa, quorum patres et ex quibus est Christus secundum carnem" (Rom. 9, 4-5), filius Mariae Virginis. Recordatur etiam ex populo iudaico natos esse Apostolos, Ecclesiae fundamenta et columnas, atque plurimos illos primos discipulos, qui Evangelium Christi mundo annuntiaverunt.

Etsi Iudaei magna parte Evangelium non acceperunt, tamen, Apostolo testante, Deo, cuius dona et vocatio sine poenitentia sunt, adhuc carissimi manent propter patres.[9] Una cum Prophetis eodemque Apostolo Ecclesia diem Deo soli notum expectat, quo populi omnes una voce Dominum invocabunt et "servient ei humero uno" (Soph. 3, 9).[10]

Cum igitur adeo magnum sit patrimonium spirituale Christianis et Iudaeis commune, Sacra haec Synodus mutuam utriusque cognitionem et aestimationem, quae praesertim studiis biblicis et theologicis atque fraternis colloquiis obtinetur, fovere vult et commendare. Praeterea iuniurias hominibus ubicumque inflictas severe reprobans, Synodus, huius patrimonii communis memor, odia et persecutiones contra Iudaeos, sive olim sive nostris temporibus perpetratas, deplorat et damnat.

Ideo curent omnes ne in catechesi impertienda seu in Verbi Dei praedicatione aliquid doceant, quod in cordibus fidelium odium aut despectionem erga Iudaeos gignere possit; numquam populus iudaicus ut gens reprobata vel maledicta aut deicidii rea exhibeatur. Ea enim quae in passione Christi perpatrata sunt minime toti populo tunc viventi, multo minus hodierno populo imputari possint. Ceterum semper tenuit et tenet Ecclesia, Christum voluntarie propter omnium hominum peccata passionem suam et mortem immensa caritate obiisse. Ecclesiae praedicantis ergo est annuntiare crucem Christi tamquam signum universalis Dei amoris et fontem omnis gratiae.

---

6   Cf. Gal. 3, 7.
7   Cf. Rom. 11, 17-24.
8   Cf. Eph. 2, 14-16.
9   Cf. Rom. 11, 28-29.
10   Cf. Is. 66, 23; Ps. 65, 4; Rom. 11, 11-32.

5. *(De fraternitate universali, quavis discriminatione exclusa.)* Nequimus vero Deum omnium Patrem invocare, si erga quosdam homines, ad imaginem Dei creatos, fraterne nos gerere renuimus. Habitudo hominis ad Deum Patrem et habitudo hominis ad homines fratres ita connectuntur: qui non diligit, non novit Deum.[11]

Fundamentum ergo tollitur omni theoriae vel praxi quae inter hominem et hominem, inter gentem et gentem, discrimen quoad humanam dignitatem et iura exinde dimanantia inducunt.

Abstineat ergo necesse est omnes homines et praesertim Christiani a quavis hominum discriminatione aut vexatione propter stirpem eorum, colorem, condicionem vel religionem. At contra, Christifideles Sacra Synodus, vestigia Sanctorum Apostolorum Petri et Pauli premens, ardenter obsecrat ut, "conversationem inter gentes habentes bonam" (1 Petr. 2, 12), si fieri potest, quod in eis est cum omnibus hominibus pacem habeant,[12] ita ut vere sint filii Patris qui in caelis est.[13]

TEXT IV

The final text of the declaration, October 1965: Declaratio de Ecclesiae habitudine ad religiones non-christianas:

1. Nostra aetate, in qua genus humanum in dies arctius unitur et necessitudines inter varios populos augentur, Ecclesia attentius considerat quae sit sua habitudo ad religiones non-christianas. In suo munere unitatem et caritatem inter homines, immo et inter gentes, fovendi, ea imprimis hic considerat quae hominibus sunt communia et ad mutuum consortium ducunt.

Una enim communitas sunt omnes gentes, unam habent originem, cum Deus omne genus hominum inhabitare fecerit super universam faciem terrae;[14] unum etiam habent finem ultimum, Deum, cuius providentia ac bonitas testimonium et consilia salutis ad omnes se extendunt,[15] donec uniantur electi in Civitate Sancta, quam claritas Dei illuminabit, ubi gentes ambulabunt in lumine eius.[16]

---

[11] Cf. 1 Io. 4, 8; 2, 9-11; Lc. 10, 25-37.
[12] Cf. Rom. 12, 18.
[13] Cf. Mt. 5, 44-45.
[14] Cf. Act. 17, 26.
[15] Cf. Sap. 8, 1; Act. 14, 17; Rom. 2, 6-7; 1 Tim. 2, 4.
[16] Cf. Apoc. 21, 23-24.

Homines a variis religionibus responsum exspectant de reconditis conditionis humanae aenigmatibus, quae sicut olim et hodie corda hominum intime commovent: quid sit homo, quis sensus et finis vitae nostrae, quid bonum et quid peccatum, quem ortum habeant dolores et quem finem, quae sit via ad veram felicitatem obtinendam, quid mors, iudicium et retributio post mortem, quid demum illud ultimum et ineffabile mysterium quod nostram existentiam amplectitur, ex quo ortum sumimus et quo tendimus.

2. Iam ab antiquo usque ad tempus hodiernum apud diversas gentes invenitur quaedam perceptio illius arcanae virtutis, quae cursui rerum et eventibus vitae humanae praesens est, immo aliquando agnitio Summi Numinis vel etiam Patris. Quae perceptio atque agnitio vitam earum intimo sensu religioso penetrant. Religiones vero cum progressu culturae connexae subtilioribus notionibus et lingua magis exculta ad easdem quaestiones respondere satagunt. Ita in Hinduismo homines mysterium divinum scrutantur et exprimunt inexhausta foecunditate mythorum et acutis conatibus philosophiae, atque liberationem quaerunt ab angustiis nostrae condicionis vel per formas vitae asceticae vel per profundam meditationem vel per refugium ad Deum cum amore et confidentia. In Buddhismo secundum varias eius formas radicalis insufficientia mundi huius mutabilis agnoscitur et via docetur qua homines, animo devoto et confidente, sive statum perfectae liberationis acquirere, sive, vel propriis conatibus vel superiore auxilio innixi, ad summan illuminationem pertingere valeant. Sic ceterae quoque religiones, quae per totum mundum inveniuntur, inquietudini cordis hominum variis modis occurrere nituntur proponendo vias, doctrinas scilicet ac praecepta vitae, necnon ritus sacros.

Ecclesia catholica nihil eorum, quae in his religionibus vera et sancta sunt, reicit. Sincera cum observantia considerat illos modos agendi et vivendi, illa praecepta et doctrinas, quae, quamvis ab iis quae ipsa tenet et proponit in multis discrepent, haud raro referunt tamen radium illius Veritatis, quae illuminat omnes homines. Annuntiat vero et annuntiare tenetur indesinenter Christum, qui es "via, veritas et vita" (Io. 14, 6), in quo homines plenitudinem vitae religiosae inveniunt, et in quo Deus omnia Sibi reconciliavit.[17]

Filios suos igitur hortatur, ut cum prudentia et caritate per colloquia et collaborationem cum asseclis aliarum religionum, fidem et vitam christianam testantes, illa bona spiritualia et moralia necnon illos valores socio-culturales, quae apud eos inveniuntur, agnoscant, servent et promoveant.

3. Ecclesia cum aestimatione quoque Muslimos respicit qui unicum Deum adorant, viventem et subsistentem, misericordem et omnipotentem,

---

[17] Cf. 2 Cor. 5, 18-19.

Creatorem caeli et terrae,[18] homines allocutum, cuius occultis etiam decretis toto animo se submittere student, sicut Deo se submisit Abraham ad quem fides islamica libenter sese refert. Iesum, quem quidem ut Deum non agnoscunt, ut prophetam tamen venerantur, matremque eius virginalem honorant Mariam et aliquando eam devote etiam invocant. Diem insuper iudicii expectant cum Deus omnes homines resuscitatos remunerabit. Exinde vitam moralem aestimant et Deum maxime in oratione, eleemosynis et ieiunio colunt.

Quodsi in decursu saeculorum inter Christianos et Muslimos non paucae dissensiones et inimicitae exortae sint, Sacrosancta Synodus omnes exhortatur, ut, praeterita obliviscentes, se ad comprehensionem mutuam sincere exerceant et pro omnibus hominibus iustitiam socialem, bona moralia necnon pacem et libertatem communiter tueantur et promoveant.

4. Mysterium Ecclesiae perscrutans, Sacra haec Synodus meminit vinculi, quo populus Novi Testamenti cum stirpe Abraham spiritualiter coniunctus est.

Ecclesia enim Christi agnoscit fidei et electionis suae initia iam apud Patriarchas, Moysen et Prophetas, iuxta salutare Dei mysterium, inveniri. Confitetur omnes Christifideles, Abrahae filios secundum fidem,[19] in eiusdem Patriarchae vocatione includi et salutem Ecclesiae in populi electi exitu de terra servitutis mystice praesignari. Quare nequit Ecclesia oblivisci se per populum illum, quocum Deus ex ineffabili misericordia sua Antiquum Foedus inire dignatus est, Revelationem Veteris Testamenti accepisse et nutriri radice bonae olivae, in quam inserti sunt rami oleastri Gentium.[20] Credit enim Ecclesia Christum, Pacem nostram, per crucem Iudaeos et Gentes reconciliasse et utraque in Semetipso fecisse unum.[21]

Semper quoque prae oculis habet Ecclesia verba Apostoli Pauli de cognatis eius, "quorum adoptio est filiorum et gloria et testamentum et legislatio et obsequium et promissa, quorum patres et ex quibus est Christus secundum carnem" (Rom. 9, 4-5), filius Mariae Virginis. Recordatur etiam ex populo iudaico natos esse Apostolos, Ecclesiae fundamenta et columnas, atque plurimos illos primos discipulos, qui Evangelium Christi mundo annuntiaverunt.

Teste Sacra Scriptura, Ierusalem tempus visitationis suae non cognovit,[22] atque Iudaei magna parte Evangelium non acceperunt, immo non pauci diffusioni eius se opposuerunt.[23] Nihilominus, secundum Apostolum, Iudaei

---

[18] Cf. S. Gregorius VII, Epist. III, 21 ad Anazir, regem Mauritaniae; PL 148, 451 A.
[19] Cf. Gal. 3, 7.
[20] Cf. Rom. 11, 17-24.
[21] Cf. Eph. 2, 14-16.
[22] Cf. Lc. 19, 44.
[23] Cf. Rom. 11, 28.

Deo, cuius dona et vocatio sine poenitentia sunt, adhuc carissimi manent propter Patres.[24] Una cum Prophetis eodemque Apostolo Ecclesia diem Deo soli notum expectat, quo populi omnes una voce Dominum invocabunt et "servient ei humero uno" (Soph. 3, 9).[25]

Cum igitur adeo magnum sit patrimonium spirituale Christianis et Iudaeis commune, Sacra haec Synodus mutuam utriusque cognitionem et aestimationem, quae praesertim studiis biblicis et theologicis atque fraternis colloquiis obtinetur, fovere vult et commendare.

Etsi auctoritates Iudaeorum cum suis assec-lis mortem Christi urserunt,[26] tamen ea quae in passione Eius perpetrata sunt nec omnibus indistincte Iudaeis tunc viventibus, nec Iudaeis hodiernis imputari possunt. Licet autem Ecclesia sit novus Populus Dei, Iudaei tamen neque ut a Deo reprobati neque ut maledicti exhibeantur, quasi hoc ex Sacris Litteris sequatur. Ideo curent omnes ne in catechesi et in Verbi Dei praedicatione habenda quidquam doceant, quod cum veritate evangelica et spiritu Christi non congruat.

Praeterea, Ecclesia, quae omnes persecutiones in quosvis homines reprobat, memor communis cum Iudaeis patrimonii, nec rationibus politicis sed religiosa caritate evangelica impulsa, odia, persecutiones, antisemitismi manifestationes, quovis tempore et a quibusvis in Iudaeos habita, deplorat.

Ceterum Christus, uti semper tenuit et tenet Ecclesia, propter peccata omnium hominum voluntarie passionem suam et mortem immensa caritate obiit, ut omnes salutem consequantur. Ecclesiae praedicantis ergo est annuntiare crucem Christi tamquam signum universalis Dei amoris et fontem omnis gratiae.

5. Nequimus vero Deum omnium Patrem invocare, si erga quosdam homines, ad imaginem Dei creatos, fraterne nos gerere renuimus. Habitudo hominis ad Deum Patrem et habitudo hominis ad homines fratres adeo connectuntur, ut Scriptura dicat: "qui non diligit, non novit Deum" (1 Io. 4, 8).

Fundamentum ergo tollitur omni theoriae vel praxi quae inter hominem et hominem, inter gentem et gentem, discrimen quoad humanam dignitatem et iura exinde dimanantia inducit.

Ecclesia igitur quamvis hominum discriminationem aut vexationem stirpis vel coloris, condicionis vel religionis causa factam tamquam a Christi mente alienam reprobat. Proinde, Christifideles Sacra Synodus, vestigia Sanctorum Apostolorum Petri et Pauli premens, ardenter obsecrat ut,

---

[24] Cf. Rom. 11, 28-29; Conc. Vat. II, Const. dogm. de Ecclesia, Lumen Gentium, AAS 1965, 20.

[25] Cf. Is. 66, 23; Ps. 65, 4; Rom. 11, 11-32.

[26] Cf. Io. 19, 6.

"conversationem inter gentes habentes bonam" (1 Petr. 2, 12), si fieri potest, quod in eis est cum omnibus hominibus pacem habeant,[27] ita ut vere sint filii Patris qui in caelis est.[28]

---

[27] Cf. Rom. 12, 18.
[28] Cf. Mt. 5, 44-45.

APPENDIX B

DISCUSSION IN THE
INTERNATIONAL BULLETIN OF MISSIONARY RESEARCH
IN 1990

This appendix consists of Miikka Ruokanen's article based on the book at hand, published in the *International Bulletin of Missionary Research* (vol. 14, no. 2, April 1990, pp. 56-61) and the successive comments by *Paul Knitter* (ibid., pp. 62-63) and *William R. Burrows* (ibid., pp. 63-64). In addition, Ruokanen's "Author's Reply" (vol. 14, no. 3, July 1990, pp. 122-123) and Knitter's "Author's Reply" as well (vol. 14, no. 4, October 1990, pp. 178-179) are included. All articles are republished here by permission.

Miikka Ruokanen:

CATHOLIC TEACHING ON NON-CHRISTIAN RELIGIONS AT THE SECOND VATICAN COUNCIL

Nostra aetate (NA), the declaration of the Second Vatican Council on the relation of the Church to non-Christian religions, marks an authoritative change in the Catholic approach to other religions. For the first time, there is a recognition of non-Christian religions as entities that the Church should respect and with which the Christians should enter into dialogue.

The NA declaration and the other parts of the Conciliar documents dealing with the question of non-Christian religions are intended to be positive in tone: criticism of religions is absent. Classical terminology like "pagan," "idolatry," or "error" is totally missing when the Council speaks about religions.[1] The Council introduced a totally new atmosphere of respect and recognition. The possible criticism is expressed by silence rather than by open critical statements.

There are many commentators of the Second Vatican Council who maintain that the Catholic Church recognized non-Christian religions as ways of divine revelation and salvation. These religions, it is said, may be seen as expressions of the universal christological grace, though less perfectly manifest than in Christianity. Paul F. Knitter summarizes: "The majority of Catholic thinkers interpret the Conciliar statements to affirm, implicitly but clearly, that the religions are ways of salvation."[2] According to Thomas F. Stransky, the NA declaration "proposes that religions as such are not outside but within the history of salvation;" religions "incarnate sufficient 'religious beginnings' of a supernatural response to the revelation in Christ."[3] In Pietro Rossano's interpretation of the Council "Christ is seen as the origin, center, and destiny of the various religions, as the One who brought them to birth, takes them up, purifies them, and fulfills them."[4]

This line of interpretation, however, reflects more the creativity of individual theological thinkers than the solid doctrinal teaching of the Council. The Church did not accept any divinely approved alternative ways of revelation and salvation, or any reinterpretation of the standard doctrine in christology and soteriology. The Council did not recognize the salvific efficacy of other religions in particular; but it did recognize the general salvific presence of God's grace in all the universe he created. The Conciliar teaching about non-Christian religions is rooted in the theology of creation and in the Roman Catholic natural law tradition; furthermore, it is placed in a missiological context.

---

[1] It is remarkable that the word *paganus* or its derivatives do not appear in the documents of the Council at all. Neither does the adjectival form *gentilis* occur. The word *idolatria* appears in the documents only once, and even then not in regard to non-Christian religions but when the Council speaks about "a kind of idolatry of the temporal" in the modern context of science and technology (see *Apostolicam actuositatem* 7, 3). The old terminology about pagan religions and their errors is radically left out. The respectful words *religio* and *gens* are normally used by the Council when speaking about the non-Christians.

[2] "Roman Catholic Approaches to Other Religions: Developments and Tensions," *International Bulletin of Missionary Research* 8, no. 2 (April 1984), p. 50. Knitter gives detailed information on the Catholic theologians representing the modern line of interpretation in: *No Other Name? A Critical Survey of Christian Attitudes Toward the World Religions* (London: SCM Press, 1985), pp. 124-135, 249-251.

[3] "The Church and Other Religions," *International Bulletin of Missionary Research* 9, no. 4 (October 1985), pp. 156-157.

[4] "Christ's Lordship and Religious Pluralism in Roman Catholic Perspective," in *Christ's Lordship and Religious Pluralism*, ed. Gerald H. Anderson and Thomas F. Stransky (Maryknoll, N.Y.: Orbis Books, 1981), p. 108.

In my study, I exclude the analysis of the history of the NA declaration that was originally initiated by the need to make a reconciliatory statement concerning the relation of the Catholics to the Jews. I have gone through the details of the history of the NA in my not-yet-published monograph "The Catholic Doctrine of non-Christian Religions according to the Second Vatican Council." Furthermore, I do not intend to address the context in which we today discuss interreligious relations. I concentrate solely on the documents of the Second Vatican Council. My emphasis is on the NA declaration, but additional reference is made to other documents of the Council for a wider exposition of the themes.

The Progress of Humanity towards Unity

When trying to find elements which unite all religions, the focus of the Council is on the possible spiritual and moral good of religions expressing the value of human life and especially that of human dignity. Religions are seen as spheres of life contributing to the general progress of humanity and human culture. All this is well in accord with the Council's general tendency in seeking positive points of connection between the Christian faith and the modern world with its rapid cultural, scientific, technical, and social development, as well as its growing sense of the unity of mankind.

The NA declaration and Conciliar statements about non-Christian religions are framed with that concept of the development of unity within mankind. The very opening sentence of NA contains the idea of the progress of humanity towards unity: "In this age of ours, when men are drawing more closely together and the bonds of friendship between different peoples are being strengthened, the Church examines with greater care the relation which she has to non-Christian religions." (NA 1, 1.)[5] The NA declaration ends with a reference to the same kind of theology, introducing the theme of human dignity and human rights (NA 5, 1-3).

The Conciliar belief in the positive progress of humanity is based on the positive implementation of natural moral law, given by the Creator of all peoples. The pastoral constitution *Gaudium et spes* (GS) confirms the

---

[5] I refer to the official texts of the Council, *Sacrosanctum Oecumenicum Concilium Vaticanum II, Consitutiones, Decreta, Declarationes, Cura et studio Secretariae Generalis Concilii Oecumenicii Vaticani II* (The Vatican City: Typis Polyglottis Vaticanis, 1964-1966). The number of the section and the number of the paragraph referred to within that section are indicated. The English translation used is from the edition by Austin Flannery, *Vatican Council II, The Conciliar and Post Conciliar Documents* (Collegeville: Liturgical Press, 1975).

permanent and universal validity of natural moral law within the development of the modern world. Being aware of the problems of the world, like the savagery of war, the Council fathers confirm the ever increasing relevance of natural moral law: "the Council wishes to remind men that the natural law of peoples and its universal principles still retain their binding force; the conscience of mankind firmly and ever more emphatically proclaims these principles" (GS 79, 2). Recalling the teaching of Thomas Aquinas, the constitution states: "Deep within his conscience man discovers a law which he has not laid upon himself but which he must obey. Its voice, ever calling him to love and to do what is good and to avoid evil, tells him inwardly at the right moment: do this, shun that. For man has in his heart a law inscribed by God." (GS 16, 1.)

The Church sees the progress towards unity to be fully in accordance with her mission: "The Church, moreover, acknowledges the good to be found in the social dynamism of today, particularly progress towards unity, healthy socialization, and civic and economic cooperation. The encouragement of unity is in harmony with the deepest nature of the Church's mission, for it 'is in the nature of a sacrament – a sign and instrument – that is of communion with God and of unity among all men.'" (GS 42, 3; the reference is to the dogmatic constitution on the Church, *Lumen gentium*, LG, 1, 1.) The decree on the Church's missionary activity, *Ad gentes* (AG), declares that "brotherly concord" of all men is a part of God's plan of salvation in Christ, and consequently, it is a part of the Church's mission. This "answers to a profound longing in all men" (AG 7, 3). The explicit work of salvation is in accordance with the basic truths of natural moral law.

The Second Vatican Council leans heavily on the Thomistic axiom: grace does not refute nature but perfects it (gratia non tollit naturam, sed perficit). The Thomistic principle is combined with missionary motivation. This axiomatic mode of thought is most clearly put forward in the central document of the Council, the dogmatic constitution on the Church: "The faithful must, then recognize the inner nature, the value and the ordering of the whole creation to the praise of God. Even by their secular activity they must aid one another to grater holiness of life, so that the world may be filled with the spirit of Christ and may the more effectively attain its destiny in justice, in love, and in peace." (LG 36, 2.) The same motive is strongly applied to the mission of the Church: "The effect of her (the Church) work is that whatever good is found sown in the minds and hearts of men or in the rites and customs of peoples, these not only are preserved from destruction, but are purified, raised up, and perfected (sanetur, elevetur et consummetur) for the glory of God, the confusion of the devil, and the happiness of man." (LG 17, 1; the same wording is given also in AG 9, 2.)

The Conciliar declaration on non-Christian religions is given in the same framework of the Church's missionary vocation to promote the unity of mankind in terms of the theology of creation and natural moral law, and in terms of perfecting it by God's explicit plan of salvation in Christ. The second sentence of NA declares that it is a special duty of the Church to foster the unity of mankind. "Ever aware of her duty to foster unity and charity among individuals, and even among nations, she (the Church) reflects at the outset on what men have in common and what tends to promote fellowship among men." (NA 1, 1.)

Religious or Moral Truth in Religions?

The NA declaration begins a closer examination of the religions of the world by defining what is common to all people: "All men form but one community. This is so because all stem from the one stock (unam habent originem) which God created to people the entire earth, and also because all share a common destiny (unum habent finem ultimum), namely God. His providence, evident goodness, and saving designs (consilia salutis) extend to all men against the day when the elect are gathered together in the Holy City which is illumined by the glory of God, and in whose splendour all peoples will walk." (NA 1, 2.)

In terms of the theology of creation, all human beings live the sphere of the Creator's providence and enjoy the goodness of created things. But, in addition to this, God himself is the ultimate goal of all people, even though they may not be aware of that. Through his "saving designs," God offers the possibility of salvation and of citizenship in the eschatological Holy City. This is the soteriological-eschatological offer of grace, mediated through the Church. This is the vocation of all men to become members of the people of God.

There exists a certain kind of duality in the theology of NA: On the one hand, all men live in the sphere of God's good creation – this is their human vocation; on the other hand, the means of salvation are extended to all but meet their fulfillment only in the elected – this is the divine vocation of man. The human vocation is understood very much in terms of the theology of creation and natural moral law, and the divine vocation in terms of *media salutis* and divine grace. The first aspect is the fundamental fact of existence; the second aspect is a call which may become a reality in the life of anybody. As all are redeemed by Christ, they are offered the same divine calling and destiny.

The idea of God's voice in the human conscience is not limited to moral questions but it also touches the question of truth. "His conscience is man's most secret core, and his sanctuary. There he is alone with God whose voice echoes in his depths." (GS 16, 1.) There are "elements of truth and grace" among all peoples; this is based on "the secret presence of God" in all of his creation. (AG 9, 2.) On the basis of creation and the Creator's voice in the conscience, every human being is involved in the search for the religious truth. The inclination of humankind to religion belongs to the created goodness of nature. People cannot avoid seeking the religious truth of existence; this orientation towards religion is a part of their nature as human beings.

The NA declaration affirms the full appreciation of all religions as expressions of the human search for truth. In this respect, both the moral and the religious aspects of any religion are recognized: "The Catholic Church rejects nothing of what is true and holy in these religions. She has a high regard for the manner of life and conduct, the precepts and doctrines which, although differing in many ways from her own teaching, nevertheless often reflect a ray of that Truth which enlightens all men (radium illius Veritatis, quae illuminat omnes homines)." (NA 2, 2.)

The *Veritas* referred to here is the Christian truth. The validity of non-Christian religions is measured by the Christian criteria. The following sentence reveals who this personified Truth is: "Yet she (the Church) proclaims and is in duty bound to proclaim without fail, Christ who is the way, the truth and the life. In him, in whom God reconciled all things to himself, men find the fullness of their religious life." (NA 2, 2.) Religions contain seeds of truth insofar as they reflect something of the Christ-centred truth, or at least seek the truth which became plane in Christ.[6]

Here again the idea of grace perfecting nature is evident: the universal human search for truth meets its fulfillment and perfection in God's explicit revelation through Christ. Christological grace purifies and perfects what is naturally good, reflecting the truth and the grace of the Creator. Jesus Christ is the ultimate embodiment of both the religious and the moral truth. If there is to be any development in religions towards "the fullness of religious life," it must be a movement towards Christ. So non-Christian religions do not

---

6   In the Council documents, the term *veritas* is a concept of the Christian truth. Christ himself is the embodiment of the truth, which is *veritas revelata*, *veritas catholica*, or *veritas evangelica*. The Council documents employ the word *veritas* only twice to mean truth possibly discerned outside the revealed Christian religion, and even then truth is presupposed to be an indication of the secret presence of that God who is fully revealed in Christianity: in the quoted passage of NA 2, 2 and in AG 9, 2 which speaks about "those elements of truth and grace which are found among peoples" and are "a secret presence of God."

seem to have an independent status of revelation of the divine mystery; their religious truth is measured by and related to the truth of Christianity.

It is important to note that when the NA declaration speaks about religions in general, the concept of revelation is not employed. Theologically speaking, the recognition of *notitia Dei* in religions does not belong to the sphere of revelation. Significantly, the Council's dogmatic constitution on revelation, *Dei verbum* (DV), although it reinforced the principle of the general knowledge of God, the term *revelatio* was not used outside the explicit events and documents of the salvation history, the history of Israel, Christ and, correspondingly, the Old and the New Testaments. When speaking of revelation, in all its documents the Council always means *revelatio divina* in the sense of *revelatio Veteris Testamenti* or *revelatio christiana*.

In fact, the constitution on revelation does not teach anything new about the natural knowledge of God. The document only quotes the statement of the First Vatican Council (1870) and thus repeats the classical Catholic doctrine on the natural recognition of God by reason through analogy in created nature: "God, the first principle and last end of all things, can be known with certainty from the created world, by the natural light of human reason." (DV 6, 2.) The providential influence of the Creator is present in all created beings and things. Human beings can understand all this by reason – nothing specifically religious is needed for that understanding. DV does not make any reference to any non-Christian religion.

The NA declaration states that "there is found among different peoples a certain awareness of a hidden power, which lies behind the course of nature and the events of human life" (NA 2, 1). Connected with the progress of culture, various religions endeavour to answer the questions about the mystery of life "with better defined concepts and more exact language" (NA 2, 1). Non-Christian religions are various expressions of humanity's natural consciousness of the existence of divinity.

Consequently, religions contain seeds of truth, not on the basis of what they are as religions proper, but on the basis of what they are as expressions of the universal human consciousness of God. This consciousness is based on reason and is in no way dependent on religions – it exists within and outside them. Thus non-Christian religions are understood as a part of human culture in general; their validity is on the same level with the validity of any aspect of human culture. Religions are seen as an inherent part of human experience and culture, without giving them any special status either in a negative or in a positive sense.

The Value of the World Religions

When speaking about the non-Christian religions of the world, the NA declaration divides the religions into four groups. Commenting on the religions by rank shows that the criteria of evaluation are those of Christianity: a religion with a concept of personal monotheism gets a higher rank than another type of religion.

First, the most appreciated religion is Judaism, which is not only historically but also theologically intimately connected with Christianity. Furthermore, taking into consideration the birth process of the document, it is natural that Judaism takes much more space in NA than any other religion.

Judaism is evaluated on premises different from the rest of the non-Christian religions. The Jews are a people of covenants and promises. The Jews still are the elected people, dear to God for the sake of the fathers. The Council confesses the deep spiritual dependence of the *mysterium* of Christianity on Judaism: "Sounding the depths of the mystery which is the Church, this sacred Council remembers the spiritual ties which link the people of the New Covenant to the stock of Abraham." (NA 4, 1.) The revelation and grace of God are effective in both of the salvation historical covenants, the Old and the New Covenants. An unbroken continuity exists between these two covenants.

Further, NA speaks about "the common spiritual heritage" of the Jews and the Christians (NA 4, 5).[7] This kind of concession to the mystery of true religion is made only in regard to Judaism. NA also expresses belief in the reconciliation and unification of Jews and Christians into one people of God as a part of the eschatological hope of the Church (NA 4, 2 & 4; LG 6, 3).

Islam, the austere book-religion, occupies the second rank. The Muslims are appreciated because of their strict monotheism and strict morals; "they highly esteem an upright life." Allah is not mentioned by name, but NA speaks about the God of Islam with respect as the true God. "They worship God, who is one, living and subsistent, merciful and almighty, the Creator of heaven and earth." (NA 3, 1.) The Council says the Muslims worship God "who has also spoken to men," but a major element of Islam, however, is overlooked: there is no word in the Council texts about the Prophet Muhammad. It is interesting how the text speaks of God's "hidden decrees"

---

[7]   The text uses the word combination *patrimonium spirituale*. The concept of *patrimonium* is a term used throughout the Council documents to describe the treasure of the revealed truth in Christianity. The relationship between Judaism and Christianity is of a profound spiritual and theological nature. The concept *revelatio* is also used when the Council speaks about "the revelation of the Old Testament" (NA 4, 2).

which the Muslims "strive to submit themselves" (NA 3, 1). But the Council does not admit that God has openly spoken to mankind in Islam or through Muhammad. Islam is not recognized as a religion of divine revelation; there is no incarnated economy of reconciliation and grace in Islam.

The third rank is given to two great East Asian religions, Hinduism and Buddhism, which are also historical book-religions containing wisdom and values of human life appreciated by Christians. It is admitted by the Council that Muslims honour and worship the one true God, but those who follow Hinduism or Buddhism still are seekers of God, "exploring" the truth and seeking to answer the deepest questions of human existence.

The Hindus "explore the divine mystery" and "seek release from the trials of the present life by ascetical practices, profound meditation, and recourse to God in confidence and love" (NA 2, 1). All this indicates clearly that the Hindus are still seekers of the divine truth. The Council admits that they may be directing their exploration and questioning into the right direction, *ad Deum* – to the true and one God as revealed in Christianity; the polytheistic nature of Hinduism is ignored. No acquisition of religious truth is recognized.

Buddhism in its various forms teaches the way of life "by which men can attain (acquirere) a state of perfect liberation and reach (pertingere) supreme illumination" (NA 2, 1). With positive intensity, Buddhists attempt to reach the truth; but from the point of view of the Catholic faith, they still remain seekers of the truth.

All the rest of the non-Christian religions fall into the fourth category summarized by NA: "So, too other religions which are found throughout the world attempt (nituntur) in their own ways to calm the hearts of men by outlining a program of life covering doctrine, moral precepts, and sacred rites." (NA 2, 1.) Various religions represent human endeavour in the search for God; the Council does not say anything about the possible result, finding the truth in them. The dogmatic constitution *Lumen gentium* is in line with NA by stating, "nor God is remote from those who in shadows and images seek the unknown God" (LG 16, 1). The true God, revealed in Christ, remains unknown in those religions.

The Possibility of Salvation extra Ecclesiam

The Council fully acknowledges the moral good that can be found in the doctrinal concepts and moral practice of non-Christian religions. Religions are good to the extent that they teach what Christianity reaches about God and to the extent that they help in the process of achieving a morally just universal human community. But in regard to the divine mystery, non-Christian religions – though Judaism is an exception – are still seekers of the truth. The NA declaration does not make any specific statement about whether and how non-Christians can be saved outside the Christian Church. The concept of grace does not become a theme when the Council teaches about non-Christian religions, although the concept of grace is connected with the Conciliar teaching about God's creation.[8] *Lumen gentium* and *Gaudium et spes* make a contribution to that.

LG 16, 1 states: "Nor is God remote from those who in shadows and images seek (quaerunt) the unknown God, since he gives to all men life and breath and all things, and since the Saviour wills all men to be saved (salvos fieri). Those who, through no fault of their own, do not know the gospel of Christ or his Church (sine culpa ignorantes), but who nevertheless seek (quaerunt) God with a sincere heart, and, moved by grace, try in their actions (operibus) to do his will as they know it through the dictates of their conscience (per conscientiae dictamen agnitam) – those too may achieve eternal salvation. Nor shall divine providence deny the assistance necessary for salvation to those who, without any fault of theirs (sine culpa), have not yet arrived at an explicit knowledge of God, and who, not without grace, strive to lead a good life (rectam vitam)."

This long passage gives a clear definition of the conditions for the possibility of being saved *extra Ecclesiam* and the explicit gospel of Christ, offered in the Church. First, these candidates of extra-ecclesiastical salvation have not yet heard about the revealed christological way of salvation, and therefore they are personally innocent for not knowing Christ. Second, they sincerely seek the truth, the still unknown God. Third, they practise the moral good that they recognize on the basis of their conscience.

God's grace as the mercy of the Creator may assist these kind of non-Christians in their search for the truth and right life. In a way not plain to us, God's grace perfects and strengthens what is already given in human nature and in natural moral law, inherent in human life. These non-Christians may become saved and attain eternal life in a way that is hidden to us.

Immediately after the above statements, the LG constitution emphatically states that whatever good or truth is found amongst the adherents of non-Christian religions, it "is considered by the Church to be a preparation for the gospel" (LG 16, 1). This *praeparatio evangelica* does not in any measure lessen the urgency of the Church's mission. Quite on the contrary, it challenges the Church to make an even greater effort in her mission: "Hence to procure the glory of God and the salvation of all these, the

---

8 The term *gratia* appears only once in the declaration (NA 4, 8), and even then clearly meaning the christological grace proclaimed by the Church.

Church, mindful of the Lord's command, 'preach the gospel to every creature,' takes zealous care to foster the missions." (LG 16, 1.)

The pastoral constitution defines the divine calling of all people: "All this holds true not for Christians only but also for all men of good will in whose hearts grace is active invisibly. For since Christ died for all, and since all men are in fact called to one and the same destiny, which is divine (vocatio hominis ultima revera una sit, scilicet divina), we must hold that the Holy Spirit offers (offerre) to all the possibility of being made partners, in a way known to God, in the paschal mystery." (GS 22, 5.) All are called, salvation is offered, but not yet guaranteed. The text does not speak about the finality of salvation, but about the call extended to all men to become participants of God's grace. Willing that good that is written by God into every human heart unites men and women with the grace of the Creator, and the sufferings of life may unite any human being with the sufferings of Christ.

Many commentators of the Second Vatican Council have understood the quoted passage of GS 22, 5 as a Catholic concession to the salvific efficacy of non-Christian religions. This, however, is *not* the case. The possibility of salvation outside the Church is defined in a context where the Council does not speak at all about other religions but about human and ethical problems in terms of the theology of creation: the nature and dignity of humankind, sin, death, conscience, freedom, and atheism. God's hidden grace may work in those – even atheists – who, guided by their God-given conscience, seek the truth and work for that what is truly good in human life. In this case, it is the grace of the Creator, making an impact on all his creation. This grace may work in any human being without regard for their religiosity or non-religiosity. This line of understanding, expressed in GS 22, 5 is in line the Pauline teaching about the possibility of the pagans to have a relationship with the Creator on the basis of God's law written in every human heart (Rom. 2:14-16).

The religious substance of non-Christian religions have no specific role as a medium of hidden salvation in terms of the theology of creation and natural moral law. A sincere seeker of the truth and the doer of good may be an adherent of any religion or of none. Non-Christian religions are neither demonized nor divinized; they are seen as naturally good. They are neutralized and relativized: religions are a part of human life and culture, and as such they offer – if compared with other aspects of human culture – neither any particular hindrance nor any special advantage in a non-Christian's relation to the Creator.

Conclusion

Although the Second Vatican Council demostrated unforeseen openness to the progress and problems of the modern world, it did not make the least compromise in respect to the Catholic faith. All the good evolution in human culture, no matter whether it be secular or religious, is welcomed. But in spite of that, all developments need to be purified, strengthened, and elevated by the revealed divine truth, given to the world in Christ and incarnated and transmitted in his Church. The urgency of the Church's mission is in no way lessened by the Second Vatican Council: the Church has received the explicit revelation of divine grace in Christ; she possesses the *plenitudo mediorum salutis*, and, consequently, it is her mission to establish the bodily presence of the people of God, that is, of the Church herself, among every nation and to add people from all nations to the number of the elected (see AG 6, 2 & 7, 3 & 9, 2).

Many of the modern interpreters of the Second Vatican Council propose a line of interpretation which cannot be supported by the Conciliar texts. There may be other authoritative documents, and certainly there is a legion of individual Catholic authors, who recognize non-Christian religions as ways of divine revelation and salvation or as expression of the universal christological grace. But the official statements of the Council do not let us make such a conclusion.

Paul Knitter:[*]

INTERPRETING SILENCE: A RESPONSE TO MIIKKA RUOKANEN

With Miikka Ruokanen, I admit that the documents of the Second Vatican Council ar silent about the issue of whether other religious traditions can be *viae salutis* or ways of salvation. But to interpret this silence, as he does, to

---

[*] Paul Knitter, formerly a Divine Word missionary, is Professor of Theology at Xavier University in Cincinnati and serves as General Editor for the Faith Meets Faith series published by Orbis Books.

mean that the Council fathers implicitly *denied* that there can be authentic revelation and salvation through other religious paths is even less warranted than to conclude that they implicitly affirmed such salvific value. It seems to me that Ruokanen's analysis moves *beyond* the evidence of the texts themselves and *contrary* to the broader Roman Catholic theological context in which these texts were fashioned. Within this broader context of Catholic experience and tradition, there are, I suggest, even clearer and more persuasive reasons to interpret the Council's silence in a *positive* sense and to conclude, with the majority (not just "many") of contemporary Roman Catholic theologians that Vatican II implicitly affirms the salvific potential of other religions.

1. Dualism between Nature and Grace

Ruokanen's main thesis seems to be based on his understanding of Catholic theology of creation and natural moral law: "The religious substance of non-Christian religions has no specific role as a medium of hidden salvation in terms of the theology of creation and natural moral law." But especially since the discussions of the "nouvelle théologie" during the 1950's and de Lubac's revision of the "supernatural," together with Rahner's early writings on "nature and grace," Catholic theology, during the Conciliar years and now, would have great difficulty seeing itself reflected in Ruokanen's overly dualistic distinction between the orders of creation and of redemption, or between nature and grace, or "human vocation" and "divine vocation." While nature and grace are clearly and necessarily to be distinguished, they cannot be neatly separated into "here and there" or "then and now." As Rahner puts it, there really is no such thing as *natura pura* – "only nature." Nature is imbued with saving grace; grace cannot work except through the natural. Therefore if "*gratia non tollit naturam sed perficit*," it is because God has already been active in nature and so the grace of Christ can perfect the grace within nature.

2. Revelation

Ruokanen, of course, recognizes the clear thing of Vatican II that saving grace is operative beyond the visible confines of the Church, throughout creation. But because of his dualistic understanding of the orders of creation and salvation, he too neatly designates where "grace" is operative within creation and where "only nature" reigns. This is especially clear in the way he argues that, according to the Council, the religions are bereft of authentic *revelation*. He would interpret the explicit statement of NA that within the religions there is "a ray of that truth which enlightens all men" to mean only that this is the "natural knowledge" of God that Vatican I said is available to all people. The religions are therefore only "expressions of the *human* search for truth" (emphasis mine).

Such conclusions are based, I suspect, on an incomplete reading of Vatican I. While the fathers of that Council opposed the fideists and insisted that a natural knowledge of God is possible, they did not deny that a "supernatural knowledge" was also possible for all. In fact, to know God through reason is not yet to know the God who saves. Therefore, if Catholic theology affirms the genuine possibility of salvation outside the visible Church, it also, *a fortiori*, affirms the possibility of authentic, "supernatural" revelation. For this reason, the "rays of truth" recognized by NA within the religions are more correctly understood as rays of the *Logos spermatikos* – "seeds of the Word" – as *Ad gentes* and the 1984 Vatican Statement on "The Relation of the Church to Non-Christian Religions" clearly state (AG 11, 15; see the 1984 Statement in *International Bulletin of Missionary Research* 9, no. 4 [October 1985], pp. 187-191). Where the Divine Word is active, there is real revelation.

But Ruokanen may ask, if they were talking about authentic revelation in the religions, why did not the Council fathers use the word *revelatio*? Why is this term reserved only for the Jewish Scriptures and the New Testament, as is evident in *Dei Verbum*? Here a Roman Catholic *sensus theologicus* might help. The traditional teaching has been that revelation *sensu stricto* ended with the death of the last apostle. Within creation and within the religions we are speaking about another kind of divine revelation ("general" or "transcendental" as Rahner terms it). Out of a respect for tradition, official statements limit the term *revelatio* to its stricter, traditional meaning.

Ruokanen's straining to deny the Council's recognition of revelation within the religions is evident, I think, in his comments on the individual traditions. To hold that Islam, "the austere book religion" (that is *not* the language of NA) "is not recognized as a religion of divine revelation" contradicts NA's explicit recognition that Muslims "worship God" and "submit wholeheartedly to his inscrutable decrees, just as Abraham did" (NA 3). One cannot worship the living God unless that God has been revealed. Were not the decrees that Abraham submitted to authentically revealed? Further, to say that in Hinduism there is "no acquisition of religious truth" is to miss the full content of NA's recognition that Hindus "scrutantur - - mysterium divinum." *Scrutantur* means not just to search for, but to explore more deeply what one grasps. If this were not the case, Hindus could not *exprimunt* (express) the divine mystery (NA 2). And to hold that Buddhists are only "seekers," not finders, of truth is to misread the Latin verb *valeant*. NA states that Buddhists are "able" to "reach supreme illumination."

In general, when NA states that the religions "seek" (nituntur) to know God, Ruokanen interprets that to mean that they never succeed. That is neither logically certain nor consistent with the evident positive tone of the text.

3. Salvation

Even more adamantly Ruokanen argues that according to the Council, although, grace is universally available, it doesn't operate through the religions; the religions contain only a natural search for God. Again, he fails to appreciate the bonds between grace and nature within Catholic theology. Grace must always have a medium in *nature* and history; it cannot operate, as Ruokanen seems to suggest, purely in an interior or individualistic manner. It has to take some natural or sacramental shape. And with Rahner and the majority of Catholic theologians, I ask, would not the religions provide one such sacramental mediation of grace? Unawares, Ruokanen suggests a positive answer to this question as he lists the three conditions for the operation of saving grace outside the Church: besides not having really heard the Word of Christ, persons have to "sincerely seek the truth" and also "practice the moral good." These last two elements are precisely what the religions are about!

But then why didn't the Council come out and say that the religions are ways of salvation? Again, I appeal to my Catholic theological "sensus" and suggest that the main reason may have been that such a statement represents a genuine change or "development" in the teaching of the magisterium. And because of our traditional notion of the "inerrancy" of the magisterium, all changes (like those concerning usury or religious liberty) are usually introduced cautiously, implicitly – *silently*!

4. Conclusion

I cautiously venture an interpretation of Ruokanen's assessment of Vatican II. A number of times, he points out something that is really not the issue of his study – namely, that the Council did not intend to lessen "the urgency of the Church's mission." My sense is that this is the deeper concern of his analysis – to protect the urgency of the missionary mandate. I would strongly agree with him that any new theological view that jettisons or jeopardizes the missionary nature of the Church runs contrary to Christian identity and must be abandoned. I would suggest, however, that in his further research, Ruokanen study not whether the Council affirms the salvific potential of other religions but, rather, whether there is any validity to the claim made by the majority of Catholic theologians that to hold such a position does not lessen the urgency of the missionary mandate but, on the contrary, strengthens it by clarifying it. Here, I suggest, there would be an even more fruitful ecumenical dialogue between Christian neighbors concerned about mission and dialogue.

William R. Burrows:[*]

COMMENTS ON THE ARTICLES BY RUOKANEN AND KNITTER

Miikka Ruokanen's summary of the doctrine of Vatican Council II concerning the theological status of non-Christian religions and their role in salvation is, in my judgment, the most accurate account of that doctrine I have seen in print. As one who spent five years preparing a dissertation on the topic, I admire Ruokanen for getting to the heart of the Conciliar teaching so concisely. Paul Knitter, though, has raised absolutely important issues, and no one should think the problems are solved because the Conciliar teaching is elegantly laid out by Ruokanen.

Knitter's and Ruokanen's disagreement points to a need for the liberal and evangelical traditions they represent to continue the conversation. I believe that Ruokanen is right in his central thesis on the magisterium's teaching; but Knitter's development of the "silence" of the Council draws on important currents in the formation of the magisterial teaching. Two things should be said. First, there simply *are* unresolved tensions in the Vatican II magisterium, and both authors employ the resources they are convinced are right. But official teaching since the Council has tended to reinforce the conservative things that were explicitly *said* in the documents instead of reinforcing ideas liberals find attractive. Second, the problem is deeper than who is winning.

---

[*] William R. Burrows, Managing Editor of Orbis Books in Maryknoll, New York, is also working on a book on reconceptualizing evangelization in a postmodern key.

In that connection, Ruokanen seems to me accurate in explicating; 1. the recourse of the Council to the natural law tradition to locate salvation (outside of visible Christianity and faith in Jesus as Christ) in the depths of human conscience; and, 2. the Council's "silence" about the value of other religious traditions as *means of salvation* or as *valid revelations*. Liberal Catholics have almost universally missed the first point and have interpreted the second as silence giving consent to viewing other traditions as such means. They should have been more cautious.

In the rest of this response, I want to try to unpack two insights that neither author attends to sufficiently: 1. a deep "theoanthropology of *true* conscience" inviting development; and, 2. ambiguity about what constitutes "revelation" in the light of the several major religiocultural characterizations of true conscience, an ambiguity often overlooked in the rush to be for or against extra-Christian revelation.

In my own thinking, I have come to see the crucial issue as one of assessing whether God's graciousness: 1. is available universally in an act of "conscientization" aiding humans to overcome false, sinful consciousness and to affirm their creaturely status before God; or, 2. is available only in an explicit act of faith in Jesus as Christ and as a result of his work. (I think it important to retain the criteria for the authenticity of both – at-one-ment with God and our fellows, however diversely that result is expressed or conceptualized – if dialogue is to have a necessary critical edge.) The Council takes the first position, while teaching also that all grace comes through Jesus as the Christ.

Liberal interpretations of revelation and salvation tend to see other religious ways mediating salvation, but are vague about what salvation means. We need to overcome that lack of clarity. We also need to see that the "act of conscience" wherein the Council locates justification is more like conscientization as Paulo Freire puts it (an existential and social appropriation of true consciousness and overcoming alienating false consciousness) than doing what one *thinks* or *believes* is best or obligatory.

Conscience, in an almost forgotten Stoic metaphysics underlying the natural law tradition, means more than ethical activity springing from sincerely held convictions. That is only one aspect of conscience. Viewed holistically, conscience is the total spiritual, mental, and volitional side of human beings. When that is seen, the real *crux theologicus* is the Council's implicit conjunction of justification and conscientization, and seeing the complex process as one that involves a total rooting of human beings and their communities in a single divinized reality. They become grounded in God the creator and redeemer. On such a view, whether it occurs inside or outside the sphere of visible Christianity, justification/conscientization is not a nominal but a real and radical transformation of people: *no cheap grace inside or outside Christianity*! Much of the talk of extra-Christian salvation and revelation, it seems to me, misses the crisis dimension of conversion. This oversight undercuts the urgency of witnessing to the gospel that people's eternal destiny is secured in grace by conversion from false consciousness to true consciousness. It shortcircuits the Christian conviction that Jesus is the manifestation of the single authentic way of rooting ourselves in reality's theonomous depths.

What needs to be investigated by both liberal and evangelical traditions is twofold: 1. What is meant by the encounter with God in the depths of conscience? 2. Is this conceptuality acceptable in the light of what we know about pluralities of logics and religiocultural syntheses?

Rather than in terms set out in the clash between Knitter and Ruokanen, it seems to me that a development of the Catholic magisterium ought to articulate both "Christian" and "extra-visible-Christian" salvation as one and the same process of gaining a divine empowering center for life, and dialoguing with other traditions to see if they have potential for helping achieve deeper understanding of justification-as-conscientization.

This may seem far removed from missiology. It is not. It involves gaining clarity about the salvation Christians believe mission-as-evangelization must make manifest. And interreligious dialogue can be the very important task not of asserting that a vague form of salvation is offered in other traditions, but the urgent effort to clarify what light can be cast and resources offered by other traditions to overcome human misery. We are only at the beginning of such a dialogue. Both Ruokanen's caution on overstating what the Council has said and Knitter's urgency about getting into the business of overcoming the barriers to human liberation caused by religious division are important aspects of a multifaceted effort to clarify Christian mission.

Miikka Ruokanen:

AUTHOR'S REPLY

In his response to my article "Catholic Teaching on Non-Christian Religions at the Second Vatican Council" (April 1990), Paul Knitter stresses "the bonds between grace and nature within Catholic theology." "Grace must always have a medium in *nature* and history." (P. 63.) As Knitter points out,

Karl Rahner is the major Catholic theologian who suggested that non-Christian religions could be understood as incarnated or sacramental media of God's supernatural salvific grace.

In his well-known article "Das Christentum und die nichtchristlichen Religionen" (published in *Schriften zur Theologie*, Bd. 5 [Einsiedeln & Zürich & Köln: Benziger Verlag, 1962], pp. 136-158), Rahner offers a new way of thinking by emphasizing that non-Christian religions are not only reflections of the natural human cognition of God, but they also contain a mediation of grace that adds something to our natural relation as creatures to the Creator. According to Rahner, a non-Christian religion "not only contains elements of natural knowledge of God," but "also supernatural instances of the grace which God presents to man because of Christ." For people who do not know the gospel, their own religions are "legitimate religions," that is, God uses them as channels of supernatural saving grace.

Rahner did indeed introduce a somewhat novel Catholic approach to non-Christian religions. His concept is founded on the principle of incarnation: God does not offer supernatural saving grace "directly;" grace is always incarnated in concrete elements or matter. Rahner extends the idea of the sacramental mediation of grace through natural matter from the explicit Christian media to the concrete material and historical elements of other religions as well. He created a theoretic model but did not go into detail about *how* supernatural grace is present in other religions.

Certainly Rahner was one of the main theological figures who affected the theological substance of Vatican II. But Rahner himself – much more than his students and followers – was aware that his particular idea about the non-Christian religions as a sacramental mediation of supernatural grace did *not* gain Conciliar recognition. He expressed his disappointment with the issue in his article "Über die Heilsbedeutung der nichtchristlichen Religionen" (*Schriften zur Theologie*, Bd. 13 [Einsiedeln & Zürich & Köln: Benziger Verlag, 1978], pp. 341-350).

Rahner says that in the *Nostra aetate* declaration, "the proper theological quality of non-Christian religions remains undefined." With profound insight into the Conciliar teaching, Rahner notes that the text does not acknowledge any specific status of the salvific mediation in other religions. He expressed his astonishment at the Conciliar teaching and asked how atheists – lacking the incarnated mediation of grace – could be in the same position as the religious non-Christians: how could "explicit, verbalized, and institutional religiosity be superfluous in all human life for the relation of man to God?"

In general, Rahner's understanding of the Conciliar teaching on non-Christian religions is in line with the analysis I offered in my article. On the whole, the Second Vatican Council clung to the traditional Catholic interpretation of other religions, the natural cognition of God (Rom. 1:20) and natural moral law (Rom. 2:14-16).

The strong emphasis of sacramentalism was generally adopted by the Conciliar teaching in ecclesiology: the Church is the sacrament of the whole world (see *Lumen gentium* 1, e.g.). But the idea of sacramentalism was not extended to the Conciliar understanding of non-Christian religions. Neither did the Council's teaching on religions acknowledge the idea of cosmic christology, as presented in pre-conciliar theology by Henri de Lubac.

One of the most interesting and promising lines of interpretation that has not yet been worked out very much in relation to non-Christians is the classical idea of the indivisibility of the works of the Holy Trinity. The *opera ad extra* of the Trinity may be distinguished but not separated from each other. According to this, for instance, creation is not only the work of the Father, but all was created through, in, and for Christ (cf. Col. 1). Furthermore, the Holy Spirit as *Spiritus Creator* works in the very act of creation (cf. Gen. 1:2; 2:7). The Holy Trinity is always present in all that God does; consequently, God's "natural" creative grace and God's "supernatural" salvific grace are simultaneously present.

This line of Trinitarian theology has its foundation in the fathers of the Church, especially Irenaeus. In modern times Lubac and some others have attempted to develop this interpretation. But there is a need for further clarification on the Trinitarian effect on non-Christians. This approach does not necessarily place any special emphasis on *religions* as media of grace. Even if it is admitted that God uses other religions as a mediation of supernatural grace, there exists an urgent need for an analysis of *modus gratiae*, that is, of how this grace works in the religions.

As I understand it, the classical line of Trinitarian theology is implied by William R. Burrows in his comment on Knitter and me, as he seeks a more profound understanding of "what is meant by the encounter with God in the depths of conscience" (p. 64). This certainly includes the encounter of human beings with the Holy Trinity.

Two final remarks: First, Knitter blames me for a "dualistic understanding of the orders of creation and salvation." In my article, I attempt to demonstrate how the classical Catholic idea of grace perfecting nature is the backbone of the Conciliar teaching. *Eo ipso* this means that nature and grace are inseparable. But this does not mean that nature and grace could not be distinguished from each other. Quite on the contrary, it is the essential basic skill of every theologian to be able to make a distinction between "natural" and "supernatural" (Catholic) or "law" and "gospel" (Protestant). Without this distinction we lose the uniqueness of the gospel, humankind being saved *sola gratia*.

Second, I do not believe that the Council limited the term *revelatio* to the explicit Christian meaning only "out of a respect for tradition," as Knitter suggests. A conclusion like that is truly an argument *ex silentio*. I am much more inclined to believe in the theological consistency of the Conciliar teaching.

Paul Knitter:

AUTHOR'S REPLY

To the Editors:

I want to thank Miikka Ruokanen for the clarity and sensitivity with which he replied (July 1990) to my comments on his April 1990 article concerning the teaching of the Second Vatican Council on non-Christian religions. His reply enables me to focus, I hope with equal clarity and sensitivity, on what remains the fundamental difference in the way each of us understands the contents and significance of what the Council had to say about other religious traditions.

His interpretation of Karl Rahner's essay "On the Importance of the Non-Christian Religions for Salvation" (*Theological Investigations*, vol. 18, pp. 288-295) illustrates, I believe, how he continues to misread both Rahner and the Council. Ruokanen claims that "Rahner's understanding of the Conciliar teaching on non-Christian religions is in line" with his own. *Concedo* – yes, Rahner would agree with Ruokanen's claim that Vatican II did not explicitly declare the religions to be "ways of salvation." But *nego* – no, Rahner would not agree when Ruokanen argues that the view of other religions as ways of salvation, proposed by Rahner and the majority of Roman Catholic theologians, "cannot be supported by the Conciliar texts" (April 1990, p. 61). This was the point of Rahner's essay: that when the Council left the issue of the salvific role of other religions open, as a *quaestio disputata*, it need *not* have done so! The Council itself, Rahner points out, established the premises for a conclusion it did not draw!

For some reason, the conclusion contained in these premises is not clear to Ruokanen. The first premise is the Council's clear and pervasive declaration of the universal saving activity of God's grace, which means the universal availability of authentic revelation. (As Rahner himself puts it in the essay Ruokanen refers to: "- - the history of supernatural revelation and the history of supernatural salvation [beyond Christianity] are necessarily co-extensive and co-existent" [p. 292].) The second premise is what Ruokanen calls "sacramentalism." For Roman Catholic theology in general, and for Vatican II in particular, the principle that God's saving grace cannot operate in an exclusively interior or individualistic manner but must take some kind of sacramental – that is, historical-social form – is not limited to ecclesiology (as Ruokanen suggests) but is fundamental to the way Catholics understand the divine-human relationship. Therefore, once you recognize that God's saving grace operates beyond the borders of the historical-social forms of Christianity (the first premise), you're going to have to admit *other* historical-social forms through which it operates (the second premise).

Therefore, Rahner is, as Ruokanen rightly describes, "astonished" that "this conclusion from the premises of the Council is not drawn by the Council in *Nostra aetate*" (Rahner, p. 290) – namely, that the religions can be counted among the sacramental expressions/mediations of this universal grace. As Rahner states, such a conclusion is "really obvious" (ibid.). For Rahner and most Roman Catholic theologians, the Council supports, though it does not explicitly draw, such a conclusion.

The reason why Ruokanen cannot see how this conclusion flows necessarily from these premises gets back to what I termed his dualistic notion of nature and grace. I agree with him that "nature and grace are clearly and necessarily to be distinguished" (from my first response, p. 62). And he agrees with me that, especially in light of the Trinitarian *opera ad extra*, the "natural and the supernatural," or "law and gospel," are "simultaneously present" and are "inseparable" (Ruokanen's words). Yet he seems to contradict himself when he so clearly, adamantly, and dualistically separates nature from grace in the realm of religion. He insists that for the Council the religions represent only "the natural cognition of God" or "natural moral law." He seems to fear that unless the religions are kept to the natural order, we jeopardize *sola gratia*. I don't understand why. If "sola gratia" can operate within/despite the Christian religion, why can't it do so within/despite other religions? Ruokanen continues not only to distinguish but to separate nature and grace much too facilely. This runs contrary to the spirit, if not to the words, of the Council.

But why did not the Council explicitly affirm in words what it was implicitly holding in spirit? Ruokanen misunderstood the explanation I tried to give in my response: "out of a respect for tradition." *Nostra aetate*'s positive view of other religions, implying their salvific role in God's plan, represents a change, something new, in Catholic teaching. Such changes are admitted only slowly, often indirectly, seeking to avoid the impression that mistakes were made in the past. (I am merely describing this reality, not defending it.) This accounts for what many have called the "schizophrenic quality" of many Vatican II teachings. Often, in areas that signified change or a development in Catholic consciousness, the Council would state something in one context, but not follow through, or would even contradict itself, in another context (e.g., admitting that salvation is possible for atheists yet holding to the necessity of the Church for salvation, or affirming the collegiality of the episcopate but allowing the Pope to act "without consent" of the bishops); or the Council would declare something new without explicitly recognizing how this corrected previous teaching (e.g. religious liberty). Thus, for Catholic theologians, it is both "astonishing" and yet understandable that, in the 1960's the Council fathers could lay out the premises, could conclude to the positive values in other religions, but could not draw the final conclusion of recognizing their possible salvific role.

The editors of IBMR received another letter (unpublished) that asked what I meant in the last paragraph of my response to Ruokanen when I stated that the new views recognizing the salvific potential of other religions do "*not* lessen the urgency of the missionary mandate but, on the contrary strengthen it." This is the pivotal question I would like to discuss with my Protestant (and Catholic!) colleagues, whose missionary commitments *I do share*. Here I can only outline what calls for a much lengthier discussion. The pluralistic theology of religions that I and others have been trying to work out, while it questions the exclusive uniqueness of Jesus, continues to affirm his *universal and relational uniqueness*. Most pluralist theologians who recognize the possible salvific validity of other paths continue to affirm that what they as Christians have experienced and known in Jesus the Christ is meant for all peoples of all times. This means that not to know of this Jesus is to have, in some manner, an "incomplete" or "unfulfilled" understanding of humanity, the world, and the Ultimate. Therefore, Christians must go forth to make known to others what has been made known to them. And the motivation to do so is much more impelling than the motivation provided by the so-called theory of "anonymous Christianity." Such a theory called the missioner to bring to full consciousness in others what they may well have already known unconsciously or anonymously. The pluralistic perspective I am suggesting recognizes that what has been revealed in Jesus may well be something "brand new," not yet known, or lived by the Buddhists or Hindus, and without which their understandings and spirituality are incomplete. (What this "brand new" might be cannot be discussed here.)

A pluralist theology of religions can offer even greater missionary inspiration than traditional, conservative views that deny any salvific role to other faiths. By recognizing the possible saving content of other religions, the pluralists understand the uniqueness of Jesus to be *relational*: the message of Jesus must be related to the possible message God gives through others. Christians are therefore motivated to go forth unto all nations not just to teach what others need to know, but also to learn from others what God may wish to reveal to us through others. Missionary work, from this perspective, is essential to Christianity not just that the Church may bring about the conversion of others but also to bring about its own conversion – and thus to remain the authentic Church of Jesus Christ.

SOURCES AND ABBREVIATIONS

Sacrosanctum Oecumenicum Concilium Vaticanum II. Constitutiones, Decreta, Declarationes. Cura et studio Secretariae Generalis Concilii Oecumenicii Vaticani II. The Vatican City 1964-1966.

The Conciliar documents referred to:

AA   Apostolicam actuositatem, Decree on the Apostolate of Lay People (November 18, 1965).

AG   Ad gentes, Decree on the Church's Missionary Activity (December 7, 1965).

DH   Dignitatis humanae, Declaration on Religious Liberty (December 7, 1965).

DV   Dei verbum, Dogmatic Constitution on Divine Revelation (November 18, 1965).

GE   Gravissimum educationis, Declaration on Christian Education (October 28, 1965).

GS   Gaudium et spes, Pastoral Constitution on the Church in the Modern World (December 7, 1965).

LG   Lumen gentium, Dogmatic Constitution on the Church (November 21, 1964).

NA   Nostra aetate, Declaration on the Relation of the Church to Non-Christian Religions (October 28, 1965).

OE   Orientalium Ecclesiarum, Decree on the Catholic Eastern Churches (November 21, 1964).

PC   Perfectae caritatis, Decree on the Up-to-date Renewal of Religious Life (October 18, 1965).

PO   Presbyterorum ordinis, Decree on the Ministry and Life of Priests (December 7, 1965).

SC   Sacrosanctum Concilium, Constitution on the Sacred Liturgy (December 4, 1963).

UR   Unitatis redintegratio, Decree on Ecumenism (November 21, 1964).

AS   Acta Synodalia Sacrosancti Concilii Oecumenici Vaticani II. The Vatican City.

DS   Enchiridion symbolorum, definitionum et declarationum de rebus fidei et morum, Edidit H. Denzinger & A. Schönmetzer. Editio 32. Barcione 1963.

PL   S. Gregorii VII Epistula ad Anazir regem Mauritaniae. Patrologia Latina 148, 450-452.

AAS   Pius XII, Evangelii praecones (June 6, 1951). - Acta Apostolicae Sedis 1951, 497-528.
John XXIII, Princeps pastorum (November 28, 1959). - Acta Apostolicae Sedis 1959, 833-864.
John XXIII, Mater et magistra (May 15, 1961). - Acta Apostolicae Sedis 1961, 401-464.

John XXIII, Pacem in terris (April 11, 1963). - Acta Apostolicae Sedis 1963, 257-304.
Paul VI, Nuntius radiophonicus (March 29, 1964). - Acta Apostolicae Sedis 1964, 391-396.
Paul VI, Ecclesiam Suam (August 6, 1964). - Acta Apostolicae Sedis 1964, 609-659.

L'Osservatore Romano.

LITERATURE

Allen, E.L.
1960   Christianity Among the Religions. London.

Amstutz, Josef
1973   Über die Religionen. Nostra Aetate, Art. 1 und 2. - Neue Zeitschrift für Missionswissenschaft 1973, 81-92.
1982   Über die Allgegenwart der Gnade. - Neue Zeitschrift für Missionswissenschaft 1982, 81-109.

Anawati, Georges C.
1967   Exkurs zum Konzilstext über die Muslim. - Lexikon für Theologie und Kirche, Das Zweite Vatikanische Konzil 2, 485-487.

Anderson, Gerald H.
1981   Response to Pietro Rossano. - Christ's Lordship and Religious Pluralism. Ed. by G.H. Anderson & T.F. Stransky. Maryknoll. Pp. 110-120.

Armstrong, R.A.
1966   Primary and Secondary Precepts in Thomistic Natural Law Teaching. The Hague.

Augustine
     De spiritu et littera. - Corpus Scriptorum Ecclesiasticorum Latinorum 60, 155-229.

Balthasar, Hans Urs von
1962   Karl Barth. Darstellung und Deutung seiner Theologie. Zweite Auflage. Köln.
1965   Wer ist ein Christ? Einsiedeln.

Bea, Augustin
1966a   La Chiesa e il popolo ebraico. Brescia.
1966b   Der Weg zur Einheit nach dem Konzil. Freiburg & Basel & Wien.
1967   The Church and Mankind. London & Dublin & Melbourne.

Becker, Werner
1966   Die Erklärung über das Verhältnis der Kirche zu den nichtchristlichen Religionen. - Catholica 1966, 108-135.

Benz, Ernst
1961   Ideen zu einer Theologie der Religionsgeschichte. (Akademie der Wissenschaften und der Literatur, Abhandlungen der geistes- und sozialwissenschaftlichen Klasse, Jahrgang 1960, Nr. 5.) Mainz & Wiesbaden.

Bouquet, A.C.
1958   The Christian Faith and Non-Christian Religions. London.

Brechter, Heinrich Suso
1968   De principiis fundamentalibus dialogi cum religionibus non-christianis. - Acta congressus internationalis de theologia Concilii Vaticani II. Ed. A. Schönmetzer. The Vatican City 1968. Pp. 340-347.

Bsteh, Andreas
1966   Zur Frage nach der Universalität der Elösung. Unter besonderer Berücksichtigung ihres Verständnisses bei den Vätern des zweiten Jahrhunderts. (Wiener Beiträge zur Theologie 14.) Wien.

Bürkle, Horst
1965   Die Frage nach dem kosmischen Christus als Beispiel einer ökumenisch orientierten Theologie. - Kerygma und Dogma 1965, 103-115.
1977   Einführung in die Theologie der Religionen. (Die Theologie.) Darmstadt.

Cardinale, Igino
1967   Religious tolerance, freedom and inter-group relations in the light of Vatican Council II. London.

Christentum innerhalb und außerhalb der Kirche
1976   Christentum innerhalb und außerhalb der Kirche. Hrsg. v. E. Klinger. (Quaestiones disputatae 73.) Freiburg & Basel & Wien.

Congar, Yves
1957   Salvation and the Non-Catholic. - Blackfriars 1957, 290-300.
1961   Außen der Kirche kein Heil? Essen.

Cottier, G.M.-M.
1966   L'historique de la déclaration. - *Vatican II, Les relations de l'Église avec les religions non chrétiennes* 1966, 37-78.

Daniélou, Jean
1950   The Salvation of the Nations. New York.
1956   Vom Geheimnis der Geschichte. Stuttgart.
1962   The Advent of Salvation. A Comparative Study on non-Christian Religions and Christianity. (Deus Books.) New York.

La dichiarazione su Le relazioni della Chiesa con le religioni non cristiane
1966   La dichiarazione su Le relazioni della Chiesa con le religioni non cristiane. Torino.

The Documents of Vatican II
1966   The Documents of Vatican II. Ed. by W.M. Abbott & J. Callagher. Chicago.

Dumoulin, Heinrich
1967   Exkurs zum Konziltext über den Buddhismus. - Lexikon für Theologie und Kirche, Das Zweite Vatikanische Konzil 2, 482-485.

Eckert, Willehad Paul
1976   Richtlinien und Hinweise für die Konzilserklärung Nostra Aetate, Art. 4. Einleitung. (Nachkonziliare Dokumentation 49.) Trier.

Elders, L.
1965   Die Taufe der Weltreligionen. Bemerkungen zu einer Theorie Karl Rahners. - Theologie und Glaube 1965, 124-131.

Eminyan, Maurice
1960   The Theology of Salvation. Boston.

Evers, Georg
1979   Die anonymen Christen und der Dialog mit den Juden. - Wagnis Theologie. Erfahrungen mit der Theologie Karl Rahners. K. Rahner zum 75. Geburtstag. Hrsg. v. H. Vorgrimler. Freiburg & Basel & Wien. Pp. 524-536.

Fahlbusch, Erwin
1969   Theologie der Religionen. Überblick zu einem Thema römisch-katholischer Theologie. - Kerygma und Dogma 1969, 73-86.

Federici, Tommaso
1966   Il Concilio e i non cristiani. Declaratio, testo e commento. Roma.

Feiner, Johannes
1964   Kirche und Heilsgeschichte. - Gott in Welt 2. K. Rahner zum 60. Geburtstag. Hrsg. v. J.B. Metz & W. Kern & A. Darlapp & H. Vorgrimler. Freiburg & Basel & Wien. Pp. 317-345.

Fischer, Klaus
1974   Der Mensch als Geheimnis. Die Anthropologie Karl Rahners. (Ökumenische Forschungen 2, 5.) Freiburg.

Fisher, Eugene J.
1985   Interpreting Nostra Aetate through Postconciliar Teaching. - International Bulletin of Missionary Research 1985, 158-165.

Fransen, Piet
1973   Dogmengeschichtliche Entfaltung der Gnadenlehre. - Mysterium Salutis IV, 2. Hrsg. v. J. Feiner & M. Löhrer. Einsiedeln & Zürich & Köln. Pp. 631-765.

Fries, Heinrich
1965   Das Christentum und die Religionen der Welt. - Das Christentum und die Weltreligionen. (Studien und Berichte der Katholischen Akademie in Bayern 27.) Hrsg. v. K. Forster. Würzburg. Pp. 13-37.

Gilbert, Arthur
1968   The Vatican Council and the Jews. Cleveland.

Graham, Robert A.
1966   Introduction to the Declaration on non-Christians. - *The Documents of Vatican II* 1966, 656-659.

Greiner, Friedmann
1978   Die Menschlichkeit der Offenbarung. Die transzendentale Grundlegung der Theologie bei Karl Rahner. (Münchener Monographien zur historischen und systematischen Theologie 2.) München.

Grillmeier, Aloys
1966   Dogmatische Konstitution über die Kirche. Kommentar zum II. Kapitel. - Lexikon für Theologie und Kirche, Das Zweite Vatikanische Konzil 1, 176-209.

Hallencreutz, Carl F.
1977   Dialogue and Community. Ecumenical Issues in Inter-Religious Relationships. (Studia Missionalia Upsaliensia 31.) Uppsala & Geneve.

Hamm, Berndt
1977   Promissio, pactum, ordinatio. Freiheit und Selbstbindung Gottes in der scholastischen Gnadenlehre. (Beiträge zur historischen Theologie 54.) Tübingen.

Hebblethwaite, Peter
1984   John XXIII, Pope of the Council. London.

Heck, Erich
1971   Der Begriff religio bei Thomas von Aquin. Seine Bedeutung für unser heutiges Verständnis von Religion. (Abhandlungen zur Philosophie, Psychologie, Soziologie der Religion und Ökumenik, N.F. 21-22.) München.

Heislbetz, Josef
1967   Theologische Gründe der nichtchristlichen Religionen. (Quaestiones disputatae 33.) Freiburg & Basel & Wien.

Karrer, Otto
1934   Das Religiöse in der Menschheit und das Christentum. Freiburg.
1955   Die Weltreligionen im Lichte des Christentums. - Theologische Quartalschrift 1955, 295-319.

King, Ursula
1981   Towards a new mysticism. Teilhard de Chardin and eastern religions. New York.

Knitter, Paul F.
1984   Roman Catholic Approaches to Other Religions: Developments and Tensions. - International Bulletin of Missionary Research 1984, 50-54.
1985   No Other Name? A Critical Survey of Christian Attitudes Toward the World Religions. London.

Korbacher, Joachim
1963   Außerhalb der Kirche kein Heil? Eine dogmengeschichtliche Untersuchung über Kirche und Kirchenzugehörigkeit bei Johannes Chrysostomus. (Münchener theologische Studien, II. Systematische Abteilung 27.) München.

Küng, Hans
1965   Christenheit als Minderheit. Die Kirche unter den Weltreligionen. Einsiedeln.
1974   Christ sein. München & Zürich.

Lais, Hermann
1951   Die Gnadenlehre des heiligen Thomas in der Summa Contra Gentiles und der Kommentar des Franziskus Sylvestris von Ferrara. (Münchener theologische Studien, II. Systematische Abteilung 3.) München.

Lambert, Bernard
1964   De Rome à Jérusalem. Itinéraire spiritual de Vatican II. (L'Église en son temps.) Paris.

Lapide, Pinchas E.
1967   Rom und die Juden. Freiburg & Basel & Wien.

Laurentin, René
1967   L'Église et les juifs a Vatican II. Tournai.

Laurentin, René & Neuner, Joseph
1966   The Declaration on the Relation of the Church to Non-Christian Religions. (Vatican II Documents.) Glen Rock.

Lazar, Elmer B.
1978   The story of the century. Jews absolved from blame of Jesus Christ's death. New York.

Leclercq, J.
1955   La philosophie morale de Saint Thomas devant la pensée contemporaine. Paris & Louvain.

Lilienfeld, Fairy von
1969   Römisch-katholische und Orthodoxe Kirche nach dem Zweiten Vatikanischen Konzil und Orientalium Ecclesiarum. - Materialdienst des Konfessionskundlichen Instituts Bensheim 1969, 21-27.

Lonergan, Bernard J.F.
1971   Grace and Freedom. Operative Grace in Thought of St. Thomas Aquinas. London.

Lubac, Henri de
1946   Surnaturel. Études historiques. (Théologie 8.) Paris.
1965   Le Mystère du Surnaturel. (Théologie 64.) Paris.
1966   Mistica naturale e mistica cristiana. - *Federici* 1966, 13-39.
1969   Teilhard de Chardins religiöse Welt. Freiburg & Basel & Wien.
1970   Glauben aus der Liebe. Catholicisme. Einsiedeln.

Masson, J.
1965   La Déclaration sur les religions non-chrétiennes. - Nouvelle Revue Théologique 1965, 1066-1083.

Mission Trends No. 5
1981   Mission Trends No. 5. Faith Meets Faith. Ed. by G.H. Anderson & T.F. Stransky. New York & Ramsey & Toronto & Gran Rapids.

Morency, Robert
1950   L'union de grace selon Saint Thomas. (Studia Collegii Maximii 8.)
        Montréal.

Müller, Karl
1968   Die Kirche und die nichtchristlichen Religionen. Kommentar zur
        Konzilserklärung über das Verhältnis der Kirche zu den nichtchristlichen
        Religionen. (Der Christ in der Welt 17, 8.) Aschaffenburg.

Nelson, Claud
1966   A Response. - *The Documents of Vatican II* 1966, 669-671.

Nys, H.
1966   Le salut sans l'Évangile. Étude historique et critique du problème du
        salut des infidèles dans la littérature théologique récente (1912-1964).
        Paris.

O'Connor, D.J.
1967   Aquinas and Natural Law. London.

Oesterreicher, Johannes (John M.)
1964   Das Konzil und die Judenfrage. - Zweites Vatikanisches Konzil. 2.
        Sitzungsperiode. Dokumente, Texte, Kommentare. (Fromms Taschenbücher,
        Zeitnahes Christentum 30.) Osnabrück. Pp. 201-204.
1967   Die Erklärung über das Verhältnis der Kirche zu den nichtchristlichen
        Religionen. Kommentierende Einleitung. - Lexikon für Theologie und
        Kirche, Das Zweite Vatikanische Konzil 2, 406-487.
1971   The rediscovery of Judaism. A re-examination of the conciliar statement
        on the Jews. South Orange.

Ohm, Thomas
1957   Die Liebe zu Gott in den nichtchristlichen Religionen. Die Tatsachen der
        Religionsgeschichte und die christliche Theologie. Zweite Auflage.
        Freiburg.

Papali, Cyril B.
1967   Exkurs zum Konzilstext über den Hinduismus. - Lexikon für Theologie
        und Kirche, Das Zweite Vatikanische Konzil 2, 478-482.

Poncins, Léon de
1967   Judaism and the Vatican: an attempt at spiritual subversion. London.

Rahner, Karl
1950   Über das Verhältnis von Natur und Gnade. - Orientierung 1950,
        141-145.
1962   Schriften zur Theologie 5. Neuere Schriften. Einsiedeln & Zürich &
        Köln.
1965   Schriften zur Theologie 6. Neuere Schriften. Einsiedeln & Zürich &
        Köln.
1977   Grundkurs des Glaubens. Einführung in den Begriff des Christentums.
        Freiburg & Basel & Wien.
1978   Schriften zur Theologie 13. Gott und Offenbarung. Einsiedeln & Zürich
        & Köln.

Ratzinger, Joseph
1964   Der christliche Glaube und die Weltreligionen. - Gott in Welt. K.
        Rahner zum 60. Geburtstag 2. Hrsg. v. J.B. Metz & W. Kern & A.
        Darlapp & H. Vorgrimler. Freiburg & Basel & Wien. Pp. 287-305.
1968   Pastorale Konstitution über die Kirche in der Welt von heute.
        Kommentar zum I. Kapitel. - Lexikon für Theologie und Kirche, Das
        Zweite Vatikanische Konzil 3, 313-354.
1972   Das neue Volk Gottes. Entwürfe zur Ekklesiologie. (Topos-Taschenbücher
        1.) Düsseldorf.

Ricken, Friedo
1965   Ecclesia...universale salutis sacramentum. Theologische Erwägungen zur Lehre der Dogmatischen Konstitution De Ecclesia über die Kirchenzugehörigkeit. - Scholastik 1965, 352-388.
Riesenhuber, Klaus
1964   Der anonyme Christ, nach Karl Rahner. - Zeitschrift für katholische Theologie 1964, 286-303.
Rossano, Pietro
1981   Christ's Lordship and Religious Pluralism in Catholic Perspective, - Christ's Lordship and Religious Pluralism. Ed. by G.H. Anderson & T.F. Stransky. Maryknoll. Pp. 96-110.
Ruello, Francis
1987   La christologié de Thomas d'Aquin. (Théologie historique 76.) Paris.
Ruini, Camillo
1971   La transcendenza della grazia nella teologia di San Tommaso d'Aquino. (Analecta Gregoriana 180.) Roma.
Rynne, Xavier (pseudonym)
1964   The Second Session. The Debates and Decrees of Vatican Council II. September 29 to December 4, 1963. London.
1965   The Third Session. The Debates and Decrees of Vatican Council II. September 14 to November 21, 1964. London.
1966   The Fourth Session. The Debates and Decrees of Vatican Council II. September 14 to December 8, 1965. London.
Rütti, Ludwig
1972   Zur Theologie der Mission. Kritische Analysen und neue Orientierungen. (Gesellschaft und Theologie, Systematische Beiträge 9.) München & Mainz.
Röper, Anita
1963   Die anonymen Christen. Mainz.
Schillebeeckx, Edward
1968   De Ecclesia ut sacramento mundi. - Acta congressus internationalis de theologia Concilii Vaticani II. Ed. A. Schönmetzer. The Vatican City 1968. Pp. 48-53.
Schlette, Heinz Robert
1964a   Die Konfrontation mit den Religionen. Eine philosophische und theologische Einführung. Köln.
1964b   Einige Thesen zum Selbstverständnis der Theologie angesichts der Religionen. - Gott in Welt 2. K. Rahner zum 60. Geburtstag. Hrsg. v. J.B. Metz & W. Kern & A. Darlapp & H. Vorgrimler. Freiburg & Basel & Wien 1964. Pp. 306-316.
1964c   Die Religionen als Thema der Theologie. Überlegungen zu einer Theologie der Religionen. (Quaestiones Disputatae 22.) Freiburg & Basel & Wien.
1970   Aporie und Glaube. Schriften zur Philosophie und Theologie. München.
Schreiner, Peter
1969   Roman Catholic Theology and Non-Christian Religion. - Journal of Ecumenical Studies 1969, 376-399.
Schwerdtfeger, Nikolaus
1982   Gnade und Welt. Zum Grundgefüge von Karl Rahners Theorie der anonymen Christen. (Freiburger theologische Studien 123.) Freiburg.
Sertillanges, R.P.
1947   La philosophie morale de St.Thomas d'Aquin. Paris.

Shivute, Tomas
1980   The Theology of Mission and Evangelism in the International Missionary Council from Edinburgh to New Delhi. (Annals of the Finnish Society for Missiology and Ecumenics 31.) Helsinki.

Speck, Josef
1967   Karl Rahners theologische Anthropologie. Eine Einführung. (Schriften des Deutschen Instituts für Wissenschaftliche Pädagogik.) München.

Stoeckle, Bernhard
1962   Gratia supponit naturam. Geschichte und Analyse eines theologischen Axioms. (Studia Anselmiana 49.) Roma.

Stransky, Thomas F.
1985   The Church and Other Religions. - International Bulletin of Missionary Research 1985, 154-158.

Teilhard de Chardin, Pierre
1971   Christianity and Evolution. London.

Thomas Aquinas
        In II sententiarum. - Opera omnia 1, 122-257. Curante R. Busa. Stuttgart & Bad Cannstatt 1980.

Türk, Hans J.
1967   Was sagt das Konzil über nichtchristliche Religionen, Mission, Toleranz? (Kleine Konzilskommentare.) Mainz.

Vatican Council II
1975   Vatican Council II. The Conciliar and Post Conciliar Documents. Ed. by A. Flannery. Collegeville.

Vatican II: An Interfaith Appraisal
1966   Vatican II: An Interfaith Appraisal. Ed. by J.H. Miller. Notre Dame.

Vatican II, Les relations de l'Église avec les religions non chrétiennes
1966   Vatican II, Les relations de l'Église avec les religions non chrétiennes. Déclaration Nostra aetate. Ed. A.-M. Henry. (Unam Sanctam 61.) Paris.

Waldenfels, Hans
1970   Das Verständnis der Religionen und seine Bedeutung für die Mission in katholischer Sicht. - Evangelische Missions-Zeitschrift 1970, 125-159.

1984   Theologie der nichtchristlichen Religionen. Konsequenzen aus Nostra aetate. - Glaube im Prozess. Christsein nach dem II. Vatikanum. Für K. Rahner zum 80. Geburtstag. Hrsg. v. E. Klinger & K. Wittstadt. Freiburg & Basel & Wien. Pp. 757-775.

Weger, Karl-Heinz
1979   Überlegungen zum anonymen Christentum. - Wagnis Theologie. Erfahrungen mit der Theologie Karl Rahners. K. Rahner zum 75. Geburtstag. Hrsg. v. H. Vorgrimler. Freiburg & Basel & Wien. Pp. 499-510.

Wojtyla, Karol
1980   Sources of Renewal. The Implementation of the Second Vatican Council. Glasgow.

INDEX OF PERSONAL NAMES

STUDIES IN
CHRISTIAN MISSION

1. WILLIAMS, C.P. *The Ideal of the Self-Governing Church*. A Study in Victorian Missionary Strategy. 1990. ISBN 90 04 09188 2

2. STINE, P.C. (ed.). *Bible Translation and the Spread of the Church*. The Last 200 Years. 1990. ISBN 90 04 09331 1

3. OOSTHUIZEN, G.C. *The Healer-Prophet in Afro-Christian Churches*. 1992. ISBN 90 04 09468 7

4. CARMODY s.j., B.P. *Conversion and Jesuit Schooling in Zambia*. 1992. ISBN 90 04 09428 8

5. PIROTTE, J. & H. DERROITTE (eds.). *Églises et santé dans le Tiers Monde. Hier et Aujourd'hui — Churches and Health Care in the Third World*. Past and Present. 1991. ISBN 90 04 09470 9

6. BRENT, A. *Cultural Episcopacy and Ecumenism*. Representative Ministry in Church History from the Age of Ignatius of Antioch to the Reformation, With Special Reference to Contemporary Ecumenism. 1992. ISBN 90 04 09432 6

7. RUOKANEN, M. *The Catholic Doctrine of Non-Christian Religions*. According to the Second Vatican Council. 1992. ISBN 90 04 09517 9

E.J. BRILL — P.O.B. 9000 — 2300 PA Leiden — The Netherlands

BX 1787 .R86 1992   93 0585

Ruokanen, Miikka.

The Catholic doctrine of non
 -Christian religions

CABRINI COLLEGE LIBRARY
610 KING OF PRUSSIA RD.
RADNOR, PA 19087-3699

DEMCO